The Art of Anti-Racism

The Art of Anti-Racism

Aesthetics, Race, and Contemporary Political Theory

Edited by

ALIX L. OLSON AND ALEX ZAMALIN

EU GPSR Authorised Representative:
Logos Europe, 9 rue Nicolas Poussin, 17000, La Rochelle, France
contact@logoseurope.eu

For information, contact State University of New York Press, Albany, NY
www.sunypress.edu

Library of Congress Cataloging-in-Publication Data

Names: Olson, Alix L., editor. | Zamalin, Alex, 1986– editor.
Title: The art of anti-racism : aesthetics, race, and contemporary
  political theory / edited by Alix L. Olson and Alex Zamalin.
Description: Albany : State University of New York Press, [2025]. | Series:
  SUNY series in critical political science | Includes bibliographical
  references and index.
Identifiers: LCCN 2025014361 | ISBN 9798855804607 (hardcover : alk. paper) |
  ISBN 9798855804621 (ebook) | ISBN 9798855804614 (pbk. : alk. paper)
Subjects: LCSH: Anti-Racism. | Anti-Racism—Political aspects. | Political
  science—Philosophy.
Classification: LCC HT1563 .A77 2025
LC record available at https://lccn.loc.gov/2025014361

Contents

Introduction

Alix L. Olson and Alex Zamalin

In the summer of 2020, following the murder of George Floyd, the world witnessed a powerful resurgence of antiracist activism as the Black Lives Matter (BLM) movement erupted in a global wave of protest. These demonstrations marked the latest chapter in a long and enduring history of antiracist struggle—one aimed at dismantling the entrenched social, political, and economic institutions that afford material benefits to those racialized as white while oppressing those racialized as nonwhite. BLM protesters took to the streets not only to demand an end to police brutality, repressive systems of law and order, and the carceral state more broadly, but to expose racial capitalism as an enduring engine of white supremacy and social and economic injustice.

But at the heart of this movement was more than just an expansive political agenda and call for policy demands—it was a radical reimagining of how we experience and express resistance. BLM protesters brought forth an aesthetic of defiance, a visual and sensorial vocabulary that communicated their collective grief and grievances, their yearning for justice, and their visions of a liberated future. Through various modes of creative expression—dance, song, painting, poetry, slogans, hashtags, street murals, graffiti, and more—activists rendered visible both the lived experiences of oppression while articulating possibilities for freedom. In doing so, they developed an aesthetics of resistance—one that invited both participants and the broader public to feel, to imagine, and to embody racial justice in deeply visceral ways.

This mobilization of dramatic public action, prefigurative performance, and artistic messaging finds its roots within a rich legacy of antiracist struggle, which has long recognized the indispensability of creativity in sustaining collective resistance. Nineteenth-century abolitionists, for example, framed their political appeals as dramatic confrontations between the forces of good and evil, rhetorically occupying the nation's founding documents to expose the hypocrisies of racialized systems of domination. In the 1960s, civil rights activists employed ritualized acts of civil disobedience—strikes, sit-ins, boycotts, and Freedom Songs—to dramatize their position as suffering but ideal civic patriots fighting to defend the very soul of American democracy. The Black Panther Party for Self-Defense, with its stylized performances such as Huey Newton's "Executive Mandate #1," issued bold declarations to demand an end to the "terror, brutality, murder, and repression of black people." And just as prison abolitionists staged silent protests, from "die-ins" to hunger strikes, to expose the violence of the carceral state, today's BLM protestors muzzle themselves with black tape to mark the systematic erasure of their voices and of their lives.

As much as antiracist activism in the US has relied on these physical "choreographies of protest" (Foster 2003) to register claims in the public sphere—outside formal political processes and official institutions—creative expression has also been a crucial undercurrent of political organizing and solidarity building. Abolitionists like David Walker distributed polemical manifestos, such as his *Appeal* (1829), to dramatize the urgency of ending racial enslavement, while poets like Claude McKay, as in his searing poem "If We Must Die" (1919), mobilized impassioned cries against lynching and racial terror. Visual artists like Jacob Lawrence, with works like the *Migration Series* (1941), captured the joy and struggle of Black freedom during the Great Migration, offering a historical and visual roadmap for activists involved in the civil rights movement. Audre Lorde's poetry in the 1970s provided a clarion call for Black feminists and womanists in the Combahee River Collective, whose work politicized the marginalization of poor and working-class queer women of color.

While the aesthetic dimensions of antiracist struggle have been indispensable to the movement, contemporary political theory has largely overlooked this intersection. This omission, though, is hardly surprising considering the field's long-standing tendency to push both race and art to the margins of more proper or "serious" political concerns. For centuries, from the birth of modern political theory in the seventeenth century through the early twentieth century, race was treated as insignificant to political life. Even as the invention of racial taxonomies and ideologies took root, and as white supremacism entrenched itself in the political infrastructure, thinkers remained preoccupied with abstract concepts like the social contract, citizenship, and political rights, and the racial contract that underpinned these structures remained uninvestigated. Only in the twentieth century—spurred by anticolonial and decolonization movements of the Global South—did political theorists begin to reckon with race as a central political category, one that shapes power, resistance, justice, the state, and identity. The trailblazing work of scholars like Frantz Fanon, CLR James, Angela Davis, Cathy Cohen, Judith Shklar, Audre Lorde, Patricia Hill Collins, and Charles Mills, among others, helped forge new paths for Black, Indigenous, decolonial, queer, and Latinx political thought. These fields revealed intimate connections between white supremacy, racial violence, white ignorance, Black liberation, racial capitalism and intersectionality—all of which challenge the foundational assumptions and core concepts of political theory itself.

Although antiracism has steadily gained recognition as a vital subject within political theory, art has had a more ambiguous reception. Political theory has tended to regard itself as the sphere of conceptual and speculative reflection on politics while activism is construed as the more practical, historical engagement with politics. Art, on the other hand, has been primarily viewed as the realm of expression, grappling with beauty and existential meaning. This distinction is evident in the long-standing skepticism of canonical Western political theorists, from Plato to Thomas Hobbes to Karl Popper, who often dismissed it as an emotional, irrational force that undermined the pursuit of political truth and justice. Hegel's view of the "end of art" in the final developmental stages of human history, Adorno's dismissal of politically commodified art, and Marcuse's critique of "art as a tool for emancipation" all reflect a broader tendency to view political art as either irrelevant, secondary to, or a distraction from "real" political practice.

Some political theorists have attempted to reclaim art's role in politics, viewing it as a tool for empowering citizens, aiding them in journeys of self-discovery or fostering therapeutic relief. In embracing creative expression, this line of reasoning goes, citizens are capable of being moved (or more precisely to "move themselves") from immaturity to maturity in the service of personal reform. For Jurgen Habermas, "Artworks promote the maturation of the person's subjectivity and provide the motivational structures necessary for moral autonomy and scientific thinking" and thus their capacity for democratic politics. Writers like

Sartre, on the other hand, insist on the full commitment of art in service to the political realm, arguing that autonomous art is useless. For Sartre, art in its most highly evolved form is attributed with a mature agency that speaks truth to power; for this reason, he even took fault with Pablo Picasso's *Guernica,* dismissing it as inadequate because it failed to convey an unequivocal political statement. But while these theorists laud the political dimensions of art and the aesthetic dimension of politics, they stop short of theorizing how art as political practice might reconstitute the very boundaries of what counts as politics. How might art challenge the ways we conceptualize democracy, reframe our understanding of justice, or provoke deeper imaginings of freedom?

This edited collection seeks to address these gaps by offering a sustained theoretical examination of the aesthetic dimensions of antiracist struggle. We argue that political theory itself can be understood as an art—a dynamic process of claim-making, and critically analyzing and expanding our ethical, moral, and strategic visions. Politics, likewise, is the art of assembling messages, narratives, symbols, emotions, and affects in public and through collective institutions and structures. Art, in turn, can serve as a critique of existing political realities while gesturing toward a horizon beyond, reimagining the boundaries of the politically possible. Through its expressive capacity, art dramatizes subjectivity, experience, and aspirations, embodying the contestation that is central to democratic politics. Given these intersections, contemporary political theory offers invaluable resources for engaging with the aesthetics of antiracist political thought, practice, and culture. How might various accounts of power and resistance be brought to bear on evaluating the often unquantifiable political effects of creative antiracist interventions? What insights can political theory provide to strengthen ties between antiracist art and broader movement aims? How might art itself be reimagined and reconstructed to align with antiracist strategies?

Leading scholars in this interdisciplinary collection tackle these crucial questions, arguing that (1) antiracist politics has a distinct aesthetics; (2) art provides powerful theoretical insights that shape our understanding of antiracism action; and (3) art is a crucial avenue for enacting antiracist political change. In making these arguments, these essays highlight how art can revitalize and energize contemporary antiracist thinking, offering a response to the collective sense of despair so strongly felt in our neoliberal era. As cultural historian Robin Kelley reminds us, radical art has the power to "take us to another place, envision a different way of seeing, perhaps a different way of feeling." Above all, this book embraces the insight that transformational politics requires us to imagine worlds that can be otherwise.

The first half of the collection focuses on the aesthetics of antiracist performance, exploring how imaginative practices can generate new ways of organizing and understanding justice. In the first chapter, "The Robert Hungerford School and Black Speculative Counterpublics in Eatonville, Florida," Julian Chambliss and Scot French examine the structure and world-building of the Robert Hungerford Normal and Industrial School in Eatonville, Florida. Founded in 1896, the school's philosophy—"Heart, Head, and Hand"—aimed to facilitate Black self-reliance under conditions of segregation and Jim Crow in the Deep South. Chambliss and French argue that the school exemplified an Afrofuturist counterpublic, offering a a powerful rejoinder to post-Reconstruction narratives of Black deficiency and helping us think through how Black citizens can imagine alternative presents under conditions of systematic constraint.

In the second chapter, "The Civics of Suffering: The Black Freedom Movement, Social Darwinism, and the Politics of Public Health," Maxwell Burkey turns our attention to the aesthetic practices of the Black Freedom movement of the 1960s, which centered on nonviolent protest, and the dramatic enactment of civic suffering. Burkey uses this aesthetic to argue for a reimagining of public health and ethics of care, proposing that the Black Freedom movement offers an alternative vision of citizenship—one that resists the racist limitations of social Darwinism, and provides an exemplary model for rethinking state policies regarding public health.

Jane Anna Gordon's contribution, "In Using Forum Theater to Practice Anti-Racist Norms: A Case Study from UCONN Hartford," examines a theater activity orchestrated by the HartBeat Ensemble at the University of Connecticut–Hartford in order to examine theater's potentiality as a crucial site for developing antiracist modes of being. Drawing on the philosophy of Brazilian theater activist Augusto Boal, including the Theatre of the Oppressed, Gordon explores how interactive theater can serve as a space for developing antiracist norms and political engagement. Her chapter highlights the potential for theater to foster rehearsals of antiracist citizenship, serving as a powerful springboard for progressive political struggle.

In the fourth chapter, "Black Dancers Matter: Black Ballerinas, Robert E. Lee, and the Politics of Resistance," Simon Stow and Amanda Millis argue that the work of Black dancers during the 2020 Black Lives Matter protests in Virginia reflects a unique form of cultural politics as resistance. Far from a defensive posture or marked by a feeling of resignation, Stow and Millis insist, these dance performances offer a constructive role in both identity-making and the creation of liberatory political horizons, highlighting the ways in which Black dance serves as resistance within a Black counterpublic.

The second half of the volume underscores how contemporary antiracist art offers valuable frameworks for rethinking core political concepts. In the fifth chapter, "Afrofuturism and Reconstitution," Alex Zamalin explores the role of Afrofuturism in the reconstitution of the social and political order. Drawing on the long tradition of Black speculative literature, including writers like Martin Delany, W. E. B. Du Bois, Frances Harper, and Octavia Butler, Zamalin argues that Afrofuturist fiction offers a creative means of undoing historically naturalized racial inequalities and imagining utopian alternatives to the (racially unjust) status quo.

Alix Olson's "Parables of Resilience: Promising Pessimism, Octavia Butler's 'Purpose,' and the Making of Worlds" (chapter 6) extends this analysis of Black speculative literature to consider contemporary neoliberal governance. Olson demonstrates the ways in which citizens are increasingly governed through a logic of resilience that she terms "promising pessimism"—or the idea that citizens benefit from adapting to a present defined by recurrent crises, economic, racial, political, and environmental. Taking NASA/Space X's plan for interplanetary colonization as a logical endpoint of this idea, Olson juxtaposes this rationality with an emancipatory account of resilience found in Black science fiction writer Octavia Butler's *Parable* series. Unlike promising pessimism, Butler's dystopian novels mark the present—rather than the beyond—as the site to be actively revolutionized.

In the seventh chapter, " 'My Ovaries Ain't For You to Bully': Trap Feminist Rappers and The Fight for Sexual Autonomy and Reproductive Justice," Shantee Rosado suggests that Black feminist artistry around sexual autonomy and reproductive justice provides a critique and counterpoint to the political right's attack on bodily autonomy and abortion rights, symbolized by the US Supreme Court's overturning of Roe v. Wade. Rosado argues that trap feminist rappers like Cardi B, Megan Thee Stallion, and Latto unapologetically reclaim the power of pleasure and of "the erotic," issue a bold challenge to misogynoir, and offer Black feminist-centered protest anthems to movements for reproductive justice.

Closing the volume, Utz McKnight and Jared Rodriguez's "Convicted by Our Humanity: Race and the Politics of Art" (chapter 8) explores contemporary poetry, film, and photography, which address questions of "racial progress," in order to examine how the time and space of racial justice is imagined. McKnight and Rodriguez draw attention to the ways in which the art under consideration can reinforce prevailing racial ideologies but also trouble our sense of what racial solidarity entails and the meaning of shared humanity.

Taken together, these essays remind us that the failure to understand the relation between the aesthetics and the politics of antiracist struggle (indeed, of any transformative movement) limits our capacity to see, much less evaluate, the full range of tactical, strategic, and expressive challenges to power. Most crucially, such a narrowed vision impedes political thinkers from laboring fully on behalf of Black life and contributing to an antiracist future. Our hope is that this collection provides alternative lines of vision to political theorists and students of antiracist politics, helping them recognize antiracist aesthetics as invaluable texts through which to understand our historical present. Central to material struggle, creative practices can be read through the ways in which they alter structures of feeling, generate new sensibilities, bear public witness to injustice, transform what counts as social truth, sustain morale and forge solidarity, and articulate and animate the unfolding aims of racial justice movements. While far more work in this area is needed, this volume represents a snapshot of how political theory can begin to strengthen its relationship to the art of antiracist struggle.

Chapter 1

The Robert Hungerford School and Black Speculative Counterpublics in Eatonville, Florida

JULIAN C. CHAMBLISS AND SCOT A. FRENCH

In *The Education of Blacks in the South, 1860–1935*, James D. Anderson writes that two conflicting ideas have long defined the history of education in the United States. First, many Americans see a direct link between "citizenship in a democratic society and popular education," while at the same time, "schooling for second-class citizenship" has been a tradition in the United States (Anderson 1988, 1). While it would be logical to assume these ideas would be held by different people at different times, in truth, they represented ideas widely shared by Americans for decades. Moreover, these ideas shaped the nation's collective vision of progress, shaping public and private efforts toward education. While it was assumed since the founding of the republic that an educated citizenry was crucial to the future, those same calls for colonial education also embraced the denial of enslaved people's ability to learn. Central to the slave society that shaped the United States was a belief that Black people did not need to be educated (Urban and Wagoner 2013, 65–66).

The transformation of the American education system after the Civil War was the first significant shift in national policy toward education and race. During Reconstruction, the United States government pushed Southern states to create an education system to address public needs.

Under the auspices of these federal mandates, Southern states could not overtly discriminate, but the overarching concern for industrial and mechanical education was central to the vision offered for education. In the aftermath of Reconstruction, the rise of Democrat-controlled state governments saw widespread retrenchment. Beginning in the late 1870s, "Blacks were ruthlessly disenfranchised; their civil and political subordination was fixed in southern law, and statutes and social customs trapped them in an agricultural economy that rested heavily on coercive control and allocation of labor" (Anderson 1988, 2).

Despite this limitation, a growing number of educational scholars have argued in recent years how much we should engage with the ways African Americans **overcame** the system's limitations to envision an educational landscape that supported Black freedom. As historian Hilary Green noted in *Educational Reconstruction: African American Schools in the Urban South, 1865–1890,* through cooperative practice, African Americans across the South were able to forge effective learning opportunities. For formerly enslaved people, "Education and literacy symbolized full citizenship" and was crucial to a Black vision for freedom (Green 2016, 6). In an atmosphere characterized by the rising narrative of Black failure as justification for political disenfranchisement, African American activism and ideology embraced counterstorytelling through community building centered on education.

This project uses the Robert Hungerford Normal and Industrial School in Eatonville, Florida, as an example of Black counterfuture practice associated with Afrofuturism. The shift to an emphasis on Afrofuturism may seem strange, but theorizing about Afrofuturism highlights how Black cultural production acts as an oppositional ideology. In this framing, we can incorporate the ways Afrofuturist scholars have increasingly stressed the long historical practice rooted in how Black people throughout the diaspora speculate toward freedom through the creation of counterpublic spaces. These efforts created platforms that sought to establish safety and prosperity from a Black perspective. By emphasizing the intersections between speculative practice and liberatory outcomes, we may consider how African Americans created institutions they intended as the foundation for alternative futures that fostered better economic, social, and political outcomes.

While the original definition of Afrofuturism by Mark Dery focused on "signification that appropriates images of technology and a prosthetically enhanced future" theorizing around Afrofuturism quickly evolved (Dery 1994, 180).

In the introduction to a 2002 special issue dedicated to Afrofuturism in Social Text, Alondra Nelson wrote that the idea that "race (and gender) distinction would be eliminated with technology" was a "founding fiction of the digital age" (Nelson 2002, 1). Her analysis called attention to a "technological transformation" pattern that promised to eliminate difference and liberate all but could not escape the cultural weight created by racial identity. Indeed, a process of othering that marginalized Black bodies served to reinforce ideas of "Black technical handicaps and 'Western' technological superiority" (5). Nelson's advocacy for Afrofuturism prompts a different take on progress, rejecting the inherent limitation of Black people created by Western narratives of modernization and progress. Her emphasis on Afrofuturism called attention to ways modernity, defined through a European perspective, systematically disadvantaged Black people. Nelson emphasizes Afrofuturism offers a different path. As she further explained in "Afrofuturism: Past-Future Visions," Afrofuturism is a "term of convenience to describe the analysis, criticism, and cultural production that addresses intersections between race and technology" (Nelson 2000, 35). Nelson's understanding of Afrofuturism allows Black people's past and present actions to be in dialogue. Kodwo Eshun further theorizes Afrofuturism as an alternative practice system that disrupts colonial thinking. For Eshun, Afrofuturism is an opportunity to "bring Africa and its subjects into history" denied by the European mode of knowledge production. Central to this process is the gathering of "countermemories that contest the colonial archive" and creating a way for us to situate the "collective trauma of slavery as the founding moment of modernity" (Eshun 2003, 288). The contestation can take many forms, but it operates with an understanding that futurity is a tool of the powerful, allowing those in control to shape our collective vision by condemning the powerless to the past and using the latest technological ethos to shape the present and future in support of the continuation of the status quo (290). In this context, Afrofuturist practice can be understood as a process of intervention and tools building across the Black Atlantic (301). This expansive view of Afrofuturism as practice aligns with Reynaldo Anderson, who argues that Afrofuturism enables us to examine overlapping "tropes of science fiction, history, trauma, reparation, and politics" for emancipation and transformation (Anderson 2020).

In the case of Central Florida, the story of the Hungerford School offers important insight into Black aspirations rooted in post-Reconstruction speculative vision. While much has been written about the "Exoduster

Movement," which sent Black settlers west to places such as Nicodemus, Kansas, or Lincoln, Oklahoma, there are numerous examples of Black community building before and after the Civil War that highlight the consistent engagement by Black Americans to define and create space that affirmed and protected themselves and their hope for future descendants. These communities, which academics frequently refer to as freedom colonies or farming villages, encapsulated a set of actions linked to ideas about progress in the Black community (Cha-Jua 2000, 2–3). The circumstances that allowed Black communities to strive after the Civil War were abundant in Central Florida. In 1866 the Southern Homestead Act (SHA) opened land in the former states of the Confederacy to white and Black settlers. Despite research highlighting the poor quality of the land available, white resistance to Black land ownership, and the lack of government protection, African Americans sought the opportunity offered by the SHA. In Florida, the Freedmen's Bureau sought to secure land for African Americans with mixed results. Over nineteen million acres were available in Florida. The Freedmen's Bureau supported newly freed slaves in finding plots, and provided supplies for one month, transportation to the homestead site, and seeds. By 1867 there were 2,000 homesteads in the state, and by 1868 more than 3,000, more than any other Southern state (Taylor 2015). With the conclusion of Reconstruction, Florida's government was not friendly to African American aspirations. The 1885 Florida Constitution, which replaced the 1868 constitution adopted as a part of the state's reentry into the United States, allowed poll taxes as a prerequisite for voting (State Library and Archives of Florida 2017). Facing questions of political inclusion and community building in the post-Reconstruction South, African Americans navigated the changing political, social, and economic landscape to achieve the benefits of full citizenship. This pattern of "imagined affordances," according to Lonny J. Avi Brooks, enabled Black people to strive for more within a hostile environment creating through daily practice ways to see and expect more from culture and tools than were intended by the original designers (Brooks 2022, 328).

Eatonville acts as a Black counterpublic space where these imagined affordances are manifested through the active resistance of white supremacy logic by Black Americans' control of public and private space. While this action fits neatly within the Afrofuturist framework seeking to decolonize our vision of Western society, we should note that the tendency toward liberatory speculation aligns with a sociopolitical narrative documented by scholars in recent years. Recent works such as Robert Cassanello's *To Render*

Invisible: Jim Crow and Public Life in New South Jacksonville demonstrate the contested nature of political identity linked to spaces public and private, which were a crucial measure of freedom for African Americans after Reconstruction. As Cassanello suggests, the late nineteenth-century emergence of Jim Crow segregation was not inevitable nor uncontested. When we recover the story of Black community space, we see the importance of African American agency that challenged social and economic restrictions created by white supremacy. This perspective highlights how Black people in Florida brought together local concerns, alternative worldviews, and an understanding of the political identity that reflects diasporic geographies articulated by Katherine McKittrick and Clyde Woods (2007, 6–8). Their articulation of the tension created by the intersection of race and space in the context of subaltern experience offers an important way to reimagine the inspiration offered by Black institutions, especially those institutions created and supported by Booker T. Washington.

While a controversial figure in terms of the broader political narrative he cultivated to glean financial support from white donors, many of Washington's followers steadfastly believed in his vision of community-based activism. Historian David H. Jackson Jr. argues Washington's supporters in Florida thought of themselves as constructionists, a term that indicated they believed in "constructing policies and programs to deal with the imposition and problem of racism, rather than react with mere words or with the threat of retaliation" (2003, 176). African Americans across the South rallied to create spaces that supported their vision of freedom. Washington explained in *Working with the Hands* (1904) that he sought to help Black people by addressing what he could do "for the people of my race by teaching the intelligent use of hands and brains on the farm, not by theorizing, but by practical effort" (1904, 32). As a pragmatic advocate for innovative thinking and doing, Washington's vision for educational institutions as spaces for application allowed for an African American speculative vision that acknowledged the rural context as a starting point but by no means assumed it was a permanent state. Washington's world building aligns with Afrofuturist practice by leveraging cooperative programs around education and work to create narratives of Black progress that inspired Americans of all races in manners that, according to historian August Meier, "undermined the American race system." Indeed, Samuel R. Spencer argues Washington fired the imagination of the poorest Black person by offering them an "active role in a creative, dynamic program which affected him personally and directly" (Hamilton 2017, 2).

This reality is crucial to understanding the impact of the Hungerford School in Eatonville. The cofounders of the school, Russell and Mary Clinton Calhoun, developed their educational philosophy ("Heart, Head, and Hand") during their eleven combined years as boarding students and teachers-in-training at Booker T. Washington's Tuskegee Normal and Industrial Institute. The Tuskegee campus consisted of just one building when Mary Clinton arrived in 1885. Over the next five years, Mary paid her tuition and board by working "in the laundry, the teachers' dining-room, the sewing division, with Principal Washington's family, as well as with the families of other teachers." Russell Calhoun enrolled at Tuskegee in 1890, working in the carpentry shop by day and attending classes at night. "I used my spare hours making picture-frames, repairing window-shades, making flower-stands and flower-boxes, and working flower-gardens for the various Faculty families," he recalled (Calhoun 1905, 330).[1]

After graduating in 1896, Russell Calhoun moved to Tampa, where Mary Clinton lived. The two married and—after an offer to teach in South Carolina fell through—accepted an assignment to teach in the public schools of Orange County, Florida (Calhoun, 333). There, the all-white school board viewed their Tuskegee background as an asset that meshed well with the Black town-building and racial uplift mission of Eatonville.[2] "We were here but a few days when we decided that this was the place for us to begin putting into practise the lessons taught us at Tuskegee. We felt that we wanted to do something toward helping our people. We decided to cast our lot permanently at Eatonville" (Calhoun 1905, 334). Though hired as Eatonville's public school principal, Russell Calhoun saw prospects for establishing a private boarding school based on the Tuskegee model. "There are more than 4,000 negroes in the county, and over 40,000 south of us to Key West," he observed, "and not another school of its kind for colored boys and girls. We must face these facts and ask the good friends, both north and south, to change the condition of things" (Calhoun 1902, 398). To build local support, the Calhouns began modeling Tuskegee's self-help principles and "lessons in economy" for the benefit of all Eatonville residents and not just those enrolled as public school students. Calhoun explained the thinking behind their holistic approach to educating and uplifting the entire community:

> Our first "industrial" service was done with the aid of the school
> children: we cleaned the street of tin cans and other rubbish.
> We found the lessons in economy which we had received at

Tuskegee very valuable to us at this trying time. We felt that if we would properly impress the lessons most needed we should own a home, a cow, some chickens, a horse, and a garden; we felt that there should be tangible ownership on the part of the people of some of these things, at any rate. These things we started to get as soon as possible. We wanted to teach the people by example. After talking in a general way for some days of the value of industrial education, coupled with that of intelligent class-room instruction, Mrs. Calhoun succeeded in getting four girls to come to her home for sewing lessons. That was the first step. (Calhoun 1905, 334)

In expanding the Tuskegee model to the entire town, Calhoun took the imagined affordances available in Eatonville and began a process of transformation that made a more liberated future real. These small actions highlight how, according to John Jennings, Afrofuturism can be considered an aesthetic that challenges European (white) expectations linked to Blackness. By engaging in these actions, Calhoun further enhanced the community's capacity to be a platform for transformation.

These transformations matter because they allowed Calhoun to better engage outside donors. Indeed, to acquire land for the private school, Calhoun appealed to a Northern white banker and philanthropist named Edward C. Hungerford, who owned a winter home and grove in the neighboring village of Lake Maitland.[3] In 1895, Hungerford offered twenty acres to Edward Waters College, an African Methodist Episcopal church–affiliated school in Jacksonville, if it would relocate to Eatonville ("A Chester Man's Generosity" 1895; "Spirit of the Press" 1895). But Calhoun learned that the deal had fallen through. "I wrote to him [Hungerford] asking if he would give us the land," Calhoun recalled. "He replied that he would be glad to give us forty acres if we would use it for school purposes" (Calhoun 1905, 335). Hungerford pledged "forty acres for immediate use and forty more for future development of the enterprise, or to be sold and the proceeds used for the school" ("Negro Industrial School" 1899). To honor Hungerford's donation, the school would be named for his "gifted young son," Robert—a doctor who "came to Maitland years ago for his health, but finally succumbed to an incurable disease." Robert, it was reported, "took a great interest in the successful development of Eatonville as a purely negro city, and the colored people became much attached to him" ("Negro Industrial School" 1899).[4]

With eighty acres pledged by E. C. Hungerford, soon doubled by gifts from other family members, Calhoun moved to secure official recognition of his Tuskegee "branch" school from the Orange County Board of Education and Superintendent of Public Instruction. At the time, Orange County made no formal provision for the education of African Americans beyond the grade school level. Recognizing the value of having the Hungerford School as an adjunct to its public school system, the county board "consented to make the Eatonville public school a nucleus for the proposed industrial school, thus giving a full supply of pupils, and a couple of teachers paid out of the regular school funds of the state to start off with" ("Negro Industrial School" 1899). On February 24, 1899, an eight-member Board of Trustees was created, with Orange County Superintendent of Public Instruction W. B. Lynch—"under whose official supervision the school will begin operation"—as its first president ("Negro Industrial School" 1899).[5] The makeup of the board reflected Hungerford's three pillars of support: Washington's Tuskegee Institute, the independent Black township of Eatonville, and local white officials and prominent citizens sympathetic to the cause of industrial education for the Black laboring classes of Central Florida.

Representing Tuskegee on the Hungerford board were two of its officers: Treasurer Warren Logan, a graduate of Hampton Institute, who served as acting principal in Washington's absence, and Secretary Robert C. Bedford, described by Washington as "a white man from Wisconsin, who was then pastor of a little coloured Congregational church in Montgomery, Ala." Bedford served on the Hungerford board until his death in 1911, Logan until the reorganization of the board in 1938.[6] Though not a board member himself, Washington offered his public endorsement of Calhoun in the school's annual reports: "This is to state that I have known Mr. R. C. Calhoun both as a student at the Tuskegee Normal and Industrial Institute and as a worker since his graduation, and I have full faith in his honesty, and believe he is capable of building up a school in Florida that will be of help for our people, and I bespeak for him a hearing wherever he may go" (*Fourth Annual Report of the Robert Hungerford Industrial School* 1903, 24). Washington also devoted a segment of his book, *The Negro in Business* (1907), to Calhoun's work at Hungerford. "The coming of this man was the most fortunate event which has happened in Eatonville. R. C. Calhoun has proven to be one of those leaders for the creation of whom Tuskegee exists, and he was filled with the enthusiasm for unselfish and devoted service which we attempt to instill at Tuskegee. . . . The school now has six teachers, of whom three are graduates of Tuskegee. Two new dormitories have recently been added, and the future of the institute is bright" (Washington 1907, 79–80). The pattern represented by the *Negro in Business* is worth noting.

Washington's world building and transformative narrative accelerated throughout the first decade of the twentieth century. Kenneth Hamilton argues that Washington's effectiveness as an organizer and visionary extended through a cultural movement inspired by the Tuskegee philosophy he sustained. His speeches, books, and articles created formal and informal followers who understood his views and pursued his aims when possible. His efforts served to raise money and promote the Tuskegee worldview. Pairing education and economic activity together, Washington founded the National Negro Business League (NNBL) in 1900. He served as its president for sixteen years. As president, he stressed that Black business would increase Black people's status. Headquartered in Tuskegee, the NNBL had affiliate groups that included the National Negro Funeral Directors' Association, National Negro Press Association, the National Negro Insurance Men's Association, and the National Negro Retail Merchants Association. Taken together at its height, these groups provided more than forty thousand Black entrepreneurs to engage with Washington. Those groups allowed Washington to engage at the community level. It was through the effort of the NNBL that Washington's Southern Education Tours were organized. Between 1908 and 1912, members of state and local affiliates of the NNBL helped organize trips across the South that allowed Washington to celebrate the Tuskegee vision, meet with local leaders, and assess the progress made by black people and potential allies (Hamilton 2017, 27–29).

Thus, the narrative of Eatonville—a magnet for those seeking racial advancement on the Booker T. Washington/Tuskegee Institute model—was bolstered by a Black network created and sustained by Washington's activities. The Hungerford School had between one and three town representatives throughout the school's first four decades that closely aligned with this Tuskegee vision. Mayors Samuel M. Moseley and ex-Mayor/Town Founder Joseph E. Clark served as founding board members in 1899. Rev. John Hurston (whose daughter, Zora, attended the school) joined briefly, between 1901 and 1904. Postmaster Matthew B. Brazell, one of the Eatonville's original twenty-seven incorporators, appears regularly on trustee lists between 1903 and 1934. The presence of local white citizens and public school officials on the Hungerford Board of Trustees assured prospective donors of the school's standing within the white community. "The whole Board of Public Instruction for Orange County have been warm friends of the school from the very beginning of the work," Calhoun noted in his fundraising pitch. "Two of its members are on the Industrial School Board." Other prominent white citizens serving the Hungerford board included Loring A. Chase, coproprietor of the Winter Park Company; Sidney E. Ives, an Orlando merchant; Rev. Charles P. Redfield, pastor of Winter Park Congregational Church; and Mary A. Thurston, a winter resident of Maitland whose home nearly abutted the Eatonville town line. As Calhoun noted in his Fourth Annual Report, "I have not said very much regarding the difficulties, the struggles, to plant this work, but I am glad to say that from the beginning we have had the friendliest support and advice from all the white people of this section, officials and citizens alike" (*Fourth Annual Report* 1903, 24).

Northern white patronage proved critical to the financial stability of the Hungerford school in its early years. As Calhoun wrote in his Fourth Annual Report: "Our school is not supported by any society or state. We live who will listen to our story." Bishop Henry B. Whipple of Minnesota, a winter resident of Maitland and pastor of the Church of the Good Shepherd, "gave his support to the movement and secured some substantial cash donations from wealthy Northern people" ("Negro Industrial School" 1899). Bishop Whipple was reported to have secured "the first $100 for the school" from railroad magnate Cornelius Vanderbilt; his widow, Evangeline, donated $245 after his death. The Fourth Annual Report listed individual donations from nine Northern states: Pennsylvania, New York, New Jersey Connecticut, Rhode Island, Massachusetts, Vermont, Maine, and Wisconsin. Donations from Southern states, outside of Florida, were limited to three from the Tuskegee Institute in Alabama (*Fourth Annual Report* 1903, 7–13; 24).

African Americans contributed time and money as well. "Already," the Savannah *Morning News* reported in May 1899, "the colored people are donating their labor in clearing up the grounds and preparing for the erection of the needed buildings" ("Negro Industrial School" 1899). In his 1902–03 Annual Report to the Board of Trustees, Calhoun noted a "considerable increase in the donations of the colored people." Among the donors listed by name in the report were Eatonville residents/trustees J. E. Clark and S. M. Moseley, the A. M. E. Church of Daytona, and the Colored Baptist Church of Daytona (*Fourth Annual Report* 1903, 3; 7–13). Two years later, in his 1905 autobiographical sketch "A Negro Community Builder," Calhoun wrote: "The colored people have had little to give in cash but have been most liberal in their contributions of labor. They have been willing to help themselves" (Calhoun 337).

Calhoun consistently touted Hungerford's impact on the social and economic development of Eatonville and the African American community at large. Perhaps no activity better illustrated this outreach mission than the annual Negro Farmers' Conferences held at Hungerford. Modeled after the annual Tuskegee Farmers' Conferences that began in 1892, these two-day programs opened Hungerford's campus to all and featured presentations on a range of topics. "This is the people's university," a correspondent for the *Springfield* (Massachusetts) *Republican* wrote of annual Hungerford gathering in 1910.

> Parents and grown-up sons and daughters, too old to enter regularly into school, come from far and near and live at the school for two days, themselves and their mules. Teachers and students constitute the faculty, and everyone, from the principal to the youngest student, is expected to render some service to the visitors, if only to show a pleasant face and good manners.
>
> The farmers tell the story of land getting, improving homes, churches and schools. Successes and failures alike are freely recited, and out of these varied experiences all are instructed, warned or inspired. In the eight years the conference has been in operation many have bought homes, improved their schools and churches and sent their children away to learn trades and to get education beyond that of their home schools.

Resolutions passed at the close of the two-day meeting—"printed and sent out into all the country round as a sort of chart and guide to action during the year"—embodied the Hungerford Farmers' Conferences' guiding principles and moral code:

> The encouragement of thrift, industry and temperance.
> The putting forth of every effort to extend the school term, everywhere, to eight months and to keep every child possible in school throughout the entire term.
> The greatest possible stress on land ownership and home improvement.
> More attention to farming and especially to the raising of meat, butter, chickens and eggs.
> Opposition to lawlessness and punishment of law-breakers.

The conference, in effect, served as an informal extension service that extended the Hungerford curriculum to the people of Eatonville and beyond ("A Negro School and Conference" 1910).

From the beginning, Hungerford School welcomed Eatonville's public school students, serving a hybrid public-private school function. During the 1902–03 school year, nearly two-thirds of its students came from within town. "We have had, during the year, 39 students in the boarding department, coming from seven counties, and 66 coming from the town of Eatonville," Calhoun reported, "making 105 students under our care." Calhoun was under no illusions about the inequality of a system that funded white schools and left private Black schools, without state appropriations, to fend for themselves. "Already," he wrote, "a petition has been made to our representative from this district, Hon. W. L. Palmer, to ask the state for a small appropriation. We shall also make special effort to have the county aid us, because of the fact that we have students coming from other parts of the county, some of whom have attended public schools and others [who] have no school advantages" (*Fourth Annual Report* 3, 7–13).

The sudden and unexpected death of Russell Calhoun in November 1910 presented an administrative and fiscal crisis for the school. It clouded its future as both a private residential boarding school and a site of public education for Black students in Eatonville and neighboring communities. It also lessened worldbuilding linked to the Tuskegee network created by Booker T. Washington. Where Calhoun had personally traveled the country on behalf of the school, tapping into networks of philanthropic support, the task of raising funds now fell to his wife, Mary, and a predominantly white Board of Trustees based in the Central Florida area. In a letter addressed to the Friends of Robert Hungerford Industrial School, the white leadership of the Board promised a smooth transition and appealed to donors for their continued support.

> You have hitherto shown your interest in the school by con-
> tributing to its support. It needs your help and assistance
> during this trying time. Whoever the successor of Russell
> C. Calhoun may be, it will take many months to gather up
> threads so suddenly broken. The work will be continued under
> the direction of his wife, Mary C. Calhoun, who has been his
> co-laborer since the beginning; the work will not suffer at her
> hands. While Professor Calhoun was methodical in his habits
> and careful in his bookkeeping, we know that he frequently

received assurances of help which did not take definite form. If you have pledged anything for the following year will you kindly advise. If not, will you not in this time of great need assist a most worthy object.

Tellingly, this appeal was signed by three white Orange County school officials who doubled as Hungerford School Board members—W. B. Lynch, board president and superintendent of public schools, Sidney E. Ives, board treasurer and president of the Orange County Board of Public Instruction, and William R. O'Neal, board auditor and president of Orlando Schools. Florida's system of "separate but equal" education depended on private, quasi-public schools like Hungerford to fill the gap in communities where no public schools for Blacks existed ("Principal Calhoun's Death").

To ensure a succession plan beyond the original trustees, Mary Calhoun and several board members successfully petitioned to have Hungerford School incorporated as a nonprofit educational institution, with a maximum indebtedness of $10,000. The charter, as approved by the Circuit Court in 1911, "provided that the board should consist of five to nineteen members, with power to fill vacancies in their number and power to enact by-laws to provide for the method of electing trustees and fixing their terms in office" (State Archives of Florida 7). This act of incorporation inaugurated a new era of self-governance by a larger, predominantly white board, increasingly removed from the Black communities the school served. Despite this reality, under the leadership of Principal Mary Calhoun and several Tuskegee-affiliated successors, Hungerford School remained a destination for African Americans in Florida and throughout the United States. A well-publicized visit by Booker T. Washington in March 1912 signaled continued support and patronage from Tuskegee.[7] Meanwhile, advertisements in publications such as the National Association for the Advancement of Colored People's (NAACP) *The Crisis Magazine* touted the school's location in "Eatonville, Florida, The Only Incorporated Negro Town in Florida. AN IDEAL HOME FOR YOUR BOY AND GIRL." By 1922–23, the school's name—Robert Hungerford Normal and Industrial School—reflected an expansive educational mission that included vocational, high school, and teacher training (*The Crisis* 278). "By teaching each student a practical trade and a high school academic course," a local news item noted, "they become substantial citizens when they return to their homes and thus the state and nation are amply repaid" ("Colored School is Under New Management").

Despite reports of major gifts, local fundraising activities, and institutional progress, Hungerford struggled to sustain itself financially through the 1920s and 1930s. In 1924, two of the original Hungerford trustees, claiming legal authority as surviving members, conveyed legal ownership of the Hungerford Trust property to the nonprofit educational corporation formed shortly after Calhoun's death. "Thereafter," court records affirm, "the said non-profit corporation proceeded to subject itself to an indebtedness far in excess of the legal limit of indebtedness set in its charter." In 1931, the nonprofit corporation amended its charter to allow up to $25,000 of indebtedness "and, thereupon, executed a mortgage to three of its creditors"—Hungerford Principal John C. Jordan chief among them—"mortgaging the entire trust property . . . to secure said indebtedness."

When the mortgage fell into default, Jordan, his wife Eula, and a third creditor initiated foreclosure proceedings, placing a legal cloud over the school's future. Six years would pass before the Florida Supreme Court, siding with State Attorney General Cary D. Landis, ruled that the original founders had no basis for creating a nonprofit corporation to replace the original trust—thus canceling the 1931 mortgage and preventing foreclosure on the school's core property. In its ruling, the court declared that the Hungerford School was widely recognized as "a public trust and charity," supported by private gifts, donations, and endowments, and that its "assumption of a recognized and important place in the function of educating of negroes" entitled it "to be considered a part of an educational system for the vocational education of negroes as a public undertaking in this state." With this ruling, the Supreme Court endorsed the creation of a new successor board (all white) that answered directly to an Orange County chancery court judge. Any African American input would come, thereafter, from school officials and a Bi-Racial Advisory Board.[8]

These challenges coincide with a broader retrenchment around race and identity in the 1920s and 1930s, which marred the supposed progressive impulses of the era. The fate of education for African Americans was considered by W. E. B Du Bois, who, in 1935, wrote that "there is no room for argument as to whether the Negro need separate schools or not." For him, there was little cause to believe that white schools and their teachers would treat Black children in a way that would see them safely educated (Du Bois 329). Indeed, he advocated that African American attitudes toward Black schools must change, recognizing that Black teachers "be decently paid; that his schools were properly housed and equipped; that his colleges be supplied with scholarship and research funds; and he would be far more interested in the efficiency of these institutions of learning, than in forcing himself into other institutions where he is not wanted" (Du Bois 331).

Hungerford's experience in this period mirrored Du Bois's call for Black support for educational resources for Black children. Throughout the 1930s, Hungerford was able to weather its legal and financial troubles thanks to a new principal, Capt. Lorenzo E. Hall, timely gifts from private donors, institutional patronage from nearby Rollins College, and a renewed effort "to arouse the interest of the colored people of the State to the feeling this is Our School, with the slogan Hungerford, Our School, we are behind it with our money, patronage, and influence." In the fall of 1931, The *Hungerford Co-Operator* newspaper announced the "reorganization" of the curriculum to emphasize "a more thorough and practical course of studies that will fit the young people for a more useful and successful life." Though no longer Tuskegee-affiliated formally, Hungerford remained committed to the "Head, Hand, Heart" philosophy of Booker T. Washington. The elementary (4–8) and high school (8–12) grades mirrored a standard public school curriculum, with state-adopted textbooks and state-outlined courses of study. For practical training ("Hands"), the school offered home economics for young women, vocational/mechanical/agricultural training for young men, and commercial/office management training for all. To enhance moral development ("Heart"), Bible study was required of all students. "Send us your boys and girls, then watch their character grow as it finds expression in the better performance of each common task" (*The Hungerford Co-Operator* 1931; Rollins College Hungerford School Committee Minutes and Reports 1932–1935; Hungerford School Vertical File, Rollins College Library Special Collections).

These efforts came in the context of a city-county decision to have Black public high school students from neighboring Winter Park attend Hungerford, beginning in fall 1936. This decision intensified Hungerford's demographic shift from boarding school, drawing Black students from across the state inspired by the vision of education and as a tool for uplift, to an institution defined by students attending daily and returning home.[9] By 1941–42, Hungerford enrolled 172 students—160 from Florida, the vast majority from communities within commuting distance. Most of the day students came from Eatonville (18) and neighboring Winter Park (48). Others traveled from nearby Orlando (8), Forest City (8), Winter Garden (6), Maitland (4), Kissimmee (4), Oviedo (3), Deland (3), Oakland (2), Apoka (2), Sanford (1), Christmas (1), and Zellwood (1). The remainder were boarding students from more distant Florida locales (such as Miami, Jacksonville, and St. Petersburg) and out-of-state (Mississippi, Alabama, Georgia, and New York).[10]

Post–World War II civil rights activism, fueled by the rise of Black voting rights in the North, dramatically transformed the social and legal context within which Hungerford operated. While Hungerford continued to fill a vital role in Florida's dual education system, serving as a magnet school for Black students across the region, NAACP legal challenges and community demands to equalize public school facilities across the South prompted Orange County school officials to initiate discussions with Hungerford's court-appointed Trustees about taking the school public. In 1947–48, the Florida State Legislature adopted a Minimum Foundation Program "to provide minimum educational opportunities for all children regardless of their racial identity or where they live." The statewide school building program that ensued made Hungerford's recruitment of out-of-region boarding students increasingly difficult, as Black parents now had local options for tuition-free public schools. Meanwhile, the Florida State Citizens Committee Survey targeted the Hungerford property as an ideal site for "a first-class center of Negro education for the north and west areas of the County" ("Trustees Recommend Turning Hungerford into Public Negro High School" 1950).[11]

For the court-appointed Trustees, Hungerford stood at a crossroads: either it must become a fully private boarding school, with a church or private school affiliation, or a fully public high school, owned and operated by Orange County Board of Public Instruction. To do nothing, they argued, would ignore historical trends and render Hungerford increasingly obsolete. "Hungerford is at present a public charitable trust organized over fifty years ago," they wrote. "At that time no public schools at the high school level were available to Negroes in Orange County and Hungerford did a great service in filling such a need." But times had changed. "With the building of Jones High School in Orlando in 1925, and many other high schools throughout the state, and with the awakening of a public consciousness of the necessity for providing equal educational opportunities for the Negro, conditions have materially changed" ("Trustees Recommend Turning Hungerford into Public Negro High School" 1950). Though unstated, the threat of equalization lawsuits against public school officials undoubtedly contributed to the "awakening of a public consciousness." Under pressure from the NAACP and Black parents, many localities were forced to build or upgrade African American schools to meet the then-prevailing standard of "separate but equal." In Orlando, for example, a "group of local Negroes" filed suit in Federal Court "seeking an injunction against the expenditure of further school funds until Negro schools are brought up to par with white schools" (*Orlando Evening Star* 1950).[12]

For localities that relied on private schools like Hungerford to fill a public function, equalization suits forced a reckoning with the true cost of maintaining "separate but equal" educational facilities to support segregation. As historian Joseph A. Tomberlin observes:

> During the late 1940s and early 1950s many Southern states, Florida included, launched strong efforts to equalize their educational facilities for Blacks and whites. This development was not, however, a matter of altruism, nor did it flow from any new or more enlightened racial attitude in the South. The drive to equalize was part of an attempt to preserve segregated education. The South believed that if it, after so many years of observing only the "separate" portion of the 'separate but equal' doctrine, now tried to live up to the "equal" segment as well then it might succeed in keeping the races separated in its schools. (457–67)

The years 1947–50 marked a critical turning point for Hungerford. With declining boarding school enrollment and the impending loss of day students to newly constructed and materially "equalized" public schools, Hungerford's court-appointed Trustees concluded that the school needed a lifeline to survive. When negotiations to affiliate the school with the Presbyterian Church US fell through, Hungerford heir Constance Fenske and other prominent Friends of the Hungerford School persuaded the court-appointed Trustees to consider a last-minute proposal from Bethune Cookman College at Daytona. Under that plan, as presented to the board, Hungerford would become a preparatory school for the four-year college, but without any firm financial or administrative commitment. Ultimately, the Trustees concluded that Hungerford could not survive as a self-financed private boarding school and—with authorization from the supervising chancery court judge—voted to transfer the property to Orange County for use as a "Public School for Negroes." The school would retain the name Hungerford, in recognition of its origins as a private school and its historic place within the community ("Trustees Recommend Turning Hungerford into Public Negro High School" 1950). Efforts to block the sale, led by Hungerford heir Constance Fenske and Rollins College professor emeritus Edwin Osgood Grover, failed when the Florida Supreme Court ruled that the successor Trustees—"appointed by the Chancellor and under his supervision and control"—had authority to transfer the property (*Fenske vs. Coddington* 1952).[13]

In July 1953, less than a year before the Supreme Court's landmark *Brown v. Board of Education* ruling, the Orange County school board released architectural drawings for a new and enlarged "Hungerford School for Negroes" in Eatonville. "Plans call for construction of a combination auditorium-gymnasium, several additional classrooms and remodeling of existing buildings. It is estimated the project will cost about $315,000" ("New Hungerford School" 1953). For local white segregationists, the Hungerford school improvements represented a shrewd investment, serving as a bulwark against parental demands for the integration of previously all-white schools under an anticipated *Brown* ruling. "It will be a long time before we will have any change in Orange County, regardless of how the Supreme Court rules," local officials told *Orlando Sentinel* courthouse reporter Walter P. Jones in September 1954. "They believe this because they will tell you with pride that school facilities for Negroes in Orange County are just as good and modern as those for white children." The *Sentinel* reporter cited the recently modernized Hungerford School and "a new elementary school for Negroes" in Winter Park as prime examples of county-wide school equalization efforts that, officials hoped, would slow the push for school integration" (Jones 1954). Ironically, the transformation of Hungerford from a relatively small, privately funded day and boarding school to a taxpayer-funded public school, serving students throughout the region, only broadened and intensified the African American community's attachment to the campus as a cultural space that would prepare their children for free and equal citizenship in a desegregated, post-*Brown* society.

As a result of Orange County's foot dragging on court-ordered desegregation, Hungerford's student body remained all-Black from the time of the school's transfer to Orange County in 1952 until its closure as a public high school in 1967 and reopening as a desegregated technical-vocational school. Throughout that time and for decades beyond, Hungerford remained an educational touchstone for African Americans in Central Florida. Zora Neale Hurston highlighted this through her protest about the *Brown vs. Board of Education* desegregation decision. Hurston argued for a "race pride" that leaned heavily on her long-established advocacy for grassroots Black culture. In this consideration, the Black-centric community logic of the Hungerford School was central to what Hurston described as the "self-respect of my people" (Hurston 1955). Rejecting the idea that proximity to whites provided equality, Hurston's argument recognized a deeper division created by race that shaped political discourse. While Washington's grassroots constructionist view emphasized Black institutions imagined by Black people for Black people, the biracial activism of groups such as the National Association for the Advancement of Colored People (NAACP) advocated for legal protections under the law (Marcucci 18–19). While the former could not fundamentally protect Black people from anti-Black violence and destruction of public property central to Jim Crow segregation, the latter allowed anti-Black sentiment to mutate within the colonial system inherent antithetical to Black people.

Despite the challenge of white control, the Hungerford School continued to be associated with the Black vision of independence and freedom, largely due to its centrality to the narrative of Eatonville's history. The permanent closure of the Hungerford school complex in 2009 marked the beginning of a new phase of speculative imagining.

In the years after the closure, the Town of Eatonville and Orange County School System have clashed over the educational vision attached to the property. For many residents, the original deed restriction, which instructed that the land must be used to educate Black children, is the guiding principle for the property. This position celebrated the founders' legacy and the school's history within the community and the region. Yet, the wider white community has consistently resisted this vision. In 2016, The Town of Eatonville and the Orange County Public Schools entered into a settlement agreement that allowed the deed restriction on the land to be lifted. In 2019, Eatonville and the school district entered into a sale agreement that allowed the Hungerford property to be sold. Still, notably that agreement saddled Eatonville with having to repay the $1 million from the previous payment the county made related to the payment to the Robert Hungerford Chapel Trust to release the deed restrictions. In March 2023, the Association to Preserve Eatonville, with the help of the Southern Poverty Law Center, filed suit in Florida state court to ensure that the Hungerford property continues to be used for educational and related purposes that benefit the community (Southern Poverty Law Center).

While the ultimate resolution remains unknown, the return to focusing on education at the Hungerford School property highlights that the liberatory vision behind the founding of Eatonville continues to matter in the current political climate. Indeed, the persistence highlights how Afrofuturism engages with questions of how power can and should be understood as a tendency within the Black experience to seek freedom by creating alternative pathways within a colonial system. Those systems have often relied on creating space that supports Black knowledge and cultural production. As the residents of Eatonville advocate for a future that aligns the Hungerford property with their vision, they demonstrate how a long legacy of Black speculative practice continues to guide contemporary action.

Notes

1. Poor health forced Mary Clinton to leave Tuskegee before completing her degree.

2. "The board, on learning I was from Tuskegee, sent me and my wife, who is also a Tuskegee student, to Eatonville, Florida, which is a negro town with its mayor and city council all colored men." Russell C. Calhoun, "Negro Towns in the South," *Friends' Intelligencer* 58 (1902): 398.

3. A news item in the *Orange County* (Orlando, Fl.) *Reporter*, May 15, 1884, notes that E. C. Hungerford had made gifts of library books to "residents of the colored village at Maitland," which was incorporated three years later as Eatonville. "In response to the gift the colored young men have formed themselves into a library association, for the proper distribution and preservation of the books."

4. In later years, Hungerford School boosters told the story that Robert Hungerford died "of yellow fever contracted while caring for a negro patient." While the specific details of Robert Hungerford's death have not been fully verified, this particularly claim is not supported by evidence from contemporary news reports or will and probate records. For a version of this legend, see the *Robert Hungerford Vocational High School Bulletin #2*, ca. February–March 1935; Florida Vertical File, Hungerford, Rollins College Library.

5. The eight trustees are listed by name in the Orange County deed conveying the initial forty acres from Edward C. Hungerford to the Robert Hungerford Industrial School of Eatonville, dated April 20, 1899: R. C. Bedford, Warren Logan, Mary A. Thurston, J. E. Clark, S. M. Mosely, W. B. Lynch, S. E. Ives, R. C. Calhoun.

6. Early newspaper reports misidentified Bedford as "colored"; thanks to researcher Sarah Boye for catching this error and locating accurate biographical/census information via FamilySearch and other sources. For Washington's quote on Bedford, see Booker T. Washington, *Up from Slavery: An Autobiography* (New York: Doubleday, Page & Co., 1907), 157.

7. For a detailed description of Washington's visit, see Nathalie Lord, "At Home and Afield: Washington at the Hungerford School," *Southern Workman* 41 (1912): 387–88. Washington's death in 1915 marked the loss of a powerful patron and advocate. "Memorial Services to B. T. Washington; Memory of Booker T.

Washington Will Be Honored at Eatonville," *Orlando Evening Star*, December 11, 1915.

8. School letterhead from 1944 listed five court-appointed Trustees and a seventeen-member Bi-Racial Advisory Board; see John E. Hall, Hungerford Principal, to Miss Clara B. Adolfs, Assistant to the Dean of the Chapel at Rollins College, July 4, 1944, Hungerford School Vertical File, Rollins College Library Special Collections.

9. On the decision to transport "colored high school pupils" from Winter Park School District Number 4 to the Robert Hungerford School in Eatonville, see correspondence between Frederick H. Ward, Secretary, Winter Park School Board, and Judson B. Walker, Orange County Superintendent of Public Instruction, Aug. 3 and 18, 1936; Hungerford School Vertical File, Rollins College Library Special Collections.

10. For a breakdown of Hungerford Vocational High School Enrollment, ca. 1941–42, see Clyde W. Hall, *An African-American Growing Up on the West Side* of *Winter Park, Florida 1925–1942* (Savannah: Savannah State University Press, 2005): 96–97.

11. On the Bethune Cookman offer, see "Hungerford School Eyes Bethune College Alliance," *Orlando Sentinel*, February 19, 1950.

12. The authors thank researcher Casey Wolf for locating this and other articles related to equalization and desegregation in Central Florida.

13. For case files, see SC22,558, Series S49, Box 2235, Florida State Archives.

Works Cited

"A Chester Man's Generosity." 1895. *Hartford Courant*, May 3, 1895.

Anderson, James D. *The Education of Blacks in the South, 1860–1935*. Later Printing edition. Chapel Hill: University of North Carolina Press, 1988.

Anderson, Reynaldo. Interview of Dr. Reynaldo Anderson, Associate Professor of Communication at Harris-Stowe State University. Sound recording. January 1, 2020. Vincent Voice Library, Voices of the Black Imaginary, MSU Libraries. https://d.lib.msu.edu/vbi/2.

"A Negro School and Conference; Florida Institution Modeled After Tuskegee and Named for Dr. Robert Hungerford of Chester, Ct." *Springfield* (Mass.) *Republican*, March 3, 1910.

Brooks, Lonny Avi. "From Algorithms to Afro-Rithms in Afrofuturism." In *The Black Experience in Design: Identity, Expression & Reflection*, edited by Anne H. Berry et al., 324–41. New York: Simon and Schuster, 2022.

Calhoun, Russell C. "A Negro Community Builder." In *Tuskegee & Its People: Their Ideals and Achievements*, 317–37. New York: D. Appleton & Co., 1905.

Calhoun, Russell C. "Negro Towns in the South." *Friends' Intelligencer* 58 (1902): 398.

Cha-Jua, Sundiata Keita. *America's First Black Town: Brooklyn, Illinois, 1830–1915.* Urbana: University of Illinois Press, 2000.

"Colored School is Under New Management." *Orlando Sentinel*, May 30, 1923.

Dery, Mark, ed. "Black to the Future: Interviews with Samuel R. Delany, Greg Tate, and Tricia Rose." In *Flame Wars: The Discourse of Cyberculture*, edited by Mark Dery, 179–222. Durham: Duke University Press, 1994.

Du Bois, W. E. Burghardt. "Does the Negro Need Separate Schools?" *The Journal of Negro Education* 4, no. 3 (July 1935): 329, https://doi.org/10.2307/2291871.

Eshun, Kodwo. "Further Considerations of Afrofuturism." *CR: The New Centennial Review* 3, no. 2 (2003): 288. https://doi.org/10.1353/ncr.2003.0021.

Fenske v. Coddington 57 So. 2d 452 (Fla 1952).

Fourth Annual Report of the Robert Hungerford Industrial School, Eatonville, Florida (Near Maitland). Orlando: Sentinel Reporter Print, 1903.

Green, Hilary. *Educational Reconstruction: African American Schools in the Urban South, 1865–1890.* 1st ed. New York: Fordham University Press, 2016.

Hamilton, Kenneth M. *Booker T. Washington in American Memory.* Urbana: University of Illinois Press, 2017.

Hungerford School Vertical File. Rollins College Library Special Collections.

Hurston, Zora Neale. "Court Order Can't Make Race Mix" *Orlando Sentinel*, August 11, 1955, Main edition.

Jackson, David H. "Booker T. Washington's Tour of the Sunshine State, March 1912." *The Florida Historical Quarterly* 81, no. 3 (2003): 176.

Jones, Walter P. "County Policies Diminish Integration Problem," *Orlando Sentinel*, September 19, 1954.

Marcucci, Olivia. "Zora Neale Hurston and the Brown Debate: Race, Class, and the Progressive Empire." *The Journal of Negro Education* 86, no. 1 (2017): 18–19. https://doi.org/10.7709/jnegroeducation.86.1.0013.

McKittrick, Katherine and Clyde Adrian Woods. *Black Geographies and the Politics of Place.* Between the Lines; South End Press, 2007.

"Negro Industrial School; Branch of Booker Washington's Famous Tuskegee School to Be Established at Eatonville, Fla." *Morning News* (Savannah, Ga.), May 6, 1899.

Nelson, Alondra. "Afrofuturism: Past-Future Visions." *Color Lines*, January 2000, 34–37.

Nelson, Alondra. "Introduction: Future Texts." *Social Text* 20, no. 2 (2002): 1–15.

"New Hungerford School." *Orlando Morning Sentinel*, July 20, 1953.

"Principal Calhoun's Death; A Communication That Speaks for Itself." *Hartford Courant*, November 30, 1910.

Rollins College Hungerford School Committee Minutes and Reports, ca. 1932–1935. Rollins College Library Special Collections.

Southern Poverty Law Center. *A Timeline of Events in Eatonville, Florida.* Last modified November 18, 2022. Accessed July 9, 2023. https://www.splcenter.org/news/2022/11/18/timeline-events-eatonville-florida.

"Spirit of the Press." 1895. *Pensacola News,* July 20, 1895.

State Archives of Florida. *Case files, Jordan v. Landis [1937], p. 7.* Series 49, Box 1460, File Folder 11.769.

State Library and Archives of Florida. "Constitution of 1885." *Florida Memory.* Accessed November 19, 2017. https://www.floridamemory.com/items/show/189169.

Taylor, J. "Florida Land of the Freedman's Bureau." *Florida Historical Society.* April 15, 2015. https://myfloridahistory.org/date-in-history/august-25-1866/florida-land-freedmans-bureau.

The Crisis 24 (October 22, 1922): 278.

The Hungerford Co-Operator, September 1931.

Tomberlin, Joseph A. "Florida and the School Desegregation Issue, 1954–1959: A Summary View." *Journal of Negro Education* 43, no. 4 (1974): 457–67. https://doi.org/10.2307/2966704.

"Trustees Recommend Turning Hungerford into Public Negro High School." *Winter Park Topics,* March 24, 1950.

Urban, Wayne J., and Jennings L. Wagoner Jr. *American Education: A History.* Taylor & Francis Group, 2013. http://ebookcentral.proquest.com/lib/mich-state-ebooks/detail.action?docID=1344551.

Washington, Booker T. *The Negro in Business.* Chicago: Hertel, Jenkins, & Co., 1907.

Washington, Booker T. *Working with the Hands: Being a Sequel to "Up from Slavery," Covering the Author's Experiences in Industrial Training at Tuskegee.* Garden City, NY: Doubleday, Page & Co., 1904.

Chapter 2

The Civics of Suffering

The Black Freedom Movement, Social Darwinism, and the Politics of Public Health

Maxwell G. Burkey

In the United States, the global pandemic caused by the COVID-19 virus spurred contention over the nature of the public sphere in a democratic society. Beginning in March of 2020, a political culture anchored in quasi-mythic notions of heroic individualism and untrammeled freedom was confronted with renewed questions of responsibility, solidarity, and reciprocity. The biology of the virus, its ability to cause severe illness and death for everyone and in all communities, gave the COVID-19 pandemic the capacity to unsettle traditional answers to the most basic dilemmas of democratic citizenship: What are the interdependencies between citizens? What are the terms of the "social contract" that sustains the commonweal? What do we mean by "the public" and how does it facilitate the flourishing of all its citizens?

At the same time, as evidence COVID-19's disparate impact on some communities emerged, these questions became enmeshed in and complicated by existing political hierarchies and stratifications, especially those of race, class, and disability (Gooms et al.). If people of color were more likely to be harmed by the virus due to long-standing inequities in health insurance, shouldn't the public health response to the pandemic include policy measures aimed at universal health-care coverage? And should robust public health measures be cast as the latest chapter in America's struggle for civil rights and racial equality? If essential workers, particularly those in emergency services and in the food and agricultural industries, bore the brunt of the virus, shouldn't the pandemic usher in stronger workplace regulations from the Occupational Safety and Health Administration? And should a robust public health initiative include strengthening America's enfeebled New Deal labor protections, making it easier for workers to unionize and hold employers accountable for workplace safety? If people with disabilities, especially those with co-morbidities and the immunocompromised, are acutely vulnerable to the virus, does pandemic-informed public policy necessitate an expansive reimagining of the "reasonable accommodation" stipulation of the Americans with Disabilities Act? And is advancing public health a key plank in reckoning with the various ways ableism manifests in American society?

While the COVID-19 pandemic thrust unconventional questions of power and inequality into mainstream political discourse, it did so against the backdrop of a collective national trauma characterized by over a million American deaths and one of the worst per capita mortality rates in the world. This included millions more Americans forced to mourn from a distance, unable to provide bedside comfort to ailing loved ones. And it included the angst and anxiety of millions more who would develop a little understood condition called Long COVID (Finucane). Debates over public health measures such as social distancing, masking regulations, and vaccine mandates were not abstractions of a political philosophy seminar. Rather, such debates were touched by the pain of loss, and at times, the added pain of disregard and denial, as disinformation narratives about inflated COVID-19 deaths, and even the existence of the virus itself, took hold with significant numbers of Americans. Indeed, the pandemic transpired amid a global decline in liberal democracy, and the conversation that ensued about democracy's resilience, its capacity to meet public health challenges more effectively than authoritarian states, was in large part a conversation about the civic dimensions of human suffering; the capacity of citizens to acknowledge the suffering of the other as a meaningful claim on their agency; and the extent to which the tribalism of American politics might be mitigated by the widely shared experience of suffering.

This essay employs the COVID-19 pandemic as a point of departure, turning to the Black Freedom Movement to reframe debates about public health and American democracy. In centering the reality of suffering, and in lending suffering civic value as a meaningful form of political agency, this essay argues that the Black Freedom Movement cared for the public well-being and offers resources for remaking the politics of public health on fresh ideological terrain. Indeed, it is odd that the most thoroughgoing transformation of the public sphere in American life—that instigated by the Civil Rights Movement—has not been repurposed to illuminate the dilemmas of public health. Specifically, I argue that the ethic of willful suffering at the core of nonviolent resistance tactics employed by civil rights activists contests the commonplace construal of public health mitigation measures like social distancing and masking as tradeoffs with freedom. Rather, seen from the lens of the Black Freedom Movement, social distancing, masking, or vaccinating are examples of willful suffering, and are therefore public acts that nurture civic freedom.

This exploration of the Black Freedom Movement's reconfiguration of the public sphere contributes to two ongoing conversations relevant to political theorists and public health scholars. First, scholars of American politics have increasingly looked to social movements and resistance politics as intricate political texts and reservoirs of political meaning, putting democratizing movements into critical conversation with the classic concerns of canonical political theory (Pineda 2021; Zamalin 2017; Ferguson 2011). This project is especially important given the conservative and reactionary uses to which the memory of the mid-twentieth Civil Rights Movement has been put in the decades since the passage of the Civil Rights Act of 1964 and the Voting Rights Act of 1965. That apex of the Black Freedom Struggle has been employed as a disciplining tool to curtail contemporary iterations of racial justice agitation, such as the Black Lives Matter movement, by reducing the movement in popular memory to a moral crusade to end racial segregation, encapsulated by a few catchphrases of Martin Luther King Jr. (Dyson 2001). A key task for the political theorist, therefore, is to mine the movement for its rich meanings and critical lessons for contemporary liberal democracy. By repurposing the Black Freedom Movement's understanding of the public sphere to recast the politics of public health, this essay is one contribution to that project.

Second, scholars of American politics and political theory are positioned to add important registers of analysis to what many science journalists and members of the scientific community describe as an ongoing public health crisis and a perennial underinvestment in public health infrastructure. As scholars of political thought have long noted, public policy commitments presuppose understated ideological assumptions and ethical commitments. The challenge in relation to public health policy is twofold. On the one hand, the forces of disinformation, conspiracy theory, and other forms of post-truth propaganda, emanating largely from the political right and fueled by new forms of media, has undermined trust in scientific experts who convey public health information and seek to influence policy. On the other hand, as critics on the political left will point out, the medical and scientific establishments do not operate in a vacuum set apart from the structures of American political economy, and the incentives that reward public health practices conducive to market normalcy. Thus, the resources of political theory and American political thought can help public health scholars and officials navigate a fraught political climate, cultivate critical reflexivity, and intervene in the ideological landscape determinative of public health politics. This essay, by distilling the ethic of willful suffering from the Black Freedom Movement's attempt to both transform and care for the public, contributes to this timely project.

The first section of the essay examines the contours of public health discourse through the first few years of the COVID-19 pandemic, considering both its ideological character and the ways public health experts may have unwittingly contributed to a political discourse hostile to public health. The second section of the essay turns to the Black Freedom Movement, and specifically African American activist Bayard Rustin, whose work on "Journey of Reconciliation" in 1947 presaged the Freedom Rides of 1961, to recover notions of the public sphere, and care for the public, that are anchored in a reckoning with citizen suffering.

COVID-19 Pandemic, Public Health Discourse, and Social Darwinism

In March of 2020, as the COVID-19 pandemic took hold in the United States, the *New York Times* published a conversation between editorialist Thomas Friedman and the political philosopher Michael Sandel on the perils of the "common good" in America's "highly individualist society" (Friedman 2020). Sandel's reflections contained the kernel of reams of journalism to come lamenting America's enfeebled pandemic response, explaining that response with reference to historic features of American political culture, including social norms dominated by market rationality and a decades-long decline in social solidarity. The pandemic preyed precisely on Americans' most ingrained notions of freedom and capitalism: the idea that as individuals our fortunes and fates can be neatly compartmentalized from one another; that individuals pursuing self-interest accomplish the common good without paying governing institutions any heed; the idea that freedom is a good to be owned individually, or what the political theorist C. B. Macpherson called "possessive individualism" (Macpherson 1962). Against these entrenched ideological commitments, COVID-19 demonstrated American's actual and radical interdependencies, leaving commentators like Sandel, and public health experts like the White House's top medical advisor, Dr. Anthony Fauci, imploring citizens with feeble appeals to the "common good."

One of Sandel's remarks proved especially prescient and offers a lens through which to grapple with the politics of public health discourse in the COVID-19 era. Considering the calls of many, including President Donald Trump, to prioritize the return to economic "normalcy" early in the pandemic, Sandel commented, "The strategy of contending with the pandemic by allowing the virus to run its course as quickly as possible in hopes of hastening 'herd immunity' is a callous approach reminiscent of social Darwinism—the idea of the survival of the fittest. It allows the contagion to spike, intensive care units to be overrun, the most vulnerable to die, but with the goal of jump-starting the economy sooner rather than later" (Friedman 2020). Sandel could have gone further. Not so much rediscovered amid the pandemic, social Darwinism has always been nestled within American individualism. The basic features and rhetorical gestures of social Darwinism, even if not named as such, are interwoven with kitschy and easily digestible appeals to freedom and productivity. Social Darwinism was the primary political response to the pandemic, governing public discourse about health not only from the likes of President Trump and others invested in distorting or denying the science of the virus but also, in significant ways, from the public health industry.

When Richard Hofstadter published his seminal study *Social Darwinism in American Thought* in 1944, on the heels of the New Deal era, he emphasized the appropriation of Darwinist ideas by conservatives who opposed progressive reforms, including some of the first public health measures in American history (Hofstadter 1955). "The most popular catchwords of Darwinism," Hofstadter wrote, "'struggle for existence' and 'survival of the fittest,' when applied to the life of man in society, suggested that nature would provide that the best competitors in a competitive situation would win, and that this process would lead to continuing improvement. In itself this was not a new idea . . . but it did give the force of a natural law to the idea of competitive struggle" (6). In this way, the emergence of social Darwinism following the publication of Charles Darwin's *Origins of Species* (1859) merely weaponized long-standing American ideals of liberty, private property, capitalist enterprise, and industrious work ethic, but in a fashion that extolled unerring struggle and legitimized persistent human suffering as hallmarks of progress. In doing so, social Darwinism evacuates citizenship of political meaning, undermining the core of what political theorists have classically meant to convey by the term "public sphere": a social space marked by the shared condition of citizenship and the relative equality of its members.

While Hofstadter contended in the 1940s that the reign of social Darwinism over the American imagination was a discrete political fever that New Deal reforms had helped to break, scholarship on American political economy over recent decades has reckoned with its reemergence, if by a different name: neoliberalism (Brown 2019). A neologism for postindustrial capitalism, neoliberalism is itself a revanchist, neo-social Darwinism, cast in the empowering terms of entrepreneurism, self-ownership, free agency, and personal responsibility, and shorn of the racist history of American eugenics that was closely associated with social Darwinist appeals to "progress" and the "survival of the fittest" in the late nineteenth and early twentieth centuries (Deggler 1991; Black 2003). In this respect, the racial politics of the classic period of social Darwinism that Hofstadter chronicled and the contemporary era of postindustrial, neoliberal capitalism are different: what scholars refer to as a neoliberal political economy—in the United States, beginning in the 1980s and extending through the present, characterized the privatization of public services, the deregulation of capital, and attacks on organized labor—has accommodated formal, or de jure racial equality. This is a key pillar of neoliberalism's, or more properly, the new social Darwinism's legitimacy: it presents as a post–civil rights politics, consistent with racial equality and the historic legacy of the Black Freedom Movement.

While the surface racial politics of classic social Darwinism and today's neoliberal instantiation differ, connective tissue is found in a corrosive orientation toward everything public and thereby democracy itself. "Democracy" derives from the two ancient Greek terms: *demos*, meaning the people, and *kratos*, meaning power. Classically, "people power" entailed the cultivation of a public sphere, characterized by political equality between citizens. In the history of democratic thought, the public sphere has been conceived of as an institutional space and an ethos through which citizens engage one another as political equals, tending to the commonweal, without which democracy loses meaning—no commonweal, no people power. As such, the work of democratic citizens amid the public sphere is distinct from that of private individuals, consumers, or producers. In this respect, democracy requires the insulation of society and citizens from capitalist market dynamics: for the public sphere to be meaningful, political equality must be made real, and this stipulation of equality necessitates the mitigation of various forms of stratification and suffering that create relationships of domination supplanting citizenship, such as those associated with race, class, gender, and disability (Brown 2019, 24–53).

Social Darwinism erodes democracy by evacuating the public of meaning, substituting competitor-consumers for citizens. The "public sphere" no longer requires tending, and Sandel's appeal to the "common good" rings hollow because social Darwinism has replaced democracy's "commonweal" with an insidious notion of social progress. Of course, only the "fit" will enjoy this progress, but those who survive the rigors of competition and struggle do stand to gain, unimpeded by the other-regarding constraints of the commonweal. As Hofstadter put it, "Whatever the immediate hardships for a large portion of mankind, evolution meant progress and thus assured that the whole process of life was tending toward some very remote but altogether glorious consummation" (Hofstadter 1955, 7). Thus, social Darwinism offers society without the social, progress without a public, collective good; only those deserving survivors benefit, absent any care for the collective. As the political theorist Wendy Brown writes of social Darwinism's neoliberal cousin, "A fully realized neo-liberal citizenry would be the opposite of public-minded, indeed it would barely exist as a public. The body politic ceases to be a body but is, rather, a group of individual entrepreneurs and consumers" (Brown 2003, 15).

An important ideological current stemming from social Darwinism's dismantling of the public sphere is a discourse of freedom that accommodates the experience of human suffering. Rather than issuing in an emancipatory politics, or buttressing the institutional infrastructure of liberal democracy, freedom here cohabitates with cruelty, or at least is unable to issue any clear denunciation of cruelty. Freedom is a quasi-religious call to individual suffering. Some will suffer more than others, of course. Ingenuity and hard work will mete out the suffering appropriately. Some suffering will be redeemed as success and merit, while other suffering will go unredeemed, thinning the herd of the unfit, the unindustrious, the nonentrepreneurial. The invariability of suffering is as self-evident as God's green earth; suffering is demanded by nature, and freedom is merely the fortitude to face suffering squarely, to persist amid suffering, to suffer on one's own terms. This last point is worth emphasizing: freedom demands suffering, but like freedom in the absence of a public, suffering is always experienced individually and never shared.

In characterizing this thread in the work of William Graham Sumner, a leading light of social Darwinist thought, Hofstadter writes:

> Sumner, and no doubt after him all those who at one time or another were impressed by his views, were much concerned to face up to the hardness of life, to the impossibility of finding any easy solutions for human ills, to the necessity of labor and self-denial and the inevitability of suffering. Theirs is a kind of naturalistic Calvinism in which man's relation to nature is as hard and demanding as man's relation to God under the Calvinistic system. (Hofstadter 1955, 10)

Within this social Darwinist lens, public health policy is reduced to arbitrary power, a usurpation of freedom, a negation of the natural order. But more than this. Now "public health" is its own social disease, parasitic on the natural "strength" of the national economy. The virile metaphors mobilized by political leaders and the news media in response to COVID-19 familiarized Americans with the tenets of pandemic social Darwinism, disfiguring public health via the nationalist frame of war and peace, where the "political realism" of the "survival of fittest" in an anarchical world of nation-states with no common sovereign power to adjudicate disputes has long held sway. As *Atlantic* journalist Ed Yong brilliantly reported, American political discourse cast COVID-19 as a test of strength, a zero-sum "battle," a waging of "war" to defeat the novel pathogen (Yong 2020). President Trump was especially invested in these metaphors, celebrating his own "defeat" of the virus, and through persistent refusals to wear a mask in accordance with public health guidance, encouraging his supporters to submit to the "warrior" logic whereby donning a mask is a sign of weakness, an indication of lagging mettle. The Fox News host Greg Gutfeld unwittingly captured the social Darwinist frenzy on the right in referring to President Trump's own bout with COVID-19: "He didn't want America to hide from the virus. He was going to do the same thing; he was going to walk out there on that battlefield with you" (Garber 2020).

Freedom loses the political meaning that weds it to liberal democracy and shared citizenship, becoming in warfare metaphors a demonstration of individual virility, and more quotidianly, the freedom to choose a survival strategy. Much of the pandemic's politics, particularly in the conservative movement that most explicitly attacked public health measures, configured individualism as survivalism. "Medical Freedom" bills made their way through Republican state legislatures, signed into law by Republican governors, weakening public health tools like mandatory masking, vaccination requirements, and travel quarantines. All told, thirty states passed legislation in the three years following the start of the pandemic that restricted public health powers, including the ability of state public health officials to close restaurants or suspend schools. Without exception this legislation was presented as choice and freedom enhancing for individuals or for parents (Weber and Achenbach 2023). Governor Kristi Noem of South Dakota, for example, in responding to criticism of her hardline position against all public health measures, said that liberals and the left were "accusing us of embracing death when we're just allowing people to make personal choices" (Goldmacher 2021). The courts followed suit, hearing over a thousand cases related to public health law in the few years following the pandemic's emergence. Supreme Court Justice Samuel Alito spoke for conservatives on the federal judiciary, many of them recently appointed by President Trump, in telling a meeting of the Federalist Society that COVID-19 public health initiatives had "resulted in previously unimaginable restrictions on individual liberty." Conservative activists held rallies with signs reading FREEDOM NOT FORCE and JAB FIGHT FOR FREEDOM opposing vaccine mandates (Goldmacher 2021). And parents, some mobilized by the newfound conservative organization Moms for Liberty, opposed mask requirements in schools, wearing t-shirts proclaiming, WE DO NOT CO-PARENT WITH THE GOVERNMENT (Craig 2021).

To those who lived through the pandemic, and care about the integrity of public health, this story of the post-Trump conservative movement's marshalling of warlike metaphors and discourses of freedom to thwart sensible COVID-19 protocols, and therefore treat the resulting human suffering as a personal choice—or as fate, for which there is no alternative—is surely all too familiar. It would be a mistake, however, to complete an analysis of the perils of public health in American politics here. This is partly because social Darwinism is so suffused in the American common sense that many Americans hardly recognize it as political position at all, consuming its COVID-19 iteration through ostensibly apolitical cultural arenas like film and sports. National Football League (NFL) quarterback Kirk Cousins echoed the warfare metaphors, for example, conveying that he was unconcerned by COVID-19 because it was merely "the survival of the fittest," and therefore he presumably had little to fear; then his colleague Aaron Rodgers refused the COVID-19 vaccine, citing a personal health regime and the cause of freedom. Both athletes, while insisting on their political neutrality, nevertheless demonstrated the pervasive political nexus between strength, freedom, and survival in the American subconscious, one which NFL football crystalizes, cohering commercialized notions of American national identity, patriotism, militarism, and brute physicality (Reed 2020; Dedaj 2021). Indeed, social Darwinism is as American as football on Sunday.

The most striking examples of the pervasiveness of social Darwinism in American political discourse, and for our purposes in conversation with the Black Freedom Movement, the most illuminating come from the ranks of public health officials themselves, precisely the public figures one would least expect to countenance the social Darwinist frame and ones whose efforts as public health practitioners are directly invested in subverting that frame, which negates recognition of the public itself. The pandemic presented a particular challenge for public health practitioners: the public health official as civic educator. Explaining the science of the virus, and the technical dimensions of preventing transmission, was not the whole of the public health practitioner's task. As important as conveying these details were, and the difficulty of continually confronting COVID-19 misinformation notwithstanding, the scientific profile of the virus could not tell Americans why they should care or what they owed to one another. The public health practitioner held an irreducibly political office, wielding a certain power over American political discourse, holding what amounted to a lecture on citizenship on the nightly news for the duration of the pandemic, unpacking the nature of the *public*, reaching, whether consciously or not, for concepts like complicity, interdependence, and solidarity to ground public health imperatives in civic agency. Given COVID-19's staggering death toll, and the magnitude of the human loss, with one in three Americans having lost a family member or friend, public health practitioners often drew upon the experience of suffering to make sense of their civic charge.

This narrative of suffering is one way to see how public health discourse accommodated social Darwinism. Dr. Anthony Fauci, the de facto figurehead of public health throughout the COVID-19 pandemic as the director of National Institute of Allergy and Infectious Diseases and chief medical advisor to Presidents Trump and Biden, offers a case study. No matter how politically noncommittal Fauci wished to cast himself and public health more broadly, he was invariably made to meet the charges of a political culture informed by social Darwinism. This took a variety of forms but was most explicit in the case of the Republican Governor of Florida Ron DeSantis's use of Fauci to advance a conservative political agenda that paid little heed to public health, invoking the term "Fauci-ism" to suggest an association with fascism, proclaiming that Florida had "chose freedom over Fauci-ism" (Shapero 2023). The DeSantis freedom agenda didn't need to be fleshed out in any detail; it was successfully popularized in Florida and elsewhere by trading in the deeply internalized social Darwinist sensibilities about strength, freedom, and survival charted above; Fauci and the public health industry merely served as convenient bogeymen, as labor organizers, antiwar dissenters, socialists, communists, and civil rights activists had in other eras.

Social Darwinism, however, is not advanced by appeals to a vacuous notion of freedom stripped down to a choice of individual survival strategies alone. As Hofstadter's study of the high priest of classic social Darwinism, William Graham Sumner, suggests, social Darwinism is also an orientation to human suffering. It says that suffering is an enduring feature of the human condition; all attempts to quell suffering are inherently misguided, stymying the social progress that results from winnowing the weak; and suffering is a wholly private affair, an individual experience, meted out according to merit or nature. Appeals to suffering were common in Fauci's attempt to explain the rationale of public health. Early on, in May of 2020, Fauci testified before a Senate health committee. Without contesting the goal of returning to normalcy, Fauci told Americans that returning to normalcy too soon would cause "needless suffering and death" (Stolberg 2020). And three years into the pandemic, in reflecting on his role, and the range of criticism he confronted, Fauci drew upon the physician's mission to avert human suffering:

> I'm a physician. That's my identity. I've taken care of thousands of patients in one period of my life during the early years of H.I.V. I believe that I have seen as much or more suffering and death as anybody has in most careers. I don't mean to seem preachy, but I don't want to see people suffer and I don't want to see people die. (Wallace-Wells 2023)

Fauci draws from social Darwinism by privatizing human suffering. In explaining public health, he appeals to a professional rather than civic identity: the physician works to alleviate suffering, not the citizen. Public health is cast as the labor of professional physicians and medical technicians, who work to prevent the suffering of individuals in their care. In casting the responsibility for confronting suffering in the terms of professional ethics, Fauci inadvertently moralizes suffering, stripping it of political meaning and of its ability to summon collective action. As long as the alleviation of suffering remains encased by professional ethics, health is not a matter of the commonweal—it is not public. Fauci reiterated this point, reflecting on the tumultuous politics of the pandemic and the ways in which COVID-19 mitigation became imbricated in broader "culture wars" and preexisting political fault lines. "But I do know that the culture wars have been really, really tough from a public-health standpoint," Fauci said,

> ultimately an epidemiologist sees it as an epidemiological phenomenon. An economist sees it from an economic stand-point. And I see it from somebody in bed dying. And that's the reason it just bothers me a lot—maybe more so than some others—that because of the culture wars you're talking about, there are people who are not going to make use of an inter-vention that could have saved their lives. (Wallace-Wells 2023)

Here Fauci further privatizes suffering, locating suffering within a scheme of professional specializations, legitimizing medicalized and economistic lenses on public health, which tend to interpret COVID-19 in terms of individual medical risk assessment and economic productivity respectively. Fauci's mistake here was to cast the "culture wars" as a dis-traction from public health and the project of reducing suffering, rather than recognizing the stakes public health has in those "culture wars," rather than making an intervention into the "culture wars," and rather than offering suffering as a shared political condition or a reading of what makes our lives irreducibly public. "Culture war" is the way democratic societies mete out the norms, sensibilities, and identities that give mean-ing to the institutional frameworks of liberal democracy; "culture war" is the name we give to ongoing contestation in the public sphere; public health is *an argument about democratic culture*, not merely a professional practice akin to that of the epidemiologist or economist and not a moral campaign of the good-willed to alleviate suffering. The price Fauci and other public health spokespersons paid for political agnosticism was to leave intact the bedrock social Darwinist tenets that strike at the core of public health's raison d'être, reducing public health practice to the dissemination of individual survival strategies, or as the Centers for Disease Control (CDC) director Rochelle Walensky said of the CDC's ongoing public health work during COVID-19 pandemic: "We at the CDC will continue to be vigilant to get the message out of all the things that people can do to protect themselves" (Park 2023).

The dissemination of individual risk management information is a notion of public health consistent with the structure and ethos of American capitalism. But it is a long way from Fauci's physician's ethic of concern for suffering. It is even further from an understanding of public health that one senses Fauci gesturing toward, though he lacked the political language or the will to fully flesh out: public health as a collective reckoning with the nature and distribution of suffering in American society; public health as the willingness to share in the suffering of others as a measure of common citizenship; and public health as action exercised in solidarity with suffering citizens. Enter the Black Freedom Movement, and its care for the commonweal.

The Black Freedom Movement, Care for the Public, and Civic Freedom

On first blush, the Black Freedom Movement and public health would seem to harbor conflicting imperatives. After all, wasn't the aim of the civil rights movement to contest public authority, specifically that of the Jim Crow state? By contrast, isn't the aim of the public health establishment amid a pandemic to instill trust in public authority and the state? Isn't the lesson of the Civil Rights Movement the import of a disobedient politics to democracy, practiced in the form of sit-ins, strikes, and other deliberate violations of "law and order"? Conversely, doesn't public health do its work by building consensus, getting citizens to invest in the existing political order—its institutions, regulations, and authorities? If so, shouldn't we accept that the Black Freedom Movement offers an antistatist logic of political action that, however laudable in dislodging American racial apartheid, is nonetheless counterproductive to an enterprise premised on the credibility of the state "following the science" in a neutral manner? Must we conclude that political dissent and the "creation of tension" that

Martin Luther King Jr. heralded in his "Letter from a Birmingham Jail" threaten to hobble public health (King 2005, 330)?

This line of questioning stems from a narrow reading of the civil rights movement, one that simplifies its political meaning and distorts its contemporary lessons. On this conventional story, the Black Freedom Movement is prized for its tactical ingenuities, specifically the use of nonviolent direct action to resist racist state practices and its success in forcing the federal government to commit to a modicum of racial equality. What makes this a restrictive reading is inattention to the political *process* and *ideology* that underlay nonviolent direct action, which civil rights activists regularly insisted was not reducible to tactics or strategy and not aimed solely at reform of the state. From a tactical lens, the above questions pitting the movement's relationship to public authority against that advocated by public health appear to make sense. Indeed, the tactical reading of nonviolent direct action has given way to a variety of reactionary deployments of the movement's legacy. It is worth noting that among those deployments is the claim by antivaccine activists to inheritance the of the civil rights mantle, comparing their movement to that of African Americans in the 1960s, inveighing against the "segregation" of individuals by vaccine status, and calling themselves "Freedom Keepers" (Mays 2019). Likewise, advocates of school choice have made explicit use of the Black Freedom Movement, likening their cause to a contemporary civil rights struggle even as charter schools compete against public schools, and grounding their activism, much like the case of COVID-19 antimask mandates, in the discourse of parental freedom and choice (Ravitch 2018). Other often vague gestures to the legacy of civil rights freedom fighters have been rife in the anti–public health movement in the COVID-19 era. These are the latest in a long line of post–civil rights era conservative reframings of the Black Freedom Movement that purport color-blind individualism, not a democratized public sphere, as the movement's lasting upshot (Dyson 2000).

In all these invocations the movement is construed as consistent with social Darwinism's emptying out of the public sphere. The movement didn't resist white supremacy and challenge the pillars of American nationhood, it allowed for Black individualism; the movement didn't transform American democracy and the terms of equal citizenship, it facilitated fair competition between individuals, making way for a meritocracy of the industrious. And movement activists like Martin Luther King Jr. are heroes worthy of emulation not in light of their political thought or the civic ethics they enacted but because of their personal virtues—the strength of character they demonstrated in pursuing their cause; indeed, in many of these uses the movement's enactment of Black Freedom is reduced to a kind of Black survivalism, severed from institutional or ideological change.

Many will sense something intuitively wrongheaded about this reading of the Black Freedom Movement. While scholars of African American political thought and social movements having studied the ways racial justice movements have been appropriated to legitimate conservative politics, scholars and activists in the public health arena may not immediately notice the stakes of this development. Given the seismic place the story of the civil rights movement now holds in the American imagination, these co-options should concern those who care about public health, particularly if one of the most successful attempts to remake the contours of American public life is repurposed in ways that make that public invisible. Thus, scholars and advocates of public health may need to tell a different story about the Black Freedom Movement. Because that movement is a crucial contested terrain in American politics, with the power to lend contemporary political projects a special urgency, what we say it was contributes to what we're able to say public health is now.

Answering this challenge requires discerning how the nonviolent direct action at the core of the movement engaged in a continuous process of generating new publics and thereby reimagined the public itself. The kernel of nonviolent direction is the civics of willful suffering, and it tells an alternative story of emergent publics fashioned by civil rights activism. The movement's understanding of suffering strikes at the heart of social Darwinism, which as we have seen, depends on a particular and privatized notion of human suffering. This dimension of the movement matters for how we talk about public health because it can illuminate the ideological pitfalls public health officials fell into during the COVID-19 pandemic and offers a fresh framework for conveying the centrality of public health to American democracy.[1]

The civil rights leader Bayard Rustin is an ideal figure to explore in this context because he did more than anyone to anchor the movement in nonviolent direct action. Rustin advanced this project in conjunction with the seminal civil rights organizations Fellowship of Reconciliation (FOR) and Congress for Racial Equality (CORE) in the 1940s, as well as in the role of advisor to Martin Luther King Jr. during the Montgomery Bus Boycott of 1956, and as the central organizer of the March on Washington in 1963. Though Rustin is most remembered as a master strategist of civil rights protest, his interest in nonviolent direct action exceeded questions of movement tactics and the immediacy of political pressures. For Rustin, nonviolent direct action, or what he termed the "performance of little actions" (D'Emilio 2003, 55), was a vector for redrawing the relationships between citizens. The willful suffering invariably embedded in those little actions was a manner of caring for the commonweal. Indeed, Rustin thought of democratic citizenship as operative on the smallest of scales, and if he had lived through the COVID-19 pandemic, he might have encouraged us to think of social distancing, masking, or vaccinating as the "performance of little actions," each a tiny bit of willful suffering, each action evidence of a freedom consistent with care for that commonality we call citizenship.

Rustin was central in bringing the teachings of Mahatma Gandhi, leader of the Indian resistance movement against British colonial rule, to the American left (D'Emilio 2003, 2). For Gandhi, political resistance necessitated a spiritual ethos and discipline grounded in conscious suffering (Gandhi 2006). Rustin began advancing the Gandhian project with FOR in the early 1940s and with CORE later that decade through what each organization called interracial workshops or institutes (Mollin 2004, 120; Catsam 2009). Such interracial institutes didn't just aim to educate, they also enacted nonviolence (Wolcott 2018, 41). Over the course of a long weekend, institute participants would discuss the history of race and the ideological pillars of nonviolence before devising "action projects" to challenge racial segregation. FOR and CORE held roughly ten such institutes each year from 1943 through 1955, mobilizing a critical mass of civil rights activists with experience in direct action (Wolcott 2018, 42). One participant in a FOR nonviolent workshop called it "a magnificent laboratory of action," echoing Rustin's "performance of little actions" framing of nonviolent citizenship (Wolcott 2018, 43).

At one 1947 institute in Toledo, Ohio, Rustin and his fellow CORE organizer George Houser went out to dinner and were refused service as an interracial party. They immediately phoned the week's institute participants, spearheading an impromptu sit-in, succeeding in desegregating the restaurant (Wolcott 2018, 43). Rustin not only ran these workshops in willful suffering, he also produced literature for civil rights neophytes on what to expect and how to negotiate the fraught dilemmas nonviolence spurred from reactionary onlookers and police authorities. Indeed, CORE activists were regularly attacked, burned, kicked, and otherwise physically brutalized during sit-ins, picket lines, and freedom rides (Wolcott 2018, 47). For Rustin, the embodied nature of political life that implicated the dissenter in suffering was part and parcel of the African American experience, the lesson Black politics presented to American democracy. In a 1942 essay, entitled "The Negro and Nonviolence," Rustin wrote,

> Nonviolence as a method has within it the demand for terrible sacrifice and long suffering, but, as Gandhi has said, 'freedom does not drop from the sky.' One has to struggle and be willing to die for it . . . Certainly the Negro possesses qualities essential for nonviolent direct action. He has long since learned to endure suffering . . . He has produced, and still sings, such songs as 'It's Me, Oh Lord, Standin' in Need of Prayer' and 'Nobody Knows the Trouble I've Seen.' He follows this last tragic phrase by a salute to God—'Oh! Glory, Hallelujah.' (Rustin 2003, 9)

Around this time Rustin began preparing for what would become known as the Journey of Reconciliation, led by FOR and CORE in 1947 (Peck 1962). It was a prescient precursor to the more well-known Freedom Rides organized by CORE in the spring of 1961 that resulted in firebombed buses and federal police escorts. The journey was designed to test the nation's political will in enforcing the Supreme Court's decision in *Morgan v. Virginia* (1946) banning racial segregation in interstate travel. In consciously choosing the name Congress *of* Racial Equality, rather than Congress *for* Racial Equality, Rustin and his CORE comrades anchored their work in an approach public action with American antecedents in Quakerism, abolitionism, and the Social Gospel movement: to act *as if* racial justice already existed as a way of undermining the legitimacy of Jim Crow segregation (Tracy 1996, 29). Rustin reflected on an early iteration of this approach to nonviolent direct action, recounting a time when he was asked to remove himself from a segregated section of a bus and declined:

> 'I believe that I have a right to sit here,' I said quietly. 'If I sit in the back of the bus I am depriving that child—' I pointed to a little white child of five or six—'of the knowledge that there is injustice here, which I believe it is his right to know' . . . By this time they were impatient and angry. As I would not move, they began to beat me about the head and shoulders, and I shortly found myself knocked to the floor. Then they dragged me out of the bus and continued to beat me. (Rustin 2003, 3)

While this incident tested Rustin's individual willingness to suffer, it had not yet pushed him to wrestle with political dimensions of suffering as it takes shape in collective action, with shared suffering as a civic ethic and a manner of caring for the public. This realization was the result of CORE's Journey of Reconciliation, officially launched in 1947, travelling through segregated Virginia, North Carolina, Tennessee, and Kentucky. In Chapel Hill, North Carolina, CORE activists were arrested, one was beaten, and the group was chased out of town by white vigilantes, narrowly escaping (Podair 2009, 27–28). Rustin knew that while the journey's nonviolent campaign would move on, vigilantes and police in Chapel Hill were sure to double-down on the racial caste system, and that African Americans, as well as others perceived as sympathetic to their cause, would be left to suffer the consequences. "When we went into the buses of the South," Rustin wrote in retrospect,

> we knew that there would be some violent reactions brought to the surface . . . We also had to accept violence unto ourselves. But unless we were naïve, we also knew that the lynch mob at Chapel Hill . . . might very well wreak its vengeance upon other Negroes in the community. And the fact is that they responded with violence not only to Negro members of the community but [also] to white ones . . . You cannot take a stance for truth and justice without automatically involving other people, and causing some suffering. (Rustin quoted in Anderson 1997, 120)

We can now appreciate the ways the Black Freedom Movement tended to the public and the lessons it may hold for the politics of public health. As Rustin biographer John D'Emilio notes, implicit in the Gandhian approach to conscious suffering is the stipulation that democratic citizens tend to more than the normal business of life (D'Emilio 2003, 2). Rustin's model of the "performance of little actions," and the nonviolent institutes and seminars of FOR and CORE, drew citizens out of the routinized, dehumanizing motions of economic and social normalcy. What made this defamiliarization of normalcy potent was that it was not an abstract or intellectual exercise. Rather, nonviolent direct action rewired the calisthenics of the public, the way we employed our bodies. As Rustin put it, "To me the real question is: If not now, when do men of concern act with their whole body?" (Rustin 2012, 129). In other words, the Black Freedom Movement couldn't simply *administer* its notions of multiracial democracy to the existing public, and it couldn't merely *advocate* multiracial democracy to the public, for the structures of white nationhood made the existent public impervious to the claims of multiracial democracy. Instead, the movement had to *generate* new, racially egalitarian publics, even if fragile and transient ones, to deconstruct the normalcy of a racial caste system.

In response to COVID-19, public health reinscribed normalcy as the ideal configuration of the public, immediately introducing pandemic mitigation measures as waystations to the resumption of normal, neglecting the primary transformative power in a democracy: that of enacting a new public (Castillejo 2020). Public health lacked an articulation of the public. As the Black Freedom Movement understood, the public sphere is always in a process of construction and contestation, vulnerable to the "performance of little actions." Thus, to invoke normalcy is to surrender agency. By explicitly making "return to normal" the endgame, mitigation measures were implicitly presented as burdens on choice and freedom, to be tolerated for a time, rather than actions aimed at the realization of democratic citizenship. When "normalcy" didn't return quick enough, or when promised, as was the case with reinstated mask mandates and breakthrough infections in vaccinated individuals, public health professionals were caught in a transactional relationship to the public that left undisturbed the default settings of social Darwinism.

If the Black Freedom Movement strengthened American democracy in the twentieth century through an expansive project of public action, public health professionals and activists are likely to have an outsized role in that project in the twenty-first century (Levy and Sidel 2013; Evans 2022; Rouse 2009). Nevertheless, even those public health practitioners who readily recognize the inherently political dimensions of their work may be reticent to anchor public health in the experience of human suffering. After all, isn't suffering, as Dr. Fauci conveyed, something to be shunned—and shouldn't public health work to stamp it out? If so, how is it that suffering can be framed as a public good? As President Joe Biden noted in addressing the nation on the first anniversary of COVID-19, suffering is associated with pain and loss: "While it was different for everyone, we all lost something. A collective suffering. A collective sacrifice. A year filled with the loss of life—the loss of living for all of us," Biden said (Biden 2021). What does the Black Freedom Movement have to say to Fauci and Biden, each of whom framed their respective pandemic leadership roles in relationship to suffering? Why is Rustin right that suffering and democratic citizenship congeal together?

Answering these questions requires recalling that the *public* health we invoke today is a *modern* project, its "public" inextricable from the dilemmas and paradoxes of public life generated by modern and Enlightenment political thought (Amato 1990; Amato 2001; Wilkinson and Kleinman 2016; Gatta 2015). The modern polity's preoccupation with suffering can be seen in its earliest theorist, Thomas Hobbes, whose *Leviathan* develops an elaborate social contract theory to inaugurate legitimate state power, replacing a cruel and violent "state of nature" where human life is "solitary, poore, nasty, brutish, and short" (Hobbes 1985, 186). But modernity is also founded on a second insight on suffering that locates suffering not in nature, and therefore redressed though politics, but in man-made, modern institutions, and therefore produced by politics. "Man is born free, and everywhere he is in chains," Rousseau writes in *On the Social Contract*, the first thinker to wrestle with the concepts of "general will," "the people," and the public that undergird modern, mass democracy (Rousseau 1987, 141). Both Hobbes and Rousseau separate modernity from religious and particularly Christian formulations holding that human suffering is the work of God, and possibly a pathway to otherworldly redemption, or otherwise natural, and thus an inevitable of feature of humanity's fallen condition (Halpern 2002; Amato 1990).

But there is a paradox here, Hobbes and Rousseau are not of a piece on suffering—suffering inheres a dualism in modern politics: on the one hand, modern politics is premised on universal rights to life, liberty, and happiness, and seeks to vanquish the suffering standing in the way of universal happiness; on the other hand, modern politics is premised on peoplehood, popular sovereignty, and nationhood, and generates its own violent exclusions and arbitrary powers, producing new forms of suffering along the way.

African American political thought has always confronted this paradox of modern suffering, and the resistance movements of the Black Freedom tradition have exploited it to advance multiracial democracy (Bromell 2013; Gooding-Williams 2009). If it was not naturalized by racist tropes related to the ability of African Americans to endure pain, for example, serving to legitimate slavery and other forms of racial oppression, Black suffering was treated as an object of pity and compassion, fodder for private philanthropy or religious good works (Spelman 1997, 7; Yancy

2015). In other words, it is not just that modernity's promise to vanquish suffering is unfinished and evades old and new forms stratification that generate suffering, like those of race, class, ability, ecology, and so on. It is also that when confronted with this persistent suffering, modern politics has often responded by relocating suffering outside the purview of the public, and thereby narrowing the scope of universal rights and happiness.

To disavow suffering would be to make the original modern mistake of purporting universal equality while neglecting the power analysis that makes a mockery of that universality. To privatize suffering, however, is a subtler and more common move, as simple as locating suffering under the professional purview of the physician. Rustin's answer to the modern paradox of suffering bears the hallmarks of the Black Freedom tradition, offering an alternative path: democratize suffering; bring suffering under the umbrella of political deliberation and agency; practice citizenship as the sharing of suffering. Moreover, Rustin's answer weaves together citizenship as suffering and citizenship as freedom in the practice of nonviolent direct action, offering public health a participatory dimension, a call to collective action, and a way of contesting the discourses of freedom that often undermine it (Foner 1998). This is particularly important given that many histories, textbooks, and primers in public health uncritically reproduce the dichotomy between public health and freedom, echoing rather than intervening in American political discourse by framing that relationship as one of zero sum tradeoffs, or otherwise evading the issue altogether (Rosen 2015, 70–73; Duffy 1990, 3; Patel and Rushefsky 2005, 8; Fee 1994, 269–71; Turnock 2009, 16–17; Tulchiinsky and Varavikova 2014, 34–35; Schneider 2017, 18–20). Thus, the language of freedom generated by America's democratizing movements has much to offer public health.

As the COVID-19 pandemic wore on commitments to public health waned. Vulnerable communities were "forced to count of the rest of society to respond with empathy" and lament that "this should not be the survival of the fittest" (Kohli 2022). In the spring of 2022 a group of public health excerpts, activists, and educators calling themselves The People's C.D.C. released a manifesto critiquing a premature return to "normalcy" and "ineffectual public health policies based on individualistic approaches," summoning the "collective power" of a democratic public to redress pandemic disparities (Reed 2022; Green 2022). The manifesto didn't mention social Darwinism or the Black Freedom Movement, but it could have. In the clash between these two political movements is contained the possibilities of public health.

Note

1. My thanks to the anonymous peer reviewers of this essay for their observations on the relationship between suffering and freedom. One reviewer noted that social Darwinists tend to think of suffering as the inevitable consequence of freedom. The difference, however, between the social Darwinist and Black Freedom understanding of suffering as freedom is that Black Freedom activists democratize suffering by insisting it be made public and shared. Within this move to democratize suffering is also the hope of ameliorating suffering through collective action, and the corresponding recognition that suffering is not inevitable or impervious to political agency.

Works Cited

Amato, Joseph. 1994. "Politics of Suffering." *International Social Science Review* 69, 1/2, 29–30. http://www.jstor.org/stable/41882133.

Amato, Joseph. 1990. *Victims and Values: A History and Theory of Suffering.* New York: Praeger.

Anderson, Jervis. 1997. *Bayard Rustin: Troubles I've Seen.* Berkeley and Los Angeles: University of California Press.

Biden, Joseph. 2021. "Remarks by President Biden on the Anniversary of the Covid-19 Shutdown." *The White House,* March 11, 2021. https://www.whitehouse.gov/briefing-room/speeches-remarks/2021/03/11/remarks-by-president-biden-on-the-anniversary-of-the-covid-19-shutdown/.

Black, Edwin. 2003. *War Against the Weak: Eugenics and America's Campaign to Create a Master Race.* New York/London: Four Walls Eight Windows.

Bromell, Nick. 2013. *The Time is Always Now: Black Thought and the Transformation of U.S. Democracy.* Oxford: Oxford University Press.

Brown, Wendy. 2019. *In the Ruins of Neoliberalism: The Rise of Antidemocratic Liberalism in the West.* New York: Columbia University Press. EBSCOhost.

Brown, Wendy. 2003. "Neoliberalism and the End of Liberal Democracy." *Theory and Event,* 7, 1 (Fall). http://muse.jhu.edu/theory_&_event/.

Castillejo, Esther. 2020. "Fauci Tells David Muir U.S. Return to Normal Will Not Be Like a 'Light Switch' Turned On." *ABC News,* April 16, 2020. https://abcnews.go.com/Health/fauci-tells-david-muir-us-return-normal-light/story?id=70164631.

Catsam, Derek Charles. 2009. *Freedom's Main Line: The Journey of Reconciliation and the Freedom Rides.* Lexington: University Press of Kentucky.

Craig, Tim. 2021. "Moms for Liberty has Turned Parental Rights into Rallying Cry for Conservative Parents." *Washington Post,* October 15, 2021. https://www.

washingtonpost.com/national/moms-for-liberty-parents-rights/2021/10/14/
bf3d9ccc-286a-11ec-8831-a31e7b3de188_story.html.

Dedaj, Pauline. 2021. "Packers' Aaron Rodgers takes aim at COVID vaccine debate:
'If science can't be questioned, it's not science.'" *FOX News,* December 31,
2021. https://www.foxnews.com/sports/packers-aaron-rodgers-covid-vaccine-
debate-science-questioned.

Degler, Carl. 1991. *In Search of Human Nature.* New York: Oxford University Press.

D'Emilio, John. 2003. *Lost Prophet: The Life and Times of Bayard Rustin.* Chicago:
University of Chicago Press.

Duffy, John. 1990. *The Sanitarians: A History of American Public Health.* Urbana
and Chicago: University of Illinois Press.

Dyson, Michael Eric. 2001. *I May Not Get There with You: The True Martin Luther
King, Jr.* New York: The Free Press, 2001.

Evans, Stephanie. 2022. "Introduction: Wellness as a Social Justice Issue." In *Black
Women and Public Health: Strategies to Name, Locate, and Change Systems
of Power,* edited by Stephanie Y. Evans, Sarita K. David, Leslie R. Hinkson,
and Deanna J. Washington, 20. Albany: State University of New York Press.

Fee, Elizabeth. 1994. "Public Health and the State: The United States." In *The
History of Public Health and the Modern State,* edited by Dorothy Porter,
224–273. Amsterdam-Atlanta: Editions GA Rodopi.

Ferguson, Kathy E. 2011. *Emma Goldman: Political Thinking in the Streets.* Land-
ham, MD: Roman & Littlefield.

Finucane, Martin. 2022. "Survey Finds 4 in 10 American Adults Know Someone
Who Died of COVID-19." *Boston Globe,* May 2, 2022. https://www.boston
globe.com/2022/05/02/nation/survey-finds-4-10-american-adults-know-
someone-who-died-covid-19/#:~:text=With%20the%20nation%20poised%20
to,a%20survey%20released%20last%20week.

Foner, Eric. 1998. *The Story of American Freedom.* New York: W. W. Norton.

Friedman, Thomas L. 2020. "Finding the 'Common Good' in a Pandemic: The
Harvard political philosopher Michael Sandel offers his take." *New York
Times,* March 24, 2020. https://www.nytimes.com/2020/03/24/opinion/
covid-ethics-politics.html.

Gandhi, Mohandas K. 2005. "The Doctrine of the Sword." In *Twentieth Century
Political Theory: A Reader,* edited by Stephen Eric Bronner, 257–60. New
York: Routledge.

Garber, Megan. 2020."Donald Trump has steadily turned masks into symbols—not
of government overreach, but of government impunity." 2020. *The Atlantic,*
October 9, 2020. https://www.theatlantic.com/culture/archive/2020/10/
donald-trump-mike-pence-coronavirus-dangerous-mask-trap/616670/.

Gatta, Giunia. "Suffering and the Making of Politics: Perspectives from Jaspers
and Camus." 2014. *Contemporary Political Theory,* 14, no. 4: 335–54. https://
doi.org/10.1057/cpt.2014.52.

Goldmacher, Shane. 2021. "G.O.P. Governors Fight Mandates as the Party's Covid Politics Harden." *New York Times,* September 12, 2021. https://www.nytimes.com/2021/08/31/us/politics/republican-governors-covid-19.html.

Gooding-Williams, Robert. 2009. *In the Shadow of Du Bois: Afro Modern Political Thought in America.* Cambridge, MA: Harvard University Press.

Green, Emma. 2022. "The Case for Wearing Masks Forever." *The New Yorker,* December 28, 2022. https://www.newyorker.com/news/annals-of-activism/the-case-for-wearing-masks-forever.

Grooms, Jevay, Alberto Ortega, and Joaquin Alfredo-Angel Rubalcaba. 2020. The Brooking Institute: https://www.brookings.edu/articles/the-covid-19-public-health-and-economic-crises-leave-vulnerable-populations-exposed/.

Halpern, Cynthia. 2002. *Suffering, Politics, Power: A Genealogy of Modern Political Theory.* Albany: State University of New York.

Hobbes, Thomas. 1985. *Leviathan.* London: Penguin Books.

Hofstadter, Richard. 1955. *Social Darwinism in American Thought.* Boston: Beacon Press.

Kamb, Ava. 2020. "The False Choice Between Public Health and Civil Liberties." *Voices in Bioethics* 6: 1–3. https://doi.org/10.7916/vib.v6i.6297.

King, Martin Luther Jr. 2006. "Letter From Birmingham Jail." In *Twentieth Century Political Theory: A Reader,* edited by Stephen Eric Bronner, 329–40. New York: Routledge.

Kohli, Diti. 2022. " 'This Should Not Be Survival of the Fittest.' For High-Risk People, COVID Is Far from Over." *Boston Globe,* March 5, 2022. https://www.bostonglobe.com/2022/03/05/nation/this-should-not-be-survival-fittest-high-risk-people-covid-is-far-over/.

Levy, Barry S., and Victor W. Sidel. 2013. *Social Injustice and Public Health.* Oxford: Oxford University Press.

Macpherson, C. B. 1962. *The Political Theory of Possessive Individualism: Hobbes to Locke.* Oxford: Oxford University Press.

Mays, Mackenzie. 2019. "We Shall Overcome': California Anti-Vaccine Claim Civil Rights Mantle." *Politico,* September 18, 2019. https://www.politico.com/states/california/story/2019/09/18/we-shall-overcome-california-anti-vaccine-activists-claim-civil-rights-mantle-1188503.

Mollin, Marian. 2004. "The Limits of Egalitarianism: Radical Pacifism, Civil Rights, and the Journey of Reconciliation." *Radical History Review* 88 (Winter): 112–38. https://doi.org/10.1215/01636545-2004-88-112.

Park, Alice. 2023. " 'It's Been a Pretty Rocky Road.' CDC Director Dr. Rochelle Walensky Reflects on Her Tenure During Covid-19." *Time,* June 27, 2023. https://time.com/6290683/rochelle-walensky-interview-cdc-exit/.

Patel, Kant, and Mark E. Rushefsky. 2005. *The Politics of Public Health in the United States.* Armonk and London: M. E. Sharpe.

Peck, James. 1962. *Freedom Ride.* New York: Simon and Schuster.

Pineda, Erin R. 2021. *Seeing Like an Activist: Civil Disobedience and the Civil Rights Movement.* Oxford: Oxford University Press.

Podair, Jerald E. 2009. *Bayard Rustin: American Dreamer.* Lanham, MD: Rowman & Littlefield.

Ravitch, Diane. 2018. "Charter Schools Damage Public Education." *Washington Post,* June 22, 2018. https://www.washingtonpost.com/opinions/charter-schools-are-leading-to-an-unhealthy-divide-in-american-education/2018/06/22/73430df8-7016-11e8-afd5-778aca903bbe_story.html.

Reed, Betsy. 2022. "The CDC is Beholden to Corporations and Lost Our Trust. We Need to Start Our Own." *The Guardian,* April 3, 2022. https://www.theguardian.com/commentisfree/2022/apr/03/peoples-cdc-covid-guidelines.

Reed, Betsy. 2020. "Vikings' Kirk Cousins Says He Sees Covid-19 as 'Survival of the Fittest.'" *The Guardian,* September 2, 2020. https://www.theguardian.com/sport/2020/sep/02/kirk-cousins-minnesota-vikings-covid-19-nfl-football.

Rosen, George. 2015. *A History of Public Health.* Baltimore: Johns Hopkins University Press.

Rouse, Carolyn. 2009. *Uncertain Suffering: Racial Health Care Disparities and Sickle Cell Disease.* Berkeley: University of California Press.

Rousseau, Jean-Jacques. 1987. *The Basic Political Writings.* Cambridge: Hackett Publishing.

Rustin, Bayard. 2012. "Rustin to A. J. Muste." In *I Must Resist: Bayard Rustin's Life in Letters,* edited by Michael G. Long, 127–29. San Francisco: City Lights Books.

Rustin, Bayard. 2003. "Nonviolence vs. Jim Crow (1942)." In *Time on Two Crosses: The Collected Writings of Bayard Rustin,* edited by Deven W. Carbado and Donald Weiss, 2–5. New York: Cleis Press.

Rustin, Bayard. 2003. "The Negro and Nonviolence (1942)." In *Time on Two Crosses: The Collected Writings of Bayard Rustin,* edited by Deven W. Carbado and Donald Weiss, 6–10. New York: Cleis Press.

Schneider, Mary-Jane. 2017. *Introduction to Public Health.* Burlington, MA: Jones and Bartlett Learning.

Shapero, Julia. 2023. "DeSantis claims Florida "chose freedom over Fauciism' during pandemic among Trump attacks." *The Hill,* June 3, 2023. https://thehill.com/homenews/campaign/4033284-desantis-claims-florida-chose-freedom-over-fauci-ism-during-pandemic-amid-trump-attacks/.

Spelman, Elizabeth V. 1997. *Fruits of Sorrow: Framing Our Attention to Suffering.* Boston: Beacon Press.

Stolberg, Sheryl Gay. 2020. "Fauci Plans to Use Hearing to Warn of 'Needless Suffering and Death.'" *New York Times,* Mary 12, 2020.

Tracy, James. 1996. *Direct Action: Radical Pacifism from the Union Eight to the Chicago Seven.* Chicago and London: University of Chicago Press.

Tulchinsky, Theodore, and Elena Varavikova. 2014. *The New Public Health*. San Diego: Elsevier, Academic Press.

Turnock, Bernard J. 2009. *Public Health: What It Is and How It Works*. Sudbury, MA: Jones and Bartlett.

Wallace-Wells, David. 2023. "Dr. Fauci Looks Back: 'Something Clearly Went Wrong.'" *New York Times,* April 24, 2023. https://www.nytimes.com/interactive/2023/04/24/magazine/dr-fauci-pandemic.html.

Weber, Lauren, and Joel Achenbach. 2023. "Covid backlash hobbles public health and future pandemic response." *Washington Post,* March 8, 2023.

Wilkinson, Iain, and Arthur Kleinman. 2016. *A Passion for Society: How We Think about Human Suffering*. Berkeley: University of California Press.

Wolcott, Victoria. 2018. "Radical Nonviolence, Interracial Utopias, and the Congress of Racial Equality in the Early Civil Rights Movement." *Journal of Civil and Human Rights* 4, no. 2 (Fall/Winter): 31–61.

Yancy, George. 2015. "Through the Crucible of Pain and Suffering: African-American Philosophy as a Gift and the Countering of the Western Philosophical Metanarrative." *Educational Philosophy and Theory* 11: 1143–59. https://doi.org/10.1080/00131857.2014.991499.

Yong, Ed. 2020. "What Strength Really Means When You're Sick." *The Atlantic,* October 9, 2020. https://www.theatlantic.com/health/archive/2020/10/trump-strength-coronavirus/616682/.

Zamalin, Alex. 2017. *Struggle on Their Minds: The Political Thought of African American Resistance*. New York: Columbia University Press.

Chapter 3

Using Forum Theater to
Practice Anti-Racist Norms

A Case Study from UCONN Hartford

Jane Anna Gordon

Actually, art is indispensable to political progress. Because art knows no rules, it expands them for you. What's familiar is gone. Your imagination is liberated. Art resonates emotionally. It stimulates your moral sensibility. A temporary refuge from the world isn't an escape. It sharpens your consciousness. It opens up your heart. It refreshes your spirit.

—Alex Zamalin

Art is, and has always been, a tool for disorientation. Good. Disorientation is what's demanded in times of crisis. The right kind. Find art that makes you feel solidarity with those you'd least expect. To find courage yourself. To see anew.

—Alex Zamalin

In spring of 2022, a collection of faculty and staff organized an inaugural Anti-Racism in Education and the Community conference at the University of Connecticut (henceforth UCONN) Hartford campus. At its center was a theater activity authored and orchestrated by the HartBeat Ensemble, which I detail in what follows. Drawing as the workshop did on the Theatre of the Oppressed or Forum Theater techniques of the late Brazilian theater activist and popular educator Augusto Boal, it offered a brief, crystallized portrait of a familiar constellation of problems. Specifically, of how overwork in the neoliberal university is used as an excuse to rationalize pedagogical practices that reenforce racist and xenophobic expectations about who rightfully belongs in spaces of higher education. However, in response, diversly implicated audience members could together rehearse enacting alternatives, concretely crafting new, anti-racist norms.

The chapter that follows draws on writing of and about Augusto Boal to explore how the theatrical space created room to practice specific instances and dimensions of transformation. It then turns to the case study of UCONN Hartford and interviews with one of the HartBeat jokers, the workshop's playwright, staff that chose to and ultimately invited the ensemble, and UCONN's chief diversity officer. While focused on changing how belonging is understood and conveyed in the classroom, the implications of this workshop reach beyond it to other interactions in which radical inequality can be uncritically reproduced or interrupted and remade. My claim is that, as with this UCONN Hartford instance, where theoretical conversations about anti-racist education and activism were indispensably buttressed by *practicing modes of engagement necessary to developing the social fabric of anti-racist relations*, that Theatre of the Oppressed and Forum Theater also offer much to contemporary progressive political organizing as it deliberately responds to failures of more traditional conceptions of leadership.

Revolutionizing Revolutionary Thought and Practice

At the age of ninety-five, Chinese-American public intellectual and progressive movement activist Grace Lee Boggs coauthored, with Scott Kurashige, *The Next American Revolution*. Having participated in most of the important left-wing movements of the twentieth century, from labor and civil rights to those of Asian Americans and women and those for racial and ecological justice, she was, at this moment, *taking stock*. Reflecting on what she thought had been won and lost, she considered what could be learned in both victory and defeat.

Lee Boggs argued that conventional progressive ways of understanding revolution had become too narrow and static—even counterrevolutionary (2012, 53). Drawing on insights from Immanuel Wallerstein, she delineated a list of ideas about revolution that were treated as axiomatic from the time of the French Revolution until roughly 1968. First among these was how the relationship between means and ends in movement struggles was conceived. (Also essential was the channeling of political activity through one party; assuming that class divisions were the most salient political form of difference; treating democratic governing practices in and beyond the movement as a luxury that might eventually be enjoyed; and understanding scientific knowledge as the sole guide to revolutionary transformation.) If, from the French Revolution onward, the galvanizing aim was to do everything necessary to seize state power and then, once seized, to try to transform its exercise, from 1968 on, this "two-step strategy" had come into question (2012, 65). Even those with the most emancipatory of aims seemed to wield power in ways remarkably similar to those they had fought hard to displace.

The disappointments of "successful" revolutions made clear to Lee Boggs (and to many others) that there was a need in how one engaged in political organizing to begin to enact, to try to achieve one's ends in real time, as one built a movement. If one didn't try, there was no hope that the results would be substantively different. Importantly, Lee Boggs had made Detroit her home in the 1950s (2012, chapter 4). Completely committed to it as both a place and political project, for her, responding to radical economic disinvestment from it—its abandonment—was a prototype of challenges that would face many US cities in the years ahead. Contemporary revolutionary activity, for her, focused on creating new forms of education, work, and collective problem-solving to meet shared needs in places left vacant by the disintegration of old ways of organizing power and living and being in the world. Responsibility for this was as much the work of artists, ministers, workers, women, families, and communities as of politicians. She likened the nurturing of potential livable futures to midwifery (2012, 139).

Lee Boggs added to this focus on collapsing means and ends a related argument about leadership. Her emphatically gendered vocabulary is intentional. She observed that movements of the early and mid-1960s were still led mostly by men raised in patriarchal cultures. While there were some women among them, this mostly vertical way of organizing and mobilizing power foregrounded a small, exclusive few. Characterized by top-down, vertical leadership, charismatic male leaders, whether at conferences or rallies, made speeches to inflame angry masses (2012, 145–46). When women emerged as leaders, it was because they were as tough as these men and could occupy leadership roles as they did. One result was that these groups and efforts lacked everyone's active participation; lacked everyone listening to each other; lacked laughter and joy and a sense that the souls of those involved were growing through their participation.

For Lee Boggs, it was the women's movement of the 1970s that deliberately sought to abandon this model for one of more broadly participatory and horizontal leadership focused on hearing multiple voices and sharing ongoing responsibilities. Instead of modeling political work on the public lives of men at hierarchically organized factory plants or in the political area, their template centered his female counterpart who also did the domestic work of caring for and nurturing family and kin. In retrospect she argued that, for all its major progressive achievements, for much of the 1960s there was far too little of the love and caring that she considered an organic part of the everyday lives of women. She thought its absence reflected a failure to appreciate the diversity of activities that sustain human communities and the centuries-long efforts to humanize and liberate them (145–46).

One of the three main catalysts of Black Lives Matter (BLM), Alicia Garza (2020) made a related observation about what she considered most singular about that movement's approach to leadership. Explaining that historically Black movements in the US had been organized through the church with Black male leaders at the helm, she suggested that when early protests were ongoing in Ferguson, Missouri, in response to the killing of Michael Brown, Jesse Jackson and Al Sharpton arrived, ready to play this traditional role in which they were the focal point of attention and would speak for Black anger and despair while urging those assembled to return home and to engage in conventional electoral means of expressing their political desires (2020, 131–32).

Garza explains that this model elevated Black people selected for their acceptability and respectability in the eyes of white people. In other words, if many members of non-Black US public have criticisms of Jackson and Sharpton, they prefer engaging with them to members of angry working-class Black mobilized crowds (2020, 133). We see this assessment reflected in the careful choice of figures like Rosa Parks in what became the Montgomery Bus Boycott (Olson 2001, 110–11) and, for many in BLM, the Obamas. Both Garza and political theorist and

Movement for Black Lives scholar Deva R. Woodly argued that the racial animus and resentment that encircled the Obamas was the death knell for Black respectability politics. "One could scarcely imagine a better example of middle-class American values personified, with what was, for many, an enchanting dash of magical negro and Black girl magic thrown in, elevating this talented bunch from exemplary to magnetic" (Woodly 2022, 109–10). Still, this neither shielded them from racist hatred nor demonization. If anything, both intensified.

At the core of BLM then was a different kind of argument: to say that Black lives matter had to mean that ordinary, average, *all* Black life matters. If the aim is to highlight a criminal justice system with double standards, the move is not to claim that Michael Brown or Freddie Gray or Tamir Rice were saints. Freddie Gray had been picked up on drug charges before, and Michael Brown was rumored to have stolen a pack of cigarillos before being shot. Neither admission meant they deserved to be killed (Garza 2020, 133). They could be imperfect young US citizens like their non-Black counterparts. The point was that they deserved deescalated police treatment. If armed individual and groups of white gunmen could be arrested peacefully, remaining alive to face trial, why was that not true for their Black fellow citizens? Law enforcement could and should have used the standard repertoire of responses activated when dealing with those they see themselves as charged to protect.[1]

This attention to ordinary Black citizens had a counterpart in approaches to organization. The traditional vertical charismatic male model had real shortcomings for Black politics. Since most Black progressive movements targeted and were targeted by the state, a disproportionate number of their indispensable leaders were assassinated. When they were, it completely destabilized the relevant movement (Garza 2020, 161–62). Garza argued therefore that, as shrewd politics, self-protection, and a way of centering ordinary citizens, decentralized leadership was more sustainable. And so, while many described BLM (like Occupy) as leaderless, she insisted that it was leader-full. This was a model in which to lead was to cultivate other leaders, with special preference for those historically most excluded from centrality. It enabled sharing the work of building and sustaining a strong network through local chapters and aimed at a different practice of power where many people determined the direction of the movement (2020, 163–64).

Woodly describes the more horizontal leadership of the Movement for Black Lives as expressing a Black feminist pragmatism that embraces *democratic experimentation* (2022, 59–60), trying to figure out new ways of building relationships that break with more hierarchical and exclusionary practices (2022, 62). As with all experimentation, and especially that which deliberately interrupts how citizens have been socialized, those involved will get a lot wrong and will need to make revisions. A real onus is therefore placed on shared commentary and correction. Emphasizing those *most on the margins* since they will help name and magnify relevant categories of disadvantage, amplified is *less the language of law and rights*—though it is also there[2]—as building a *different form of intentional community* (2022, 50).

As Lee Boggs suggested in a separate context—she died before the emergence of Black Lives Matter/the Movement for Black Lives—the metaphor for this mode of leading is mothering as a social practice rather than as a biological relationship.[3] After all, if the toll of political injustice is not only unjust but damaging, healing must also be conceived as both political and personal. However, rather than continuing a long-standing pattern in which care is feminized and devalued through being framed as the natural expression of private and individualized love, universal interdependency should be integrated into how political movements organize (Woodly 2022, chap. 3). If messy and imperfect, the work of deliberately developing different kinds of human interaction involves transcending hurting and shaming and letting tensions and misunderstanding simmer only then to be displaced (Woodly 2022, 156–57). This break is to be mirrored in deliberately interrupting and departing from the cycles of burnout and partial recovery that mark so many modes of engaging in political action (Ibid.). Still, such labor is essential to the real political work of building different futures, efforts that began centuries before us and will continue long after we are gone.

Theater of the Oppressed/Forum Theater

In Augusto Boal's account, the initial hubristic aim of what became Theatre of the Oppressed and then Forum Theater was to address *all* oppression. In his home of Brazil, this focused on Indigenous peasants fighting for their land, urban Black citizens resisting dehumanizing oppression, and women contending with misogyny.[4] Quickly realizing his own arrogance and the ineffectiveness of doling out political advice since "he could not liberate anyone by making their decisions" (Boal 2001, 338–39), Boal's ensemble developed *simultaneous dramaturgy*. In it, the theater group would dramatize a problem to the critical juncture where the protagonist must make a pivotal decision. As audience members would yell out suggested directions, the actors would try to improvise them.

Boal witnessed how interactive theater excited participants. Able to intervene in the action, they began to break down the wall separating actors from spectators. Nothing that unfolded was presented as inevitable since everything was subject to potential rectification (Boal 1985, 134). These innovations moved in the Marxist direction of putting the means of theatrical production increasingly in the hands of audience members.

Still, there were remaining inadequacies. In Boal's account, he continued to seek "something beyond Brecht, who only asked the spectator to think with his head, without giving him the stage space to express that thought. No more message-bearing theater, I did not want to be postman for the unknown sender (the Party? Divine revelation?). I wanted the spectators, democratically, to use the same theatre language used by the actors. How could this be done? A good question, an answer to which would only come years later" (Boal 2001, 200–201). As he relays it, it was "the genuine intervention of a 'spect-actor,' which gave rise to Forum Theater" (Boal 2001, 205). In Peru in 1973, Boal's ensemble was acting out a scene in which a woman, who supported her husband, learned that he had a lover in the town where he claimed to be building her a new home. The middle-aged woman whose story it was wanted recommendations for how to respond when her husband would arrive the next day. The audience counseled that she should confront him, react, cry, become angry, bite him on the neck, and pretend she didn't know about his infidelities.

One plump older woman insisted that all of these approaches were wrong and that the wife should forgive him: "After she had a very clear conversation with him!" But each time the actors tried to do as she said, she repeated that they were getting it wrong. Exasperated, Boal invited her to join the actors on stage. As he tells it:

> Delighted, she came up, she took hold of a broom, and doled out a magnificent thrashing to the husband. He was an excellent actor; I shall never forget his wonderful, sincere, emotion-filled, Stanislavskian interpretation of his part when, cowering under the broom, he promised never again to betray her. . . . Only after this beating—her "clear conversation"!—did the fat woman forgive the treacherous husband, and not before sending him out to the kitchen to fetch her a plate of food, famished as she was after all that beating. (Boal 2001, 206–7)

Boal described *this* moment as the emergence of the "spect-actor." From then on, Boal would explain Forum Theater as inviting the audience to do anything they wanted beyond beating up the cast! In this version, not only was the ensemble not giving advice, the spectator was an interpreter, carrying out uniquely what came to their mind. In this approach, the debate/forum *is* the show and theater "is not didactic . . . but pedagogic, in the sense of a collective learning" (Boal 1995, 7). Crucially, the ten- or fifteen-minute skit portraying that problem is improvised, rehearsed, and then presented once and then again but now with the invitation for any participant in the audience to replace any actor enact what seems most appropriate. Treated as necessarily unfinished, everyone can and should take responsibility. As the other actors respond to the new situation and its possibilities, anyone may propose any solution, but "they are not allowed to come on the stage and talk, talk, talk. . . . Anyone may propose any solution, but it must be done on stage, working, acting, doing things . . . not from the comfort of his seat. . . . he often realizes that things are not so easy when he himself [must] practice what he suggests" (Boal 1985: 13).

Boal explains that "bourgeois theater is . . . finished theater. The bourgeoisie already knows what the world is like, *their* world, and [can] present images of this complete . . . world. The bourgeoisie presents the spectacle" (Boal 1985, 140). By contrast, "the proletariat and the oppressed classes do not know yet what their world will be like; consequently their theater will be the rehearsal, not the finished spectacle" (Ibid.). If conventional theater requires noninterference by the audience, Theatre of the Oppressed and Forum Theater give rise to "a spectator of a new kind: spect-actor. I see and I act" (Boal 1995, 72).

Delineating exercises that make participants conscious of how their bodies are governed by their work and in how they may engage them much more expressively,[5] Boal explains that domination relies not on an honest interchange of ideas and of criticism but on unilateral force and violence. As he elaborates: "The capitalist does not ask the working man if he agrees that the capital should belong to one and the labor to another; he simply places an armed policeman at the factory door and that is that—private property is decreed" (Boal 1985, 149). Defining the dominated as those who must regularly suffer constant and ongoing repression (149), particular techniques involve revisiting the specific moments when the actor began to act "in a manner contrary to his own desires" (150). Once it has been reproduced, the protagonist is asked not to accept the repression. As the other participants maintain the dynamics of the situation, the protagonist fights to impose his wishes and ideas, measuring the strength of the enemy and what would be required actually to achieve his aims.

For Boal, the rehearsal involved in Forum Theater is neither escapist nor even cathartic. Instead the goal is to dynamize and to unsettle. Participation provokes a sense of incompleteness desiring fulfillment. It evokes a desire to enact beyond what has been practiced in the theater (140). Again, Boal frames this approach as putting theatrical means of production in the hands of all: Since theater is not composed primarily of physical constructions so much as by the human capacity to observe ourselves in action and to imagine alternatives (13), its embodied language for discovering new ways of being can be used by anyone (121). With the aim of transforming passive beings into those who delegate no power to others to act or think in their place, collective ownership means trying out solutions together to build a different kind of world (122).

Anti-Racism, Education, and Community

Hosted by Academic Affairs and the Sustainable Global Cities Initiative at UCONN Hartford, with sponsorship by Africana Studies, Asian and Asian American Studies, El Instituto, the Indigeneity, Race, Ethnicity, and Politics (IREP) Graduate Certificate, Office of Diversity and Inclusion (ODI), and Women's, Gender, and Sexuality Studies, the two-day conference opened with an emphasis on the importance of coalition-building among educators, students, and community. It included a keynote by New School Provost Renée White; a session on the role of the cultural centers and ethnic institutes in educating UCONN students, advocating for anti-racism, and engaging thoughtfully in interdisciplinary or cross-disciplinary collaborations among constituents; a discussion featuring community thought-leaders reflecting on the role of their organizations in addressing anti-racism and education;[6] a panel highlighting action research bridging scholarship and community undertaken by Hartford-based faculty in Public Policy, Social Work, and History; and research presentations by IREP Graduate Certificate and the self-run graduate Philosophy of Education group students. The second day closed with a keynote, remarks, and merrymaking.

Each day was punctuated by a two-hour interactive play, "Stuck in the Tape," commissioned by UCONN Hartford through the leadership of Nadine Brennan and spearheaded by Godfrey L. Simmons of HartBeat Ensemble. (HartBeat was founded in 2001 in Hartford, Connecticut, with the express aim of using theater to speak across different generational, racial, class, and geographic groups. An ensemble of artist-activists, they create productions based on critical civic issues and lead in-school and after-school programming, including Moved to Act and the Social Studies Theater Workshop. Inspired by Augusto Boal's Theater of the Oppressed, both programs use theater as a form of conflict resolution and to nurture civil engagement and deeper learning.) Envisioned as a professional development activity focused on working competently with culturally, ethnically, and racially diverse students, its story, authored by Gineiris Garcia, drew directly from interviews conducted with students of color at UCONN through storycircles,[7] and from the central findings of the 2020 UCONN Microaggressions Survey.[8] Among them were: that classrooms were top among the thirteen spaces of learning and living that students of color experienced as hostile; that racial microaggressions perpetrated by faculty, students, and staff were widespread in living and learning spaces; that many students experienced both singling out for comment on issues of diversity *and* isolation due to the handling of students of color in predominantly white spaces; that there was a lack of awareness of UCONN's policies and reporting procedures in response to racial incidences; and lack of confidence that the university administration would respond to reports in a meaningful or effective way.

The short play (Garcia 2022a) opens in a UCONN Hartford classroom with a stressed-out white female, Professor Quinn, trying to elicit discussion from disaffected students. She is very dismissive of the one Latino student, Carl, who is perfectly happy to speak, even if he does so casually and imprecisely. When the silence lags, Professor Quinn focuses in on the one student wearing a headscarf, asking if she *really has nothing, academic or personal, to say* about the Taliban or US aid to Afghanistan. When the student quips that she is from Bethlehem, *Connecticut*, Professor Quinn presses, stating that she, Khadijah, had written an excellent paper related directly to the article under discussion. At this point, the third student of color in the room, Juno Etienne, laughs out loud and mutters something beneath her breath. Professor Quinn quickly scolds Juno for her "disruptiveness," returning to Khadijah until the class ends. As we transition to the next scene, Joker 1 reads from the 2020 Microaggressions Survey, "classrooms rank second among thirteen settings that students of color feel uncomfortable in or avoid while on campus." They later add, "30% of students of color report being singled out for discussions of diversity."

In the next scene, the three students of color from the class are talking with each other. When Khadija says that she is tired, Juno responds that what just happened in class was ridiculous. Khadijah challenges, "It's not like you were helpful. You put her on the defensive. I could have said something productive, but . . ." (Garcia 2022a). We learn that the paper attributed to Khadijah had been written by Juno, who has no interest in devoting time or energy to improving the racial environment on campus. Having been excited to attend college there, she had found that being one of few students of color left her tongue-tied and that she simply wanted to earn her degree and move on. *And she had been proud of that paper.* Carl interjects optimistically that something productive could come from this. Khadijah, as a student leader, would actually know how to respond. (Carl teases that Khadijah has the ODI telephone numbers saved and favorited and regularly lunches with the deans!) But we see Khadijah reluctant, thinking that what transpired does not reach the level of seriousness to warrant formal, institutional action. She states, "It wasn't blatant enough for that; it would need to be a slur" and that trying to do something would get her stuck in bureaucratic circles with no tangible outcomes (Garcia 2022a). Joker 2 then defines the meaning of a racial microinsult.

We then see Professor Quinn at her laptop, reading email. She has received a message from Juno and Khadijah explaining what transpired. We see, in an instant, an acknowledgment of error, realization of why the series of interactions in the class unfolded as they did, and minimization of the seriousness of her responsibility. As Joker 1 reads that the UCONN Microaggression report relates that over 40 percent of students of color experience microaggressions related to intellectual aptitude, we transition to a lounge where Professor Quinn stands at a coffee machine with Mira, an older white female guidance counselor. As Professor Quinn complains about all the responsibilities she must juggle, Mira gently but challengingly replies that other professors manage to get it all done. Professor Quinn is clearly still thinking about what has just happened and begins to recount it. Mira tells Professor Quinn to take a breath and asks if the students' names were similar. When it is clear the answer is no, Mira offers, "If you want my opinion, you probably won't like it, but knowing student names is part of your job. Teaching is a responsibility" (Garcia 2022a). Professor Quinn interrupts Mira to say that she is aware of what teaching is and has so many papers and she can't take extra time and she just misspoke. Mira, unrelenting, says, "Students don't need to worry about how hard it is for you. They are paying for their education here" (Garcia 2022a). Professor Quinn is also unrelenting: "I am paid as an expert in my field and as a human being. This was a simple error. You can understand" (Garcia 2022a).

In the following scene, Mira is meeting with Khadijah, who, after saying how tired she is with courses and family obligations, retells what occurred in Professor Quinn's course. Khadijah immediately states that worse things have happened, and she isn't even sure why she wrote to Professor Quinn. Mira implores Khadijah not to minimize her feelings and says that this is still an instance of oppression. When Khadijah asks what she is supposed to do, Mira says that she should report it, elevating responsibility for it so it doesn't rest on her shoulders. Mira suggests that maybe Juno would do it with her. Khadijah responds that, in the context of all the other institutional failures, this isn't that big a deal. After all, the university doesn't even think the Hartford campus, with its majority-minoritized students, needs its own diversity office. Both visibly frustrated, Joker 1 comments that 625 of the surveyed students of color report feeling isolated because of race.

When Professor Quinn sees Danny, a Latino professor walking to his car, she is both insistent in making conversation and avoidant of really talking. When she says that she confused two students and attributed the paper of one to another, he asks if she acknowledged her mistake. Rather than answering, she says that Mira "kind of threatened her," questioning her ability to do her job (Garcia 2022a). When he replies that that sounds like a serious response for a small mix-up, Professor Quinn confesses that both were students of color; one Black and one Muslim. When Danny asks if the papers were similar, Professor Quinn admits that they were not. As Danny then tries actually to engage her, she thanks him abruptly, saying that she has taken enough of his time, that it is cold, and that she has figured out what she will do.

As Joker 2 interjects that 70 percent of students do not know the formal procedures for handling racial incidents, we see Danny and Mira joke in the penultimate scene about coffee and overwork. They then speak about Professor Quinn. When Mira expresses her frustration with her underserved students and her sense that there is nothing, as staff, that she can do, he insists that she can talk to Professor Quinn. As a fellow white employee, she has the power to shape conversations about what students deserve and are owed.

The play ends with Professor Quinn alerting students to an email that she sent about "an incident that occurred in [their] last class" (Garcia 2022a). She says that her "history in speaking up for diversity . . . pushed

[her] to own up to this embarrassingly simple, human mistake [which she could assure them] was not motivated by race" (Garcia 2022a). She tells them that they can review her website and teaching evaluations to see "how that is in no way a part of [her] composition, as a professor or human being" (Garcia 2022a). She abruptly then says that she has one final question for Juno, who freezes in her seat. Professor Quinn continues, "A fine essay, written by our very own Juno Etienne, ties the themes of this week so seamlessly with current events. It's an urgent piece and I wanted to ask if I could include it in this season's syllabus for the rest of the class to read" (Ibid.). Aware of Juno's discomfort in being singled out in this way, Carl tries to redirect Professor Quinn to the subject of preparing for the midterm. When he asks if it's appropriate to have this conversation in class, she tells him that if he'd like to discuss class etiquette, he can save it for after class or office hours. It is only as Juno completely shuts down that the professor moves on to the midterm, as Carl had initially suggested (Garcia 2022a). And the Jokers close out the play.

Having completed the series of scenes once, the Jokers tell everyone assembled that the Ensemble will run through it a second time. In this round, audience members, now in the role of "spect-actors," should yell "stop!" when they want to interrupt the course of action or think that an interaction should be otherwise. However, rather than simply saying that something was wrong, those who interjected had to suggest an alternative course of action and were urged to step on to the stage to enact it themselves. As they did, others in the audience could stop them, making more adjustments, or more fundamental changes. In each instance, there was discussion about the potential implications of each revision.

As Joker 1 Simmons (2022) explained and playwright Garcia (2022b) affirmed, their charge was to write a play with easily observable *critical junctures*, where a key decision could go otherwise.[9] The main aim was to observe and realize what was happening and how it might be altered or undone. This group of mostly administrators, faculty, and staff, similarly situated within the institution, were to participate in a thought experiment in which they could see and engage to try to understand themselves better in a story that was necessarily incomplete (Simmons 2022).[10] They had the opportunity to try out changing roles and adjusting the script to improve what was originally enacted.

The quality of facilitation by the Jokers or "difficultators" (Boal 1995) was crucial. Charged with reading the room, in this instance it was intentional that one was Black and male-presenting and the other a white-passing, female-presenting Latine person.[11] Simmons (2022) emphasized that with two Jokers, the Ensemble increases the chance of many people feeling represented. Their role was to orchestrate the shared use of time and space, moving everyone through the objectives of the scenes, creating safety to be brave (Garcia 2022b). They introduced and enforced the rules and were to function as a voice of objectivity, here through stating findings from the survey. In Veronika Baxter's words, their job is to make it "impossible to arrive at naive, magical, or fatuous solutions to the problems posed" (2009).

Success was to be gauged not in terms of people arriving at "correct" actions, words, or outcomes but whether they connected to and grappled with the issues and whether they found compelling ways to respond. As Simmons explained, it is not a problem if things turn sour. Instead one wanted to be able to say "yes" to questions like these: Did participants step in and change the story and review, comment, see themselves in it or not, and think about those observations? Did the workshop function as low-stakes practice where participants could see ourselves getting it wrong? Did we try out new ways of exercising responsibility and relating? Did the workshop stimulate the likelihood of being more thoughtful in future comparable moments? (Simmons 2022). To facilitate these ends, the scenes, as evident in this play, are stripped down, simple, and focused on a particular situation that has gone largely unaddressed, in this case, outside of student complaints to each other or to a counselor (Garcia 2022b).

Based on the workshop's success, several ODI administrators present decided that they would employ HartBeat again, this time for UCONN Hartford's 2022 New Student Orientation.[12]

The central insight of the workshop is that if we have been largely socialized to participate in the smooth running of a deeply unequal world in which only some fully belong, we must create alternative ways of relating. For those who are committed to working at becoming effective anti-racists, not merely in principle but in the quotidian mess of institutional life, practice can be useful. Role-playing in Theatre of the Oppressed or Forum Theater creates such a space where we can critically explore conversations or events we have heard of or seen, rehearsing how we can shift their register and outcomes. Indeed, with such understanding in mind, there are groups who meet monthly to do just such work.

If, in contemporary progressive activism, as represented here by the written reflections of Lee Boggs, Garza, and Woodly, we abandon a sharp divide between means and ends, we do so through focusing on how to relate with other people in building the world we seek. Forum

Theater potentially offers ongoing opportunities to construct a different kind of social fabric through magnifying voices historically oppressed and repressed and rehearsing how to listen and to respond. In these forms of "spect-acting," those willing practice stepping back and observing, identifying a wrong, and intervening in unfamiliar ways.

When repeated, such role-playing involves learning to function as part of an ensemble that assumes that everyone has the resources they need to better address the problems they face alone and together (Garcia 2022b). As such, Forum Theater functions as a metaphor for the work of building and maintaining a democratic community in which there will always be differences and inequalities and where, when observed and engaged, these can be assets to be mined (Garcia 2022b). In theory, there are therefore no situations where role play would not be individually or collectively useful since, through it, participants actively build relational muscles, tactics of connecting and engaging in preferable, public ways.

Conclusion

In response to objections that even this democratically practiced theatrical method was, as any method, "elaborated according to a living and earthbound ideology" (Boal 2001, 339), Boal replies first, that Theater of the Oppressed/Forum Theater are not the old, evangelizing political theater. Rather than prepackaged answers, it poses disarming questions. But second and more, Boal states: "I did not invent Theatre of the Oppressed by myself, in my house, nor did I receive it as tablets of stone from God: it was in the interaction with popular audiences that the [Theatre of the Oppressed] was born, little by little. It did not come out of me ready and finished: it created itself by a process of exchange. The method was structured through decades of [shared] work . . ." (Ibid.). Even if attributed to him, as I have been doing here, Boal is not the method's singular author. As his story relays, it was generated from ongoing, collective theatrical problem-solving.

The results made available to all what was frequently only accessible to actors: the human capacity of "diving into the depths of self and emerging with undreamed-of characters, hidden potentialities submerged. . . . immersing oneself in this plunge into self, awakening the characters bubbling away in the pressure cooker of our unconscious" (Boal 2001, 321).

Sharon Green describes a Boal workshop she participated in at the Brecht Theater in New York City in 1991 as offering the "missing piece . . . to meld an activist and artistic spirit" (2001, 47). Provoking "stunning realizations," it transformed spectators into spect-actors who became active subjects rather than passive observers (Ibid.). It gave power, authority, and responsibility to them to rehearse active resistance to normalized oppression by trying out different possibilities within the relative safety of the theater.

Staging transformative opportunities of this kind has made Theatre of the Oppressed and Forum Theater wildly successful, stretching "into every aspect of engaged social life, from artist to activist, social worker to trade unionist, teacher to therapist" (Jackson 2009). If later, as Diana Taylor observes, Boal's ensembles shifted from Theatre of the Oppressed to Theatre of the Repressed, it still put theatrical means of production into the hands of those who wanted to bring about social change (Taylor 2009). Whether deliberately developing sociopolitical capacity for participatory democracy through building courage to enact feasible alternatives in everyday life (Ghoshal and Manna 2020) or as an indispensable portion of public-budgeting processes[13] or to reduce gender-based violence (Dahal, Joshi, Swahnberg 2022; Mitchell and Freitag 2011), as Baxter explained, this is "theatre that isn't literary, activism that isn't violent, learning that isn't prescriptive. Most of all, it [celebrates] seriously playful space that makes us human" (2009).

For some practitioners, this degree of success may itself be troubling. Are these methods being employed for means other than those for which they were intended—of addressing and uprooting oppression? Green, for example, suggested that the widespread uptake may be an expression of nostalgia—of artists yearning for a time when the relationship between theater and politics was more intimate (2001, 28). In opportunities that are increasingly rare, she contends, Forum Theater offers opportunities to reclaim a seemingly vanquished power of self-reflexive critique, enabling participants to enact more meaningful membership in community with others.

I would offer a different explanation of its popularity, rooted both in a reading of the prefigurative political organizing of Black Lives Matter and in engagement with Forum Theater at UCONN Hartford. Perhaps Theatre of the Oppressed and Forum Theater are so widespread because of their *timeliness*. In this reading, they better reflect the approach to understanding social transformation borne of a fundamental political disenchantment that has characterized progressive politics from the 1960s on. Such radical disappointment in traditional methods of leadership, as described by Grace Lee Boggs, have led to a reenvisioning of the responsibilities of progressive political organizing, as suggested by Alicia Garza and Deva R. Woodly. This now includes a call for nothing less than resocializing ourselves in new ways of building and sustaining relationships—charges once seen as private and psychological. Similar demands face contemporary public institutions of higher education: that faculty and staff learn *as rapidly as possible* how to make these settings ones where *all* students, including those from historically excluded communities, thrive. Doing so does not only require revisiting the nature of the classroom as a social space of learning but how we conceptualize valuable knowledge.

If we are to meet these highly legitimate demands, we need spaces for creative rehearsal of the kind that fundamentally democratized Theatre of the Oppressed and Forum Theater offer. As such, it is not that the space between politics and art has broadened. Perhaps, if conceived as suggested here, the space has narrowed or even collapsed in ways that can be generative. After all, Theatre of the Oppressed and Forum Theater treat constructing viable human relationships marked fundamentally by inequality and oppression as a matter of collective, repeated experimentation and public, concerted artistry. To achieve their stated missions, our public institutions of higher education need to foster just such ongoing incentives to further develop and hone our relevant crafts.

Notes

1. But white male sovereignty gives white men the right over life and death—in the name of "we, the people."

2. As it almost always is nowadays.

3. This helpful formulation of mothering comes from Amy Allen (2000).

4. Started in the Arena Theater in efforts to deliberately Brazilianize culture, Boal would break away to experiment with "more direct combinations of politics and art" (Jackson 2009).

5. Boal writes, "The exercises of this first stage are designed to 'undo' the muscular structure of the participants. That is, to take them apart, to study and analyze them. Not to weaken or destroy them, but to raise them to the level of consciousness. So that each worker, each peasant understands, sees, and feels to what point his body is governed by his work" (Boal 1985, 128). He continues, "In the second stage the intention is to develop the expressive ability of the body.

In our culture we are used to expressing everything through words, leaving the enormous expressive capabilities of the body in an underdeveloped state" (130).

6. The organizations included Re-Center and Shanelle Morris of Grow Hartford Youth Program.

7. In storycircles, small groups of people share stories in a practice that deliberately encourages the embrace of dialogue over debate and the value of nuances of experience over well-structured arguments. Inviting participants to abandon adversarial stances, storycircles suggest that it is listening to stories instead of arguing points that enables us to discover who we are (Lizzy Cooper Davis 128). Resonant with both global Indigenous circle practices and methods of community education and dialogue of Brazilians Paulo Freire and Augusto Boal, in the US, storycircles were developed by the Free Southern Theater (first in Mississippi and then in New Orleans). In it, John O'Neal and Doris Derby, along with Gilbert Moses, used theater as a way to engage rural Black communities in the planning of the civil rights movement. Launched with a donation from Langston Hughes and other artists as a theatrical arm of SNCC, rather than holding postshow talk backs, those present would sit in circles of audience-members to share stories evoked by the show, using them as a prompt for the collective action that would follow. The rules were and are few: no more than eight people per circle; everyone must be able to see each other; time is shared equitably among all participants; the person who just shared is timekeeper for their neighbor; participants can pass with the circle returning to them at the end; there are no interruptions or clarifying questions; the story must be personal, with a beginning, middle, and end; everyone must really listen; and the circle must end with a closing activity. There is no note-taking or recording. As O'Neal (1968) insists, participants should honor the original recording devices of our ears, hearts, minds, bodies.

8. See Csizmadia et al. (2020). The UCONN Microaggressions Research Team (UCONN MRT) was an interdisciplinary group of faculty, staff, graduate, and undergrad students who invited UCONN students of color to participate in an online survey between spring of 2019 and winter of 2020; 1,229 students of color completed the survey, which ends with many important recommendations. Among them were to fund and commission yearly racial campus climate studies to be released to the entire community along with a strategic plan with objectives for cultivating diversity; to hold annual town hall meetings across campuses to solicit feedback and suggestions about campus climate that aim to give students of color a platform and greater voice; to allocate money and incentivize faculty and staff participating in annual anti-racist training tailored and aimed at nurturing critical self-reflection to empower action; to diversify faculty and staff at UCONN and incorporate DEI in merit, tenure, and promotion criteria; to fund and develop a university-wide information campaign to promote anti-racism, DEI, and social justice; to include a permanent DEI section in UCONN's Daily Digest; to undertake a social media campaign and ongoing plan for increasing awareness on how to disrupt racism and racist microaggressions; with the aim of increased

transparency about racial bias incidents, to create a dashboard of incidents as a measure of the overall public health of the institution.

9. There are many other instances of using theater to foster anti-racist educational communities. For instance, in summer 2021 at Principia, eight student and alumni actors, under the leadership of Professor Chrissy Calkins Steele, chair of the Theater and Dance Department, used Theatre of the Oppressed techniques, image theater, and Forum Theater to create frozen pictures of real issues, inviting attendees to rearrange, join, and recast the tableau and enacted scenes in which audience members froze the action to explore practical alternatives. Those involved wanted to explore racism and how to act against it. This did not necessarily mean finding immediate solutions so much as developing better strategies for ongoing anti-racist engagement. Boal's *Rainbow of Desire* (1995), which focused on internalized oppression and how repression impinges on everyone's desires and decision-making, adapts theater for those who want to be catalysts for social and political change in a range of circumstances different from those of the Peruvian peasantry with whom these techniques were first developed.

10. In this workshop, which differed from traditional Forum Theater, there were roles for both "oppressor" and "oppressed." Green (2001) points out that traditionally Forum Theater works best with members of groups with similar investments in the issues being explored and that it is only the protagonist, identified as oppressed, who is replaced, as there is no effort to further empower oppressors (50). As Jackson comments: "Having created the remarkable worldwide operation of the Theatre of the Oppressed, having given away his secrets to all and sundry, [Boal] sometimes seemed torn between the desire to seek to regulate this potential empire, both in terms of quality and content, and the knowledge that the cat was out of the bag. The ethos demanded—the whole point of the ethos is and was—universal access to the tools, provided that their deployment was for the good of humanity. But how to ensure this? And how to avoid terrible misappropriations and misunderstandings?" (2009, 308)

11. In addition to Simmons, Zulynette [her mononym] served as Joker 2.

12. Simmons was asked to prepare an activity for the Fall 2022 New Student Orientation. The Microaggressions Survey guided the shaping of interview questions asked of juniors and graduating seniors to craft and layer narratives chiefly focused on race. It became a series of monologues that lasted for approximately forty minutes. In their assessment, which was affirmed by Chief Diversity Officer Frank Tuitt (2022), while the production likely stimulated students to realize that they would soon have peers who were not like them and that our behaviors effect everyone and that there would be different bodies on campus and that this mattered; they were not sure that the format worked in that setting. Partly due to insufficient preparation time that made it difficult to connect with enough students, the setting also required a more performative and less interactive engagement. It did feature the storytelling of actual students and, as such, was simple and evocative; however, the size of the new student audiences kept everyone in the role of

spectator. Preferable in the future, they suggested, might be training residential assistants to facilitate storycircles which they could lead regularly with students in their residence halls (Simmons and O'Rourke 2022).

13. "Since 1997, in Santo Andre, popular assemblies, which decide on the city's budget, have invariably begun with the presentation of Forum plays mounted by groups organized by the CTO, and relating to that budget. An experiment which promises to blossom" (Boal 2001, 337).

Works Cited

Allen, Amy. 2000. *The Power of Feminist Theory: Domination, Resistance, Solidarity.* New York: Routledge.

Barak, Adi. 2016. "Critical Consciousness in Critical Social Work: Learning from the Theatre of the Oppressed," *British Journal of Social Work* 46: 1776–92.

Baxter, Veronika. 2009. "Playing Seriously with August Boal (1931–2009)," *Critical Stages/Scènes critique* Issue No. 1 (Autumn).

Boal, Augusto. 1985. *Theatre of the Oppressed.* Translated by Charles A. and Maria-Odilia Leal McBrode. New York: Theatre Communications Group.

Boal, Augusto. 1995. *The Rainbow of Desire: The Boal Method of Theatre and Therapy.* Translated by Adrian Jackson. London and New York: Routledge.

Boal, Augusto. 2001. *Hamlet and the Baker's Son: My Life in Theatre and Politics.* Translated by Adrian Jackson and Candida Blaker. London and New York: Routledge.

Boal, Augusto. 2002. *Games for Actors and Non-Actors*, Second Edition. Translated by Adrian Jackson. London and New York: Routledge.

Brennan, Nadine. 2023. Interview conducted virtually with Jane Anna Gordon. February 10.

Cooper Davis, Lizzy. 2019. "The Free Southern Theater's Story Circle Process." In *Creating Space for Democracy: A Primer on Dialogue and Deliberation in Higher Education*, edited by Nicholas V. Longo and Timothy J. Shaffer, 128–39. Sterling, VA: Stylus Publishing, LLC.

Csizmadia, Annamaria, Eleanor Shoreman-Ouimet, Micah D. Heumann, and Terrence H. W. Ching. 2020. "The UCONN Racial Microaggressions Survey." University of Connecticut.

Dahal, Pranab, Sunil Kumar Joshi, and Katraina Swahnberg. 2022. *Journal of Interpersonal Violence* 37, no. 13–14 (July): NP12086–NP12110.

Garza, Alicia. 2020. *The Purpose of Power: How We Come Together When We Fall Apart.* New York: One World.

Garcia, Gineiris. 2022a. "Stuck in the Tape: A Forum Play for UConn Hartford," with assistance and research collected by HartBeat Ensemble, most notably Hannah Simms and Godfrey Simmons.

Garcia, Gineiris. 2022b. Interview, conducted virtually by Jane Anna Gordon, December 30.

Ghoshal, Shubhra, and Nirban Manna. 2020. "Dialogue for Empowerment: Jana Sanskriti's Experiment with the Method of the Theatre of the Oppressed in Rural Bengal," *NTQ* 36, no. 2 (May): 117–30.

Green, Sharon. 2001. "Boal and Beyond: Strategies for Creating Community Dialogue." *Theater* 31, no. 3 (Fall): 47–61.

Howard, Leigh Anne. 2004. "Speaking Theatre/Doing Pedagogy: Re-Visiting Theatre of the Oppressed," *Communication Education* 53, no. 3 (July): 217–33.

Jackson, Adrian. 2009. "Augusto Boal—a Theatre in Life," *NTQ* 25:4 (November): 306–9.

Lee Boggs, Grace, with Scott Kurashige. 2012. *The Next American Revolution: Sustainable Activism for the Twenty-First Century*, Updated and expanded edition. Berkeley and Los Angeles: University of California Press.

Mitchell, Karen S., and Jennifer L. Freitag. 2011. "Forum Theatre for Bystanders: A New Model for Gender Violence Prevention," *Violence Against Women* 17, no. 8 (August): 990–1013.

Moses, Gilbert, John O'Neal, Denise Nicholas, Murray Levy, and Richard Schechner. 1965. "Dialogue: The Free Southern Theatre," *The Tulane Drama Review* 9, no. 4 (Summer): 63–76.

Olson, Lynne. 2001. *Freedom's Daughters: The Unsung Heroines of the Civil Rights Movement from 1830 to 1970*. New York: Simon and Schuster.

O'Neal, John. 1968. "Motion in the Ocean: Some Political Dimensions of the Free Southern Theatre," *The Drama Review* 12, no. 4 (Summer): 70–77.

Pratt, Geraldine, and Calen Johnston. 2007. "Turning Theatre into Law, and other Spaces of Politics." *cultural geographies* 14: 92–113.

Principia News. 2021. "Acting out Against Racism," August 12.

Simmons, Godfrey L., and Patricia O'Rourke. 2022. Interview conducted virtually by Jane Anna Gordon, December 19.

Sullivan, John, Sharon Petronella, Edward Brooks, Maria Murillo, Loree Primeau, and Jonathan Ward. 2008. "Theatre of the Oppressed and Environmental Justice Communities: A Transformational Therapy for the Body Politics," *Journal of Health Psychology* 12, no. 2: 166–79.

Taylor, Diana. 2009. "Augusto Boal 1931–2009," *The Drama Review* 53, no. 4 (Winter): 10–11.

The Jane Addams Collective. 2021. *Mutual Aid: Self/Social Therapy*. Columbia, SC: Combustion Books.

Tuitt, Frank. 2022. Interview conducted virtually by Jane Anna Gordon, December 20.

Woodly, Deva R. 2022. *Reckoning: Black Lives Matter and the Democratic Necessity of Social Movements*. New York: Oxford University Press.

Zamalin, Alex. 2022. *All Is Not Lost: 20 Ways to Revolutionize Disaster*. Boston: Beacon.

Chapter 4

Black Dancers Matter

Black Ballerinas, Robert E. Lee, and the Politics of Resistance

Simon Stow and Amanda Millis

It is one thing to dance as though nothing has happened; it is another to acknowledge that something singularly awful has happened . . . and then decide to dance.

—Jonathan Lear

[Blacks] put up the Lee Monument, and should the time come, will be there to take it down.

—John Mitchell, *Richmond Planet*, June 7, 1890

Amid the urban upheaval that followed the May 2020 murder of George Floyd, a forty-six-year-old Black man, by Derek Chauvin, a white City of Minneapolis police officer, many of the public monuments to the Confederacy on display in several Southern cities were defaced or destroyed. Nowhere, perhaps, was this assault on the symbols of white supremacy more prevalent than in Richmond, Virginia, the former Confederate capital; a city where, in the years since Reconstruction, the celebration of the "Lost Cause" had become something of a fetish (Blight 37). The city's Monument Avenue—lined with statues of five Confederate grandees including

Jefferson Davis and Stonewall Jackson[1]—was a target-rich environment, and all but one of the monuments were torn down. The fifth, a twelve-ton bronze statue of Robert E. Lee, perched atop a forty-foot-tall stone plinth at the center of a large traffic circle, proved more recalcitrant. In the face of this difficulty, Black citizens claimed the plinth and the traffic circle as their own. The former was covered in graffiti proclaiming BLACK LIVES MATTER, offering slogans of empowerment and profanity-laden assaults on racism, white supremacy, and the police. At night, Black artists employed the plinth as a screen upon which to project images of George Floyd, Breonna Taylor, and other victims of police violence as well as key figures in the Black struggle including Malcolm X, John Lewis, and Angela Davis. The traffic circle upon which the Lee monument stood was renamed for Marcus-David Peters, a Black Richmonder who was shot and killed by the police. Thereafter, according to the *Washington Post*, the site became "an open-air civics forum, with gospel choirs, daily speeches, voter registration booths and a public vegetable garden" (Schneider). It was a space both created by, and made for, cultural expression, especially dance.

Dancing styles exhibited at the monument site included traditional African, hip-hop, jazz, modern—with a dancer costumed in white shirt and black pants paying homage to the great Black choreographer Alvin Ailey—and even Irish step dancing (Ritzel).[2] The dancers who drew the most attention were, however, two Black teenagers—Ava Holloway and Kennedy George—who performed classical ballet at the site. Images of their performance went viral, and the women were featured on both NBC's *Today Show* and the syndicated news magazine *Inside Edition*. The TV coverage of their performance was, nevertheless, politically anodyne. While NBC did very briefly situate the dance in the context of the 2020 protests, more attention was paid to the difficulties faced by Black women in ballet, itself an important issue but not that which had precipitated Holloway and George's performance. Beyond that, the soft-soaping of the story focused on the young women's determination to do some good with their sudden fame. George Floyd was not mentioned. *Inside Edition*'s coverage was even worse. There was no mention of the protests that precipitated the dance performance. Rather, the focus was on the statue as a historical relic, paying attention to Lee's role in the Civil War, with no contemporary political corollary. As with NBC's coverage there was some acknowledgment of the problems faced by ballerinas of color, even as it was suggested that these problems had all but been solved. Most vexing, however, was the show's description of ballet as a "sport." For although there is some discussion within dance circles about the extent to which dancers might be considered athletes, this categorization served to remove the dance's aesthetic, intellectual, and thus, its political, content (Guarino).

Working against the characterization of Holloway and George as plucky young teens employing their balletic skills to draw attention to Richmond's problematic Robert E. Lee monument without any broader political motives, this essay highlights the political dimensions of their performance, situating their work within recent debates about counterpublics and the politics of resistance. Holloway and George, it is suggested, demonstrate the important role that cultural politics play for subaltern populations who are marginalized in, or excluded from, the dominant public sphere. Their embrace of a white dance form in a historically white space served, it will be argued, to create, strengthen, and make visible, the microcosmic Black counterpublic that emerged in Marcus-David Peters Circle. Categorizing Holloway and George's performance as a form of resistance, the essay will then seek to demonstrate how it challenges a dominant contemporary understanding of the concept as an "essentially defensive" form of politics (Walzer 1960), one that, because it lacks a "politics of offense" aimed at the state, is only "half a politics" (Walzer 2017). Likewise, it will aim to show how the women's performance challenges Adolph Reed's categorization of cultural politics as a vacuous "don't-worry, be-angry politics of posture" that is, by definition, about "resignation and acquiescence" (168). The aim here is not to critique the work of Walzer and Reed, though that will obviously be part of the argument. Rather, it is to show how Holloway and George's performance embodies a complex politico-aesthetic form of resistance that surmounts such criticism. The approach is best understood not merely as a defensive "pushing back" against the white public sphere à la Walzer, but rather as what W. E. B. Du Bois characterized as a "pushing onwards" (1926). It is an understanding in which, according to Ella Myers, Du Bois "urges his audience to define their own collective aims and to work to build a society that realizes them, rather than accept the terms of the dominant social order" (112). For Du Bois, who famously observed that "all art is propaganda" (1926), culture was central to achieving this self-definition. The stakes here are suggested by Frantz Fanon's observation that "[b]y imparting new meaning and dynamism to artisanship, dance, music, literature, and the oral epic, the colonized subject restructures his own perception" (176). In their act of "restructuring perception," it will be observed, Holloway and George's performance moves beyond Walzer's characterization of resistance as a purely defensive form of politics to capture its positive role in the creation of identity as/and a pushing onward.[3] It will further be suggested that in their complexity Holloway and George's resistive acts indicate, contra Reed, that even as it employs posture for political purposes, cultural politics is considerably more than a politics of posture. For, in their embrace of the balletic form, Holloway and George problematize many of the conceits of the very dance form they are enacting, most obviously its long-standing hostility to Black female bodies. Their approach, it will be argued, not only challenges the stereotypes that have hampered Black dancers, but, in its complex self-reflexiveness, also points to the possibility of a different future. For, as Zora Neale Hurston observed, Black "dancing is dynamic suggestion . . . every posture gives the impression that the dancer will do much more" (53).

The essay will begin with a brief account of the nature of, and the relationship between, publics and counterpublics. It will then rehearse the ways in which the Robert E. Lee monument served the interests of the dominant white public from May 29, 1880, until May 31, 2022. As a precursor to the discussion of their role in claiming of the monument through dance, the essay will then offer an account of the obstacles that have traditionally hampered Black women in the world of dance, and in ballet in particular. The aim of this seeming digression is to permit the delineation in the final part of the essay of a simultaneous double movement by which Holloway and George embrace and employ an aesthetic form which "likes to think of itself as beyond politics" (Gottschild 2003) to offer positive resistance to the politics of white supremacy. First, by helping to turn the site into the microcosmic counterpublic—theirs was among the first artistic performances at the site coming only eleven days after George Floyd's murder—and second, by exposing as falsely pernicious the stereotypes that impede the progress of Black women in dance. While it is, perhaps, the former that has drawn most attention, it may be their engagement with the latter that most clearly demonstrates the power of positive resistance—of pushing onward—to "restructure perception," both of the world in which this dance form is an artifact, and of the dominant white supremacist assumptions that structure dance itself. In this, the essay seeks to demonstrate the fecundity of the relationship between art and radical politics.

Publics, Counterpublics, and Resistance

"Publics," writes Michael Warner, "have become an essential fact of the social landscape; yet it would tax our understanding to say exactly what they are" (65). Jürgen Habermas has no such concerns. For him, the public sphere is the space in which citizens debate and discuss their shared concerns through the medium of speech (1991). It is, he argues, an arena of rationality and consensus, one in which citizens come to an agreement on their values and policies. A number of theorists, including William Connolly (2005), Bonnie Honig (1993), and Chantal Mouffe (2005) have, however, taken issue with Habermas's assumption that the endpoint of democratic deliberation is consensus. Rather, they suggest, democracy is necessarily antagonistic, filled with always-ongoing conflicts, and that as such, reaching consensus is—at best—highly unlikely. For this reason, they argue, democratic theory should focus on turning antagonism into a potentially politically productive agonism, a register in which opponents are seen as rivals rather than enemies. There are, they note, multiple possible publics and that, as such, any public's claim to be *the* public sphere is inherently ideological: an expression of a desire for hegemonic cultural and/or political power. In such hegemonic spheres, notes Michael Dawson, social stratification is such that favorable outcomes are guaranteed to privileged groups, even in the absence of formal exclusions (2001, 24). Counterpublics are those publics that stand outside of, and/or in opposition to, the dominant public sphere. Noting the way in which such spheres are formed by those excluded and/or disadvantaged by the dominant public, Nancy Fraser labels them "subaltern counterpublics" (67). One of the ways in which such publics are *counter*publics, Warner suggests, is that they "try to supply different ways of imagining," offering the subaltern a space and ways in which to create their identities in the face of the hegemonic demands of the dominant public sphere (121, 57). Thus, he argues, they seek to offer "not only new shared worlds and critical languages but also new privacies, new individuals, new bodies, new intimacies, and new citizenships" (Warner 61). It is out of such publics—and especially out of what Frank Farmer calls *cultural publics*—that a mode of resistance beyond the merely defensive, a form of "pushing onwards," emerges (31).

In his book *Race Rebels: Culture, Politics, and the Black Working Class*, Robin Kelley offers a far more capacious understanding of politics than that embraced by Walzer and Reed. He rejects the idea that "the only struggles that count take place through institutions" (4). Here he anticipates Chantal Mouffe's distinction between "politics" and "the political." "By the 'political,'" she writes, "I mean the dimension of antagonism which I take to be constitutive of human societies, while by 'politics' I mean the set of practices and institutions through which an order is created, organizing human coexistence in the context of conflictuality provided by the political" (9). Thus, in Mouffian terms, by paying attention to behavior in nonstate contexts, Kelley's focus is on "the political." By way of example, he identifies Malcolm Little's—the putative Malcolm X's—adoption of zoot suits and conked hair during his years as "Detroit Red." While Malcolm's stylings have been presented as assimilationist—not least by Malcolm himself—Kelley connects his attire to resistive traditions emerging out of parts of the Latinx community, traditions in which fashion conveyed opposition to a dominant white public sphere (165). While such sartorial choices can obviously be understood as a defensive posture—a "pushing back" against the respectability norms of the dominant public sphere—such a reading is necessarily incomplete, missing as it does fashion's role in a positive construction of identity, and as a mode of communication for the subaltern in the dominant public sphere (Ford). Similarly, Kelley identifies the multiple roles that gangsta rap played in the lives of the Black underclass in the 1990s, including, but not limited to, creating identity, decrying living conditions, generating aesthetic pleasure, and detailing police abuse all the while cultivating a distinct sense of style (183–226). That none of these aspects was in any way *aimed* at the dominant white public sphere—though they were inevitably overheard and sometimes problematically embraced by whites—suggests the ways in which Black resistance is more than a strategy of defense. It is, to be sure, often a mode of survival in the face of a white hegemonic public, but Kelley's work also indicates the ways in which it is a pushing onward, cultivating a consciousness, way of being, and a sense of identity that is a thing unto itself, not a reaction to something else. It is a pushing onward located in multiple locations and expressed in multiple voices; as Foucault observes, because "power is spread throughout society . . . the struggle against power must also be diffuse" (Pickett 458). It is an account of political activity that exposes the limitations of Walzer's and Reed's understandings of resistance.

Reed's narrowness of focus would seem to be called into further question by Richard Iton's argument that it is necessary to study Black politics in and through Black culture "because of the exclusionary and often violent practices that have historically defined black citizenship and public sphere participation as problematic and because of the recognition that the cultural realm is always in play and already politically significant terrain" (17). It is an argument that finds support from Waldo Martin. "Precisely because African Americans historically have had more control over their own culture than many other aspects of their world," he writes, "culture has always been a critical battleground in their freedom struggle" (3). To look only to the state for evidence of Black agency and politics, or to prioritize that mode of politics over and above the cultural would, then, be to obscure important political activity in the Black counterpublic. Although such Black resistance is not necessarily defined in opposition to the dominant white public sphere, the form of resistance embodied by Holloway and George's performance can best be understood against the history of the Lee monument and its role in an exclusionary white public.

Look Away, Look Away

On May 29, 1890, a giant equestrian statue of Robert E. Lee was unveiled in Richmond, Virginia. Attended by an estimated crowd of between 100,000 and 150,000 people, the event was marked by a parade of some 20,000 citizens with bands playing "Dixie," and the waving of both Confederate and American flags (Blight 267–69). The intermingling of the flags was telling: the unveiling was seen as the embodiment of a reconciliation between the North and the South. Indeed, *The New York Times* declared Lee's memory "a possession of the American people, and the monument that recalls it is itself a national possession" (Savage 152). It was a reconciliation that excluded Black Americans. By making Lee rather than Jefferson Davis the southern face of the Civil War, forces both North and South emptied the conflict of any political content. The war became one of valor: a tragedy in which brother fought brother, with the issue of slavery all but forgotten. The whitewashing of Lee's reputation even extended to the claim that he had been opposed to slavery, a position not borne out by his actual statements about the nation's original sin (Savage 131). Indeed, solidifying the white reconciliationist impulse, Lee was depicted as a proponent of gradual emancipation, a position that found great favor in the North where Black participation in public life was far from popular. Indeed, the design of the monument—depicting Lee astride his horse, Traveller—was itself an embodiment of white supremacist ideology. Building on a well-known racist folktale in which a "negro boy" tried to ride Traveller but was thrown off because the horse would not permit himself to be ridden by an inferior being, the design, notes Kirk Savage, showed that "Lee did not have to spur or whip or strangle with the reins; his moral authority achieved what mere physical domination could accomplish only imperfectly" (134). In this, the monument offered a model of the benevolent master controlling the inferior races that had considerable appeal to postbellum whites both North and South.

There was, however, considerable opposition to the memorial from Richmond's Black residents. John Mitchell, editor of the Black newspaper *The Richmond Planet*, and a member of the city council—which had not yet gone full Jim Crow—voted along with the two other Black council members to refrain from approving an appropriation to fund the monument's dedication. Such was their marginality they were, nevertheless, relatively limited in what they could achieve, with silence on the issue being "their only feasible non-suicidal option" (Savage 152). Mitchell reported hearing an elderly Black man witnessing the monument's inaugural parade and its multitude of Confederate flags declare: "The Southern white folks are on top—the Southern white folks is on top!" (Blight 270). It was a lament that captured the postwar predicament of Blacks both North and South. With typical sagacity, Frederick Douglass had long railed against the sort of historical forgetting embodied by the Lee monument. In his 1865 speech, "Our Martyred President," he declared: "We were manifesting almost as much gratitude to General Lee for surrendering as to General Grant for compelling him to surrender" (Douglass 78). Nevertheless, even his fiery rhetoric and well-timed interrogative were insufficient to prevent the exclusionary reconciliationism and historical amnesia made manifest in the Lee monument. The monument was but one small part of a broader narrative that took shape after the war, but its history is suggestive of the ways in which that narrative took hold, for, as Savage notes, "A funny thing happened once the monument was built and it took over the landscape of people's lives: it became a kind of natural fact, as if it had always been meant to be. The monument's rhetorical claims of popular status became self-fulfilling prophecy" (7). The monument in effect erased its own history along with any tensions among whites that it might have embodied, cultivating a politics of consensus that excluded those who might have objected to its construction and/or the story it told about the world in which it was an artifact.

In keeping with recent work on the power of monuments to generate and/or to shape publics by thinkers as diverse as Karen Cox, Erika Doss, and Steven Johnston, Savage nevertheless offers some hope—albeit perhaps Du Bois's "hope, not hopeless, but unhopeful" (1994, 93)—that such sites might be reworked in a manner that is politically productive for subaltern groups. "The public monument," he writes, "was, after all not just a rhetorical space where people debated image and symbol but was a real physical space where public could gather and define themselves at ceremonies and rallies" (7). In a world in which art—albeit, in the case of the Lee statue, a monumental form of poshlost—helped to shape dominant political understandings, it is possible that art might also serve to signify on, reconfigure, remix, or replace such prevailing values in ways that better serve the needs and/or the interests of the subaltern. Such was the impact of those who initially claimed the Lee monument in the days following George Floyd's murder. Among those acts of claiming was Ava Holloway and Kennedy George's dance performance, one which not only engaged with the monument but also the white supremacist history of ballet itself. Delineating that history sets the stage for understanding the complexity and political import of Holloway and George's double engagement with both the white supremacist American public sphere, and the similarly tainted balletic form.

Ballet and the Racial Aesthetic

In both NBC's and *Inside Edition*'s coverage of the young women's performance, Kennedy George recounted an experience common to ballet dancers of color: that a prerequisite for her dancing with her ballet company was dyeing her pointe shoes—which usually only come in pink for women—to match her skin tone. This, she noted, required that she find foundation makeup that matched her complexion and apply to the shoes with a brush, a laborious process that, she said, took several coats (NBC). While deeply symbolic of the difficulties faced by ballerinas of color in the word of classical dance, this is but one such obstacle, many of which arise from the form's almost maniacal obsession with uniformity: a world in which a Black ballerina is seen to disrupt the desired aesthetic effect to the extent that they have sometimes been asked to color their skin (Sulcas 2020). This is one reason Black ballerinas have difficulty finding a company (Gottschild 78).[4] Such exclusions have a knock-on effect, with Black children often not taking up ballet because they have no role models, with classes largely taught by white women (Klapper 130). If these obstacles to Black participation in the ballet world are only incidentally racist—and it is not clear that they deserve such a benign ascription—then there are other more explicitly racist reasons why Black dancers are disadvantaged, most obviously in the mischaracterization of the Black body's aptitude for classical performance, and in the assumptions about the supposedly "natural" ability of Black dancers.

"On of the most prevalent and pernicious myths attached to the Black dancing body," observes Gottschild, "is that movement is not learned but inborn" (2003, 47). Connected to this is the assumption that "as 'natural movers," Black dancers are "attuned solely to rhythm and incapable of being trained" (Das 22). Such primitivist understandings of Black dance stretch back to before the founding of the nation (Thompson 23). Under slavery, dancing was taken as evidence of Blacks' intellectual vacuity; indeed, in his *Notes on the State of Virginia,* Thomas Jefferson pointed to Black dance as an indication of the primitive nature of the enslaved, a claim that served, he believed, to justify slavery itself (Jefferson 148). The "natural" Black dancer is a trope that, as Rachel Carrico points out, has had a shockingly long half-life, stretching from slavery to the present day (27). In addition to robbing Black dance of its intellectual content, the "natural" dancer trope also serves to rob the Black dancer of the recognition of the physical effort that both dance training and performance require. It is an aspect of the trope that serves to undermine the recruitment of Black dancers, especially in ballet. It does so in two ways. First, and most obviously, it continually inscribes and reinscribes upon the Black dancing body, the notion that it is unsuitable for choreography, such as ballet, that is strongly predicated upon technique; second, Black dancers often find themselves subject to stereotype threat: when faced with a widely held negative perception of group's abilities—such as a lack of technique—members of that group find themselves hampered by the stereotype in their performance of a task (Gottschild 2003, 80–81; Steele and Aronson). Most profoundly, however, the "natural" trope robs Black dancers of any agency, with their performances seen as a product of instinct, not technical acumen, creativity, and hard work. It is, furthermore, an understanding that empties Black dance of any political content. Dance, and Black dance in particular, is nevertheless inherently political. This is something that becomes evident when it is situated within a Black counterpublic: the sphere in which Black Americans both create and identify themselves as a people, that which stands outside of and/or in opposition to the dominant white public sphere, and through which they seek to cultivate productive responses to their marginalization (Dawson).

Black Swans and the Claiming of Public Space

There is no video footage of the first occasion upon which Kennedy George and Ava Holloway danced on the Lee Monument at the Marcus-David Peters Circle. The performance was, however, captured by Marcus Ingram, a Richmond-based photographer, whose pictures went viral on Instagram and elsewhere.[5] Evident in all the pictures is the way in which the monument's plinth has been tagged with graffiti. Slogans include "BLM," "Stop White Supremacy," "Fuck Pigs," "Hold Cops Accountable," and "Save Black Lives." What might be seen as defacements of the monument are, says Ella Myers, borrowing the vocabulary of Bruno Latour, better understood as "reface-ments" (127). It is an insight that captures the way in which the resistive force of claiming the site points both ways: it is to be sure a pushing back against the state—though not through its formal institutions in the manner championed by Walzer and Reed—but also a pushing onward. The tagging of the territory helps to make the monument site a space for Black lives to matter, a microcosmic counterpublic in which there is room for the flour-ishing of Black imagination and dialogue, and the cultivation of a critical Black consciousness. Renaming the site the Marcus-David Peters Circle enacts the same mechanism, a further refacement. In this, the actions of those who claimed the plinth and the traffic circle—Holloway and George among them—embodied a Black resistive tradition of claiming the streets, often those in white locales. The most obvious example of this is second lining street parades in New Orleans where participants "own" the street for the duration of their performances: a subaltern claiming of property by the propertyless, one that brings with it a sense of community and agency in the face of dispossession (Regis 2008, 756). Second lining is, as Helen Regis notes, a way for those who take temporary control of the streets to "take hold of the public imagination" (1999, 480), shaping a communal resistive ethos in the in the manner suggested, in different ways, by Du Bois and Kelley.[6] Little wonder, perhaps, that Fanon should declare that, in the face of sterile negotiations with the colonial government, "[t]he time for dancing in the streets has arrived" (32). Such engagement serves to create a Black counterpublic, says Michael C. Dawson, a space where not just the Arendtian *vita activa* but also the *vita contemplative* is made possible, not just a world of action, but a world of action imbued with thought and imagination (53). As with any aesthetic form, the process by which this happens is far from linear. Observes Iton, "[i]t is extremely rare-though not impossible-for actions undertaken by creative artists alone to bring about specific substantive public policy reorientations on the part of state authorities. Rather, the discursive disruptions artists instigate, and the meanings read into their actions and creations are most likely to have a more diffuse, symbolic impact, at least in the external domain" (28). Nevertheless, as Myers notes, characterizations of such actions as a purely symbolic politics—a characterization which would, no doubt, find favor with Reed—are mistaken (125). Rather, as Lisa Perhamus and Clarence Joldersama argue, the tearing down and the refacing of monuments "is not *symbolic* of a dismantling; it *is* a dismantling, bit by physical bit, of anti-Black racism and hierarchical racial ordering" (1322). What might be seen as a politics of symbolism by those in the dominant public sphere is, their work suggests, always more than that for those engaged in the aesthetic—and other forms of political action—in the subaltern counterpublic. Such was Holloway and Kennedy's performance in the Marcus-David Peters circle.

"This is us enforcing that we are not putting up with this anymore," observed Kennedy George about their performance, "we are not going to be discriminated against, this is unacceptable. This is us putting our foot down and making things happen . . . I knew I could use dance because it is always something I have done" (Turner). Taking their dance out of the concert hall and/or the classroom and into the streets, Holloway and George claimed both the dance form and the location for a rich form of resistance, inscribing upon both (and thus upon the audience(s) for their performance) the insistence that Black lives matter. Indeed, in a time when it has repeatedly been shown that Black bodies often do not matter—evidenced by the deaths of George Floyd, Eric Garner, Breonna Taylor, Tamir Rice, and many others—the women were able to demonstrate the political importance of their own Black bodies through dance. In so doing, they drew attention to such losses and pushed back against the attitudes and conditions that make such deaths commonplace in the American republic. For if, as Warner suggests, counterpublics create the conditions for, and are created out of, a different imaginary than the dominant public, then dance proves its worth as a subaltern political form. Writes Randy Martin, "Dance . . . makes its own politics, crafts its own pathways and agency in the world, moves us toward what we imagine to be possible and desirable" (29). Its inherent duality as a form of resistance—as both a pushing back and as a pushing onward—is further suggested by Katrina Hazard-Gordon who suggests that "the African-American dance arena has demonstrated a cultural resilience and a recuperative creativity" (xi). The recuperative creativity on show in Holloway and George's performance is suggested by how they employ their crafted bodies—disciplined through ballet's commitment to precise and proper technique—to seek to create a space where Black life not so precarious, where the threat of violence is, if not entirely diminished, at least potentially mitigated (Beausoleil 119).[7] This productive duality is evident in the way Holloway and George both employ and signify on the balletic form in their response to the death of George Floyd.

Figure 4.1 shows Kennedy George (left) and Ava Holloway halfway up the base of the plinth of the Lee Monument, dressed in black tutus. Facing the camera (*en face*), Holloway in pink pointe shoes, George in black, the women are positioned in the classical ballet position *sous-sus*, *en pointe* (on their toes), one foot behind the other—in what dancers call fifth position—their legs fully stretched.

Figure 4.1. Digital Photo, 2020. *Source:* Photo by Marcus Ingram Jr. Used with permission.

While this position is a standard part of the ballet repertoire, its degree of difficulty is elevated here because the women are posing for the camera rather than being caught in mid-movement. In this, their form—their execution of the required position—demonstrates a resistance to the racist stereotypes about the technical ability and physical unsuitability of Black female bodies for ballet and other formal dance. This is also evident in figure 4.2, where the dancer is in a *penché*—a lean—which is a position that requires considerable strength, skill, and technique.

It is a resistance that pushes two ways. First, *against* those would employ such stereotypes to justify their exclusion of Black bodies from

Figure 4.2. Digital Photo, 2020. *Source:* Photo by Marcus Ingram Jr. Used with permission.

concert dance; and second, it pushes *onward* by allowing the excluded to embrace the hitherto unseen possibilities that such a performance makes obvious. Most clearly these include the power of the aesthetic to refute, reframe, and reimagine in productive ways the supposed truisms of white supremacy. Dance thus plays its part in the Black counterpublic. In the first instance, dance pushes back against the constraints and values of the white public sphere such as, for example, by countering stereotype threat (whose pernicious effects are not, of course, confined to the world of dance). In the second, it serves to restructure the perceptions of its Black members in a productive fashion, promoting community, consciousness, and agency in ways that have little if anything to do with a response to white hegemony. It offers, that is to say, a nondefensive form of resistance. This aspect of the women's performance is made evident by their creation—along with two other Black dancers Sophia Chambliss and Shania Gordon—of the organization Brown Ballerinas for Change. In keeping with the double movement of their performance, that which focuses on injustice inside and outside of ballet, they describe their mission as "to help create advocacy, social justice, and to increase participation of underrepresented populations in ballet," and their vision as "to use ballet to promote activism, social justice, and to increase diversity in the arts by providing annual scholarships, a mentor network, and community programs" (Brown Ballerinas for Change). Characterizing dance as being about joy and collaboration, Kennedy George—no doubt inadvertently but still tellingly—channeled Du Bois when she declared: "We're moving forward" (Rendlemean). The organization suggests but one of the many possibilities enacted and enabled by the politics of their performance.

The richness of that performance is further evidenced in figure 4.1. where the dancers are positioned with one arm behind their backs, and the other in fifth position, *en haut* (stretched). Both arms in fifth position is extremely common in ballet; indeed, it is probably the position most often adopted by those trying to imitate a ballerina. Here, however, only one arm is raised, with the dancers creating a mirror effect by each holding up different arms. While arms *en haut* would normally be completed by an outstretched hand with a flat palm, here the women offer the clenched first of the Black Power salute. It is a bold refacement of both the monument site and the dance tradition they embody: both are claimed and reworked, not only as a rebuke to white supremacy but also as an appeal to a Black radical tradition. Perhaps confused by the juxtaposition of the women's youth, the balletic form, the radicalism of the gesture, or simple willful blindness, many white observers chose to ignore or bend over backward to empty their performance of its political content. Thus, a story in one of Richmond's free newspapers, *Style Weekly* referenced the photograph of the dancers "with their right *[sic]* fists raised *reminiscent* of the Black Power salute" (my emphasis). In addition to misdescribing the picture, the author seems unwilling to acknowledge that the raised fist *is* the Black Power salute, something made clear by the dancers echoing in their positioning a graffitied Black Power first salute below and between them on the plinth, and by figure 4.3. in which Holloway repeats the gesture combining, once again, *sous-sus* with a right arm in fifth position, again making the Black Power salute.

If the raised fist of the Black Power salute in figures 4.1 and 4.3 are a form of signification on the fifth position in classical ballet, then the same can be said for the dancers' gaze in both figures 4.3 and 4.4.

Figure 4.3. Digital Photo, 2020. *Source:* Photo by Marcus Ingram Jr. Used with permission.

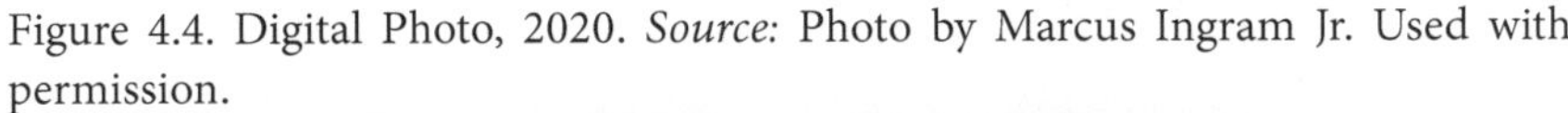

Figure 4.4. Digital Photo, 2020. *Source:* Photo by Marcus Ingram Jr. Used with permission.

Traditionally, the direction of the head follows that of the fingers, except when the dancer is facing the audience, as in figures 4.1, 4.3, and 4.4. In those circumstances, the head and eyes are directed out toward the audience, but not in a way that looks directly at them. Rather, the gaze is one that looks of into the distance. As we see in all three of these images, the dancers are looking directly at the camera that serves as their audience in this performance. In this, in balletic terms, they are said to be "breaking" the movement.

The significance of this breaking becomes clear once it is observed that a recurring practice of Black Lives Matter has been the daring look back, or the unflinching staring into the eyes of law enforcement. One of the unwritten rules of the Jim Crow era was, notes Myers, that Black people could not make eye contact with whites for fear insult, beating, or worse (122).

Thus, the direct stare as it is employed by BLM is a form of resistance to the white gaze, but also one which pushes the movement forward by raising the consciousness of, and empowering, its members. Its embrace by Holloway and George might be thought to do the same, capturing the political complexity of their performance in ways that suggest that, contrary to historical stereotypes, Black dance is action imbued with intellectual content, and is, thus, a powerful form of resistance that gives the lie to the inadequacy of Walzer's and Reed's account of the same.

Turning Mourning into Dancing

In closing, it should, perhaps, be noted that Holloway and George's is very much a dance of mourning and one that embodied a complex tradition of Black responses to loss. In *Souls of Black Folk*, for example, Du Bois's refers to an "awful gladness" arising from his son's passing: a combination of his sorrow at his loss and his simultaneous relief that his child was now free from racial oppression (1994, 95). It is a tradition that has long served as a resistive force in Black life, and one that pushes both ways—backward and forward—against the values of the dominant white public, and forward to the creation of identity and the cultivation of a Black consciousness (Stow 2017). Following Denmark Vesey's failed uprising in Charleston, South Carolina, in 1822, for example, slaves were prohibited from wearing any outward signs of mourning in the week following his execution. Many, nevertheless, chose to do so, both resisting the state, and cultivating, signaling, and sharing an identity which, will no doubt oppositional, was also directed at fellow Blacks (Robertson 98, 104). It is also a tradition of futurity and hope—in the Du Boisean sense—as is suggested by the Reverend Joseph Lowery's assertion that, at a Black funeral, "we celebrate the life of the dead, but then we challenge those who are living to pick up the mantle and carry on the work" (Stow 2010, 691). Holloway and Kennedy's dance embodied just such a sensibility, one that mourned loss but that also looked forward to, and sought to bring about, a world in which the state violence that killed George Floyd is a world of the past. For, as Elizabeth Alexander observes: "Our dancing is our pleasure, but perhaps it is also our sorrow song" (81). The duality of the sorrow songs—what Du Bois calls "the music of an unhappy people, of the children of disappointment; they tell of death and suffering and an unvoiced longing towards a truer world" (1994, 103)—is evident in Holloway and George's performance, not least in their choice of black tutus for their dance. While obviously the traditional color of mourning, in ballet the black tutu necessarily invokes Odile, the Black Swan in Tchaikovsky's *Swan Lake*. There the blackness of the costuming is meant to indicate evil and in this sense Holloway and George claim the color for good, signifying upon the balletic tradition in a way that reconfigures both it and the world in which it is an artifact. As with all their efforts, there is no guarantee that they will succeed, but the complexity of their resistive mode demands that this is not a reason to try. It is a form of resistance that seeks to move beyond the present, embodying all the while the recognition that to push back is insufficient, that such art must help its audience and protagonists push onward, embodying always the duality at the heart of Black life. Clad in black tutus of mourning, Ava Holloway and Kennedy George did just that, cultivating in the process a space for their fellow Black citizens to imagine and to create a new future.

Notes

1. The first monument, to Robert E. Lee was dedicated in 1890, and the four other Confederate statues between 1907 and 1929. A sixth monument, added in 1996, commemorates tennis player and Richmond native Arthur Ashe. A statue of Christopher Columbus not located on Monument Avenue was also torn down during the post-George Floyd unrest.

2. The step dancing was formed by a young Black Woman, Morgan Bullock, who combines traditional Irish dancing with the sounds of hip-hop (Bullock).

3. It is for this reason that Holloway and George and the Black citizens who helped to claim the site of the Lee monument as their own are not here characterized as "protestors," a nomenclature that suggests an objection to government actions or policy rather than to the foundation of that government in white supremacy. Given the broad coalition of groups organized under the headings of Black Lives Matter and the Movement for Black Lives, it is, of course, impossible to say that *none* of the participants in the post-George Floyd unrest saw themselves as lobbying the state, but it is more than clear that for many of those engaged in this resistance, their opposition was to white supremacy in all its forms.

4. Black men face some of these same difficulties, but overall dance companies are said to be more hospitable to Black male bodies than those of Black women (Klapper 130).

5. Julia Rendleman, a photojournalist, also took photographs of the dancers. She sold one of her pictures to Reuters which also helped the story go viral. It did, however, cause some confusion with Mr. Ingram and Ms. Rendleman often being credited for the other's work online and in print. This analysis draws on Mr. Ingram's work.

6. The strength of the tradition is suggested by its resistance to white attempts at appropriation (Stow 2008).

7. The women noted that they were sometimes subject to abuse by passing motorists. An aspect of their performance which suggests the women's bravery.

Works Cited

Alexander, Elizabeth. 2022. *The Trayvon Generation*. New York: Grand Central Publishing.

Beausoleil, Emily. 2014. " 'Only They Breathe': Identity, Agency and the Dancing Body Politic." *Constellations*, 21, no. 1: 111–33.

Blight, David. 2002. *Race and Reunion: The Civil War in American Memory*. Cambridge, MA: Belknap Press.

Bollock, Morgan. 2020. "Experience: I'm an Irish dancing TikTok star." *The Guardian*, July 17. https://www.theguardian.com/lifeandstyle/2020/jul/17/experience-im-an-irish-dancing-TikTok-star. Accessed November 12, 2022.

Brown Ballerinas for Change. n.d. https://www.brownballerinasforchange.com. Accessed December 15, 2022.

Carrico, Rachel. 2016. "Un/Natural disaster and Dancing. Hurricane Katrina and Second Lining in New Orleans." *The Black Scholar*. 46, no. 1, 2016, 27–36.

Connolly, William. 2005. *Pluralism*. Minneapolis: University of Minnesota Press.

Cox, Karen L. 2021. *No Common Ground. Confederate Monuments and the Ongoing Fight for Racial Justice*. Chapel Hill, NC: University of North Carolina Press.

Das, Joanna D. 2017. *Katherine Dunham. Dance and the African Diaspora*. New York: Oxford University Press.

Dawson, Michael C. 2001. *Black Visions. The Roots of Contemporary African-American Ideologies*. Chicago: University of Chicago Press.

Dawson, Michael C. 1995. "A Black Counterpublic? Economic Earthquakes, Racial Agenda(s), and Black Politics." *Public Culture*. 7, no. 1: 195–223.

Doss, Erika. 2010. *Memorial Mania. Public Feeling in America*. Chicago: University of Chicago Press.

Douglass, Frederick. 1999. *Frederick Douglass: Selected Speeches and Writings* edited by Philip S. Foner. Chicago: Lawrence Hill Books.

Du Bois, W. E. B. 1926. "Criteria of Negro Art." *webdubois.org*. http://www.webdubois.org/dbCriteriaNArt.html. Accessed September 30, 2022.

Du Bois, W. E. B. 1994. *The Souls of Black Folk*. Mineola, NY: Dover Press.

Fanon, Frantz. 2004. *The Wretched of the Earth*. New York: Grove Press.

Farmer, Frank. 2013. *After the Public Turn. Composition, Counterpublics, and the Citizen Bricoleur*. Boulder: University Press of Colorado.

Ford, Tanisha C. 2015. *Liberated Threads: Black Women, Style, and the Global Politics of Soul*. Chapel Hill, NC: University of North Carolina Press.

Fraser, Nancy. 1990. "Rethinking the Public Sphere: A Contribution to the Critique of Actually Existing Democracy." *Social Text*. 25/26: 56–80.

Gottschild, Brenda Dixon. 2003. *The Black Dancing Body: A Geography from Coon to Cool*. New York: Palgrave Macmillan.

Gregory, Stephen. 1994. "Race, Identity and Political Activism: The Shifting Contours of the African American Public Sphere." *Public Culture*. no. 7: 147–164.

Guarino, Lindsay. 2015. "Is Dance a Sport? A Twenty-First-Century Debate." *Journal of Dance Education*, 15, no. 2: 77–80.

Habermas, Jürgen. 1991. *The Structural Transformation of the Public Sphere. An Inquiry into a Category of Bourgeois Society*. Cambridge, MA: MIT Press.

Hazard-Gordon, Katrina. 1990. *Jookin'. The Rise of Social Dance Formations in African-American Literature*. Philadelphia: Temple University Press.

Honig, Bonnie. 1993. *Political Theory and the Displacement of Politics*. Ithaca, NY: Cornell University Press.

Hurston, Zora Neale. 2022. *You Don't Know Us Negroes and Other Essays*. New York: Harper Collins.

Inside Edition. 2020. "Black Teen Ballerinas Reclaim Robert E. Lee Statue's Space." *Inside Edition*, July 17. https://www.youtube.com/watch?v=AT-59bLtHrVg&t=228s. Accessed October 13, 2022.

Iton, Richard. 2008. *In Search of the Black Fantastic. Politics and Popular Culture in the Post-Civil Rights Era*. New York: Oxford University Press.

Jefferson, Thomas. 2006. *Notes on the State of Virginia*. https://docsouth.unc.edu/southlit/jefferson/jefferson.html. Accessed September 30, 2022.

Johnston, Steven. 2007. *The Truth About Patriotism*. Durham, NC: Duke University Press.

Kelley, Robin. 1994. *Race Rebels. Culture, Politics, and the Black Working Class*. New York: The Free Press.

Klapper, Melissa R. 2020. *Ballet Class: An American History*. New York: Oxford University Press.

Martin, Randy. 2011. "Between Intervention and Utopia: Dance Politics." In *Emerging Bodies: The Performance of World Making in Dance and Choreography*, edited by Gabrielle Klein and Sandra Noeth, 29–45. New Rockford, MD: Transcript Publishing.

Martin, Waldo. 2005. *No Coward Soldiers. Black Cultural Politics in Post-War America*. Cambridge, MA: Harvard University Press.

Meyers, Ella. 2022. *The Gratifications of Whiteness: W. E. B. Dubois and the Enduring Rewards of Anti-Blackness*. New York: Oxford University Press.

Mouffe, Chantal. 2005. *On the Political*. New York: Routledge.

NBC. 2020. "Black Ballet Dancers Talk about Their Powerful Protest Shoot." *Today*, July 15. https://www.youtube.com/watch?v=_fgI8ONfsGQ&t=152s. Accessed October 13, 2022.

Perhamus, Lisa M. and Clarence W. Joldersama. 2020. "What Might Sustain the Activism of This Moment? Dismantling White Supremacy, One Monument at a Time." *Journal of Philosophy of Education* 54, no. 5: 1314–1332.

Pickett, Brent L. 1996. "Foucault and the Politics of Resistance." *Polity* 28, no. 4: 445–466.

Reed, Adolph. 2000. *Class Notes: Posing as Politics and Other Thoughts on the American Scene*. New York: The New Press.

Regis, Helen. 1999. "Second Lines, Minstrelsy, and the Contested Landscapes of New Orleans Afro-Creole Festivals." *Cultural Anthropology*, 14, no. 4: 472–504.

Regis, Helen. 2001. "Blackness and the Politics of Memory in the New Orleans Second Line." *American Ethnologist*, 28, no. 4: 752–77.

Rendleman, Julia (@juliarendleman). 2020. "Ballerinas Kennedy George, 14, left, and Ava Holloway, 14, pose in front of a monument of Confederate general Robert E. Lee." *Instagram*, June 5. https://www.instagram.com/p/CBD40VCl8ju/?hl=en. Accessed November 11, 2022.

Ritzel, Rebecca J. 2020. "In Richmond, Black Dance Claims a Space Near Robert E. Lee." *The New York Times*, August 6. https://www.nytimes.com/2020/08/06/arts/dance/richmond-virginia-lee-monument.html. Accessed October 13, 2022.

Robertson, David. 2000. *Denmark Vesey: The Buried Story of America's Largest Slave Rebellion and the Man Who Led It*. New York: Vintage Books.

Savage, Kirk. 1997. *Standing Soldiers, Kneeling Slaves. Race, War, and Monument in Nineteenth-Century America*. Princeton, NJ: Princeton University Press.

Schneider, Gregory S. 2020. "Northam Proposes Major Effort to Reimagine Public Space Around Robert E. Lee Statue in Richmond." *The Washington Post*, December 11. https://www.washingtonpost.com/local/virginia-politics/northam-proposal-lee-statue-richmond/2020/12/10/10018a1c-3a3a-11eb-98c4-25dc9f4987e8_story.html. Accessed October 13, 2022.

Sehra, Rohina Katoch. 2020. "How Ballerinas of Color Are Changing the Palette of Dance." *Huffpost.com*, February 10. https://www.huffpost.com/entry/ballet-dancers-of-color_l_5e14b343c5b66361cb5b6b5f. Accessed October 17, 2022.

Steele, Claude M., and Joshua Aronson. 1995. "Stereotype Threat and the Intellectual Test Performance of African Americans." *Journal of Personality and Social Psychology* 69, no. 5: 797–811.

Stow, Simon. 2008. "'Do You Know What It Means to Miss New Orleans?' George W. Bush, the Jazz Funeral, and the Politics of Memory." *Theory & Event*. 11, no. 1.

Stow, Simon. 2010. "Agonistic Homegoing: Frederick Douglass, Joseph Lowery, and the Democratic Value of African American Public Mourning." *American Political Science Review*. 104, no. 4: 681–97.

Stow, Simon. 2017. *American Mourning. Tragedy. Democracy. Resilience.* New York: Cambridge University Press.

Style Weekly. 2022. "Kennedy George, 16, and Ava Holloway, 15. Co-founders and CEOs of Brown Ballerinas for Change." March 26. *styleweekly.com*. https://m.styleweekly.com/richmond/kennedy-george-16-and-ava-holloway-15/Content?oid=18592599. Accessed November 23, 2022.

Sulcas, Roslyn. 2020. "Black Ballerina, Playing a Swan, Says She Was Asked to Color Her Skin." *The New York Times*, December 11. https://www.nytimes.com/2020/12/11/arts/dance/Chloe-Lopes-Gomes-Ballet.html. Accessed October 17, 2022.

Thompson, Katrina Dyonne. 2014. *Ring Shout, Wheel About. The Racial Politics of Music and Dance in North American Slavery.* Chicago: University of Illinois Press.

Turner, Jasmine. 2021."Brown Ballerinas for Change' Working to Diversify the Arts." *12 On Your Side.* March 13. https://www.nbc12.com/2021/02/19/brown-ballerinas-change-working-diversify-arts/. Accessed December 12, 2022.

Walzer, Michael. 2017. "The Politics of Resistance." *Dissent.* March 1. www.dissentmagazine.org/online_articles/the-politics-of-resistance-michael-walzer. Accessed September 22, 2022.

Warner, Michael. 2005. *Publics and Counterpublics.* New York: Zone.

Chapter 5

Afrofuturism as Reconstitution

Alex Zamalin

Upon first glance, Afrofuturism and the law appear to be fundamentally at odds, on opposing sides of the conceptual spectrum.[1] Law is driven by a system of rules bound by strict standards of formal interpretation; Afrofuturism is a speculative genre of imaginative engagement, unbound and unconstrained. Law traffics in logical binaries, whereas Afrofuturism is unafraid to go into the sprawling depths of dystopia and utopia. Law is the technical language of state power—of the existing order, the status quo. Meanwhile, Afrofuturism, with its emphasis on the not-yet (which is to say, the future) is, above all, fiction, and its fictions are meant to energize, inspire, and generate new analytical categories into being and disrupt the existing orders, which is to say, the law. Law is the site of regulations, of juries and jurors, and precedent; Afrofuturism makes its own rules. The law aims to hide its creativity and inventiveness, whereas Afrofuturism embraces it.

And yet, there is more commonality between the law and Afrofuturism than originally meets the eye. Through a survey of the classic texts of Afrofuturist fiction, I briefly explore the way that the genre critiques and reconstructs modes of thinking embedded in American society and the legal system. What becomes clear, I argue, is that Afrofuturism is defined by the work of reconstitution. Reconstitution involves the breaking down, and reorganizing; disorienting and reorienting; it means opening up and expanding frames of theory and politics. By undoing in fiction what is socially familiar and naturalized in practice and in history—whether unconscious racist common sense or the sense of political and legal stasis—Afrofuturism opens up a vantage for a utopian reconsideration of the (racially unequal) status quo. Throughout its long and complicated history, the utopia Afrofuturism posits isn't characterized by a romantic notion of progress, or tranquility—American style. Mindful of the way racism and white supremacy consistently undermine Black freedom dreams and antiracist horizons, Afrofuturism imagines utopia as mindful of contradiction, tragedy, and irresolvable tensions—but one that still holds fast, with hope, to the promise of liberation. In this way, Afrofuturism isn't simply of significance as a cultural relic of the past of the present, but it is a generative frame of engagement that demands our attention in expressing strategies, standpoints, arguments and modes of thinking that can help reconstitute law in emancipatory ways.

Afrofuturism isn't law. And law isn't literature per se, even though, as the law and literature movement has attested, it's imperative to read law as a kind of literature and to examine the way law manifests itself in literary works. But Afrofuturism does have something of a law—if by this, we mean a first principle, a constitutional imperative, a grounding maxim that gives it a rationale. And that is, fundamentally, to imagine Black citizens to be in a position of autonomy and freedom beyond the reaches of white supremacy, which is inscribed in the law. Arguably the first Afrofuturist text, Martin Delany's work of speculative fiction, *Blake; or the Huts of America* (1859) articulates this vision through the story of a successful enslaved insurrection led by its formerly enslaved Black protagonist, Henry Blake, that begins in the US south, and reaches the shores of Cuba. Delany, himself one of the first black nationalists and ardent proponent of Black immigration to Canada, Central American and South Africa in the 1850s, writes *Blake* in direct response to two major legal developments. First, US Congress's passage of the Fugitive Slave Act (1850), which, for all purposes, nationalizes slavery by permitting slave catchers to travel north of Mason-Dixon line and capture escaped formerly enslaved citizens. Second, the US Supreme Court's notorious decision in *Dred Scott* (1857), which holds that people of African descent, whether enslaved or free, aren't entitled to any citizenship rights under the US Constitution. "The will of the man who sits in judgment on our liberty, is the law," Delany writes, "To him is given all power to say, whether or not we have a right to enjoy freedom" (Delany 2003, 201).

So in *Blake*, Delany puts the genre of Afrofuturism to work to dismantle racist assertions of Black inferiority, by bringing the reader into the fold of Black theoretical debate about the meaning of freedom, the scope of justice, and the nature of equality. "And these are really the people declared by American laws, to 'have no rights that a white is bound to respect'? Why have we so long submitted to them?" declares Madame Cordora, a revolutionary councilwoman whom Henry Blake meets in Cuba, "And if we say it shall, it will be so!" (Delany 2007, 264). The organizing narrative of *Blake*—from Blake's escape from bondage, to his attempt to free his enslaved wife, Maggie, from the clutches of the vicious slaveholder, Colonel Franks, to his attempt to forge a network of solidarity with indigenous citizens, to the formation of a Grand Council in Cuba—is an attempt to decenter white supremacy and center a Black perspective that is sensitive to the revolutionary possibilities that are silenced by the law—whether in the 1850s or today. After reading the novel, one is drawn into a reconsideration of whether the future must replicate the past. As Blake's narrator puts it, "The blacks have everything to hope for and nothing to fear. . . . They must and will be free; whilst the whites have everything to fear and nothing to hope for" (Delany 2007, 305). One is emboldened by a sense that collective action from below, that concerted organization, can be effective, as the book concludes with Blake and the revolutionary council preparing to revolt and build a new society. As a work of imagination, *Blake* performs a counternarrative to the racial common sense of its time—the era of enslavement, and diminished Black political possibility. By bringing the reader into the experiences and internal deliberations of its protagonists—the back and forth, the debate, the critique, the hope and hopelessness—that accomplish political and legal change, even if in fiction, *Blake* charts an alternative.

A similar counterhegemonic strategy is evident in an Afrofuturist text written by W. E. B. Du Bois in his novel *Dark Princess* (1928). Du Bois, the Harvard-educated social scientist, is well known for his prophecy that the color line would be the defining boundary of the twentieth century. Less well known is Du Bois's fiction. And yet, it's in his fiction that Du Bois tries to move past the debilitating pessimism that his analysis of American racism suggests. Against the racist idea circulating in the 1920s that Black citizens would be passive in the face of racial injustice—whether through the epidemic of lynching, racism in the early labor movement, eugenics, resurgent Klan violence, or Jim Crow segregation. This view is captured by the character Perugia, who says, "Your caution is ignorance inbred for ten generations" (Du Bois 1995, 61). Du Bois imagines and details the exact opposite through the story of a Black American, Matthew Townes and Indian princess Kautilya of Bwodpur. Together the characters work to establish a Great Council of the Darker Races to plan global emancipation for all people of color in the Global South. The novel features Townes becoming involved with a Chicago Pullman Porters strike, attempting to sabotage a Klansmen action, while Kautilya, after thwarting a sexual assault in the Pennsylvania factory where she works as a laborer, comes to lead a labor uprising. "That which began as a game and source of experience to me suddenly became life," Kautilya says, "I became an agent, organizer, and officer of the union. I knew my fellow laborers, in home and street" (Du Bois 1995, 224). By putting into fiction the struggles, paradoxes and complexities of global antiracist movement building, Du Bois brings the reader to recognize that legal and political strategy requires the consideration of social standpoint or lived experience. How would women of color benefit from revolution? How do they make democratic knowledge through everyday life? At the same time, in *Dark Princess*, Du Bois depicts the fragmented, disjointed process through which solidarity is formed, and genuine social recognition is acquired. Townes, a one-time aspiring politician and member of the middle class, shifts from up-by-the-bootstraps individualism to an enlarged sense of collective responsibility and concern for the masses. And Kautilya comes to understand the conditions of inequality, rather than seeing them as abstractions, from a distance. In this way, Du Bois emphasizes the virtue of critical self-examination as a way to move past orthodoxy and conventional political wisdom.

Afrofuturism, at its heart, like law, involves stories and narrative. Yet, it is precisely the unconventional way in which Afrofuturist narratives are structured, and what they expose, that gives them a unique status as sources of knowledge-making. Storytelling has been of central importance to the field of Critical Race Theory since its inception: whether these are stories that emphasize domination, intersectionality, or competing standpoints on power (Williams 1993; Matsuda et al. 1993). Of these, perhaps the most famous is the counterfactual thought experiment of Constitutional law scholar Derrick Bell (1992), "The Space Traders" (Bell 2018, 197–243). In a fictionalized science fiction telling, Bell imagines how the vast majority of white Americans are prepared to offer the nation's entire Black population to a group of aliens who arrive from outer space with abundant gold and nuclear power, promising to solve the nation's economic woes after years of neoliberal deregulation, privatization, and outsourcing of American jobs. As Bell writes, "As is the usual fate of minority rights when subjected to referenda or initiatives, the outcome was never really in doubt. The final vote tally confirmed the predictions. By 70 percent to 30 percent, American citizens voted to ratify the constitutional amendment that provided a legal basis" (Bell 239). Bell's story of what he, and other CRTs understand as "racial realism," is primarily illustrative of a larger dynamic he believes plagues American law—his theory of "interest convergence," which holds that racial progress is only possible when it is in the white majority's economic interest.

But Afrofuturist narratives aren't simply in place to confirm existing sociological truths, or to validate expectations around racial common sense. They question, challenge, and revise what utopian alternatives might be possible. Consider another of Du Bois's stories, a short story included in his *Darkwater*, called "The Comet" (1920), which is set in postapocalyptic New York after a comet has destroyed the city. Du Bois tells the story of two survivors, Jim, a Black worker, and Julia, an affluent white woman, who together scour the streets of the city in search of fellow survivors. For a brief few hours, Du Bois explores the possibilities of interracial utopian solidarity before they are rudely interrupted by white supremacy; it turns out, in the conclusion, that Julia's husband, a hardened racist is, in fact, alive, and accuses Jim of sexually assaulting her. While the conclusion of "The Comet," refuses a romantic resolution to racial inequality—suggesting in fact that white supremacy is a specter than haunts America in the past and future—it nonetheless describes how new ways of being seem within reach: "To both, the vision of a mighty beauty—of vast, unspoken things, swelled in their souls" (Du Bois 2007, 157). In the dozen or so pages of the story, Du Bois imagines an ethics of engagement that exists in a state of precariousness, when identity is called into question and established modes of action reworked. Not only does Du Bois dispel the idea that lawlessness will generate more lawlessness and create an ethical vacuum that would need to be filled with state power, but he thinks more broadly about what a new, future ethical language might look like. In various exchanges as they walk uptown and downtown, Julia carefully listens to Jim and quickly becomes aware of her unconscious white racism and her class position, and both Julia and Jim recognize that a new society requires a democratic ethos of responding to and cultivating a shared sensed of responsibility, which is mindful of Jim's social standpoint as a Black man who has to endure racism. In "The Comet," we see how Afrofuturism does its political work not through a set of prescriptions, or established answers to long-standing problems, but through enlisting readers to consider various possibilities, to speculate upon the idea of the future. If an ethos of responsiveness is possible, how might it exist in law? What modes of argument, receptivity, and engagement are necessary? What might an antiracist language—legal or otherwise—truly look like? What forms might interracial solidarity take without recourse to history, or precedent?

Some of the early Afrofuturist texts like Frances E. W. Harper's *Iola Leroy* (1892) sought to answer some of these questions through a reimagined Black civil society where white supremacy isn't the norm. In life, Harper was devoted to liberation politics at moments when it seemed impossible. She consoles John Brown's widow after he is hanged in 1859, is close associates with Harriet Tubman while she is the conductor of the Underground Railroad, and speaks alongside Frederick Douglass in defense of black suffrage when white redeemers are busy calling for an end to Reconstruction. So in the conclusion of her novel, Harper—writing amidst the slow solidification of Jim Crow, which is eventually formalized through *Plessy v. Ferguson* (1896)—tries to go beyond what seems possible, as she a imagines a collective of Black citizens (e.g., doctors, philanthropists, civic republicans, feminists, patriots) discussing the merits of assimilation against emigration, the role of the women's suffrage, and the potential of universal education. One character is described as "more than a successful doctor; he is a true patriot and a good citizen. Honest, just, and discriminating, he endeavors by precept and example to instill into the minds of other sentiments of good citizenship. He is a leader in every reform movement for the benefit of the community; but his patriotism is not confined to race lines" (Harper 2010, 223). Another character echoes Harper's aspiration, for the future: "We have been aliens and outcasts in the land of our birth. But I want my pupils to do all in their power to make this country worthy of their deepest devotion and loftiest patriotism" (Harper 200).

Other Afrofuturist texts, however, attempt to posit a coherent alternative to dominant ways of knowing and being. Although it's only roughly sketched out, science fiction writer Octavia Butler's two books, *Parable of the Talents* (1998) and *Parable of the Sower* (1993), accomplish this through the story of a Black woman, Lauren Oya Olamina, living in postapocalyptic Los Angeles. Olamina tries to forge an underground resistance movement against a right-wing authoritarian populist movement that is organized around the imperatives of neoliberal capital and white Christian identity politics. The two books are only a thinly veiled analysis of 1990s American racial politics when Black motorist Rodney King is viciously beaten by LAPD officers in 1992, Democratic president Bill Clinton signs the 1994 Crime Bill, which expands federal funding for police and prisons, and in 1996, along with a Republican Congress, "ends welfare as we know it." But much more so than simply speculating upon the dystopian ends of American culture, at the center of the *Parable* books is Butler's examination of what kind of philosophy could counter it. For Butler, this philosophy is the movement that Olamina begins, Earthseed, which is organized around the idea of "adaptability." Without adaptability, the novel's narrator declares, "what remains may be channeled into destructive fanaticism. Without positive obsession, there is nothing at all" (Butler 1993, 2).

Butler posits a pragmatic counterpoint to fundamentalism—or, as a counterpoint to originalism, or legal positivism. At the same time, she highlights the strategies of survival and persistence beyond the law, which communities undertake in everyday life. Adaptability, in the two *Parable* novels, involves building a sense of improvised solidarity through Olamina's Earthseed intentional interracial community living on the margins of society, named Acorn. Acorn practices unconditional generosity and an ethic of care; it resists the ravages of neoliberal capitalism (Los Angeles, in Butler's telling, is filled with private police who patrol wealthy neighborhoods) by practicing mutual aid among its members. Acorn members sabotage "slave collars," which the government uses to punish and discipline citizens, and they destroy "parateco," a popular designer drug that enhances one's ability to learn—to make workers who have jobs more productive—but has deadly side effects. And through its ethos of collaboration, improvisation, pluralism, and self-examination, Acorn forms a democratic alternative to the right-wing populist leader, Andrew Steele Jarret—in echoes of Donald Trump—who comes to power through demonizing migrants and who promises salvation and national rejuvenation to the poor, who, as the narrator puts it, "want to be fooled, need to be fooled" (Butler 1998, 281).

Just as Afrofuturism reveals the ways communities are built outside of—and sometimes, in opposition to—the law, it also outlines the clear limitations of the legal system and the rule of law in securing freedom for the most marginalized. This is, in fact, an argument it shares with legal realists who highlight the way systemic inequalities preclude legal reforms from substantially modifying the quality of life for dispossessed citizens. For Afrofuturists, power is thoroughly and unequally dispersed in ways that legal egalitarianism—equality of opportunity and nondiscrimination—cannot remedy. Take the example of George Schuyler's satirical Harlem Renaissance novel, *Black No More* (1931). The book, centered on the life of Max Disher, a Black man who undergoes a painful procedure called "Black-No-More" to change his skin color from black to white, is meant to test a hypothesis that some liberal legal theorists espouse: that racial equality would be achieved if citizens, and the law in general, were more colorblind. In *Black No More*, colorblindness becomes something of a reality precisely because, after the Black-No-More procedure becomes popular, there are virtually no citizens with black skin—as most of them, in an effort to escape the pervasive history of American anti-Black racism, now have white skin.

And yet, Schuyler suggests that postracialism is an impossible aspiration because race and racism will find new and creative ways to emerge, to become salient and flourish, and will be manipulated for instrumental reasons by those in power. Consider that after Disher becomes "white," his first order of business is to be a prominent spokesperson for a white supremacist organization, the Knights of Nordica—in order to charge lucrative fees as he goes on speaking tours defending the value of white purity and white supremacy. Later, as there are fewer and fewer citizens with black skin, there's widespread social panic that many people who appear to be white are actually, secretly Black. As a result, new organizations emerge devoted to classifying differences of whiteness. Eventually, in an even more farcical twist, a new racial category is invented, called the "New Caucasians," whose skin is of a slightly more pinkish complexion. These citizens are segregated, underpaid, and, as a result, form a "Down-With-White-Prejudice League." The rich, meanwhile, recognizing an opportunity to cement their social status, begin to find creative ways to get darker, and soon, enough, as Schuyler writes, "Everybody that was anybody had stained skin" (Schuyler 1999, 179). In *Black No More*'s telling, racial sameness doesn't magically eliminate racism and the things upon which it subsists—resentment, unconscious antipathy, fear of difference, desire for dominance, instrumentalism, greed, and exploitation. These qualities—widespread in American culture—find ways to reemerge and reconsolidate themselves.

Beyond its critique of the doctrines of colorblindness or postracialism, Afrofuturism challenges a certain idea of freedom, which asserts that maximizing individual choice will lead to greater social liberation.

In Samuel Delany's best-selling science fiction fantasy, *Triton* (1976), citizens live in a futuristic society in which individuals can change their appearances and identities—racial, gender, sexual at will—and where there isn't a legal system that denigrates marginalized citizens. In fact, the world of Triton is something of an anarchic utopia, where law doesn't legislate or constrain one's identity, opportunities or capacity to pursue a good life. Nonetheless, inequality still remains intact beyond the law. Paralleling the 1970s the subterranean white backlash to affirmative action, integration, the liberation movements of the 1960s, in Delany's telling, the white, male-blue-eyed protagonist, Bron Hellstrom, feels like his power is diminished in a society where identity is fluid. So as a result, Bron decides to undergo a sex-reassignment surgery from male to female, so he can better experience the intimacy he feels he's been denied by women, such as his love interest, The Spike—who refuses his sexual advances. This act of freedom, according to Delany, does nothing to undo Bron's entrenched misogyny: "I wish men were all strong and were all weak . . . somehow it would be easier to justify" (Delany 1976, 302). Or his deeply held racism, evident in the way he describes a Black coworker from Kenya, Miriamne, as a "typical" citizen of the unlicensed sector, the "u-l," (Delany 56) a neighborhood where there are high levels of crime. Bron's patriarchal impulses are still hidden below the surface, and her anti-Black attitudes don't make any room for a genuinely antiracist existence, let alone an intersectional framework that acknowledges how citizens like Miriamne—a Black woman—is dominated by virtue of race and gender. Just because there is no longer de jure inequality, *Triton* insists, de facto inequality is still maintained. Anticipating theorists who draw attention to unconscious racism and sexism, which can't be legislated or, often, fully comprehended with the law, Delany suggests that social inequality will persist even if formal mechanisms for equality of opportunity are maintained and overt discrimination is absent.

Rather than simply be relegated to the sphere of cultural criticism, Afrofuturist theoretical insights can deepen critiques and reconstructions of the law. We are living through an unprecedented moment where issues of race and racial inequality have become a central part of the national conversation. The Republican Party's overt embrace of white identity politics invested in an exclusionary and nostalgic conception of America, is met with movements like youthful, interracial movements like Black Lives Matter after the murder of George Floyd in 2020, which posit an antiracist alternative. Calls for defunding the police, reparations for slavery, abolishing prisons, and restoring the frayed social safety net are no longer the political nonstarters they were several decades ago—and the bipartisan consensus around "colorblindness" and "equality of opportunity" seem to be waning in significance, and instead are being replaced with more color-conscious redistributive visions. True, US federal courts—stacked with conservative justices during the Trump years—will, in the near future, likely serve as barriers against any democratically enacted antiracist policies. And racial justice advocates must contend with yet another iteration of the mainstreaming of racist fears over education and diversity—through the invented "controversy" over CRT, which is fueled by right-wing media and politicians, who know nothing about the decades-long movement in the legal academy but nonetheless recognize the salience of playing upon white Americans' fears of anything that involves either race, critique or theory. But antiracist lawyers and civil rights organizations are perfectly equipped to seize this moment, to use their expertise and training, to make compelling arguments for political reconstruction in the courtroom, in the public sphere as well as on the streets. The technical mechanisms of legal claim-making or research are only one part of the equation—what's equally important is a vivified imagination and willingness to critique and struggle against an unjust status quo. Beyond refreshing one's resolve to imagine the impossible, and work to bring it into existence, the long history of Afrofuturism offers insight into the strategies of narrative construction and standpoint theory, conceptions of utopia and democratic struggle. All of this is crucial if there's any hope for reconstituting the present, and achieving an antiracist future.

Note

1. This essay first appeared in "Afrofuturism and the Law," *Critical Analysis of Law* 9, no. 1 (2022): 1–8.

Works Cited

Bell, Derrick. 2018 *Faces at the Bottom of the Well: The Permanence of Racism.* New York: Basic Books.
Butler, Octavia. 1993. *Parable of the Sower.* New York: Seven Stories Press.
Butler, Octavia. 1998. *Parable of the Talents.* New York: Seven Stories Press.

Delany, Martin. 2017. *Blake, Or the Huts of America*. Cambridge, MA: Harvard University Press.

Delany, Martin. 2003. *Condition, Elevation, Emigration and Destiny of the Colored People of the United States*, Edited by Robert Levine. In *Martin R. Delany: A Documentary Reader*. Chapel Hill: The University of North Carolina Press.

Delany, Samuel. 1976. *Triton*. New York: Bantam Books.

Du Bois, W. E. B. 2017. "The Comet." In *Darkwater: Voices from Within the Veil*. New York: Dover.

Du Bois, W. E. B. 1995. *Dark Princess*. Jackson: University of Mississippi Press.

Harper, Frances. 2010. *Iola Leroy, or Shadows Uplifted*. New York: Penguin.

Matsuda, Mari J. Charles R. Lawrence III, Richard Delgado and Kimberle' Williams Crenshaw. 1993. *Words That Wound: Critical Race Theory, Assaultive Speech, and the First Amendment*. New York: Routledge.

Schuyler, George. 1999. *Black No More: Being an Account of Strange and Wonderful Workings of Science in the Land of the Free, A.D. 1933–1940*. New York: Modern Library.

Williams, Patricia J. 1993. *The Alchemy of Race and Rights*. Cambridge, MA: Harvard University Press.

Chapter 6

Parables of Resilience

Promising Pessimism, Octavia Butler's "Purpose," and the Making of Worlds

Alix L. Olson

Resilience is the trailblazing savior of contemporary social and political life. Politicians, scientists, self-help experts, public school and university administrators, military officials, and psychologists increasingly taught resilience-building as the only rational solution to a twenty-first-century world of unprecedented uncertainty.[1] The bestselling *Resilience: Why Things Bounce Back*, summarizes this new guiding telos: "The journey toward resilience is the great moral quest of our age. It is the lens through which we must necessarily adjust our relationships to one another, to our communities and institutions, and to our planet" (Zolli and Healy 2012, 276). The underlying promise of resilience—that people, and by extension global systems, can not only survive but flourish through crisis—gets promoted variously as ethical injunction, patriotic duty, policymaking mantra, revolutionary paradigm shift, and golden rule for local, national, and global programming. Perhaps most vitally, resilience is a prized value through which people are asked to appraise themselves, one another, and the world around them—as well as which practices and interventions are deemed both possible and desirable. As *New York Times* columnist Tom Friedman (2014) asserts, training in resilience may well be "our generation's freedom struggle."

Simply put, lives around the world—and the life of the planet itself—are being deeply impacted by what is said and done (or not) in the name of resilience. This chapter insists that to engage in political struggle over how to govern ourselves and our world, in a shared context of escalating crises, requires sustained critical investment in the ethical and political implications of this valorization of resilient life. I first provide a brief overview of the overlapping ways—across various domains—in which power is exercised, vulnerability mobilized, action taken, and possibilities for resistance refuted in the name of resilience. Here, I point toward a neoliberal rationality that I call "promising pessimism," or the idea that the only credible aim of governance—within a noncalculable future—is to facilitate a capacity for adapting, transforming, and even *thriving* within and through crisis. In order to underscore the material, ideological, and political danger that this logic poses, I examine NASA/SpaceX's plans for interplanetary colonization—a project explicitly intended to promote a resilient human species—as promising pessimism's devastating finale.

Despite this dire trajectory, I conclude by considering the cost for left thinkers and activists of reducing the concept of resilience to a neoliberal technology of power. In the context of waning grand narratives and revolutionary frameworks for working toward "another world," we cannot dismiss the inventive possibilities for sustaining hope—amidst uncertainty, disappointment, and failure—that resilience offers. To this end, I contend that Octavia Butler's prophetic diptych *Parable of the Sower* (1993) and *Parable of the Talents* (1998) counters the colonizing project of promising pessimism and recovers a liberatory account of resilience: one that refuses to exchange utopian surety for acquiescence to power but recuperates the present as a practice ground for transformation. Here, I treat the line between social reality (Mars colonization) and science fiction (Butler's cautionary observations) as an "optical illusion," contending that speculative futurity is always at work in shaping how the historical present is produced, conceptualized, and acted upon (Haraway 1991, 149). My aim is that the interplay of these competing imaginaries might defamiliarize "promising pessimism" responses to the crises that surround us and open up the present as an actionable site of/for political struggle. If neoliberalism tells us that building a more just world is "speculative fiction"—captured by its mandate that "there is no alternative"—Butler's literary social experiment shows how life beyond capitalism becomes possibility and purpose. In turn, the "scientific reality" of resilient world-extension is rendered a dystopian warning.

The Rise of Promising Pessimism:
Ready or Not, This Is Our Future!

The queer theorist Lauren Berlant (2011) characterizes the contemporary political condition since the 1980s as cruel optimism. Cruel optimism describes our individual and shared attachment to the (unachievable) organizing fantasies of the good life. These are desires for liberation, job security, financial success and class mobility, social and political equality, lasting intimacy and overall happiness—despite all evidence that liberal capitalism fails to deliver on this "cluster of promises" (23). In this sense, cruel optimism produces a kind of affective "double bind" in that these attachments work to reproduce what is destructive in the world while representing the world to which we are attached. These desires for the "moral-intimate-economic thing" called the good life are an obstacle to our flourishing, since in practice they restore us to what is actually "the bad life" (27). What has been especially cruel about contemporary life then has been our ability to slog through these deteriorating conditions rather than critically assess our stuck-ness in relation to our desires.

But the allure of this "traditional fantasy bribe"—which has guided and sustained attachments to this world—holds waning traction in the face of the accelerating destruction of life (Berlant 2016, 409): escalating terrorism, economic disparity and poverty, endless war, and the seemingly inescapable effects of climate change. This is a moment of "impasse," a breakdown of liberal infrastructures—material, economic, political, and affective—that has served to reproduce narratives of progress, security, and visions of the good life (Berlant 2016). And indeed, this dawning recognition of the cruelty of our desires does not belong to any one particular political camp. The left too has had its traditional frameworks for anchoring and sustaining political action repeatedly squashed: narratives of progress, visions of "achieving" economic and political equality, utopian dreams, and revolutionary projects. This is a collective witnessing of a malfunctioning world. The salient question then becomes: How will we be governed and govern others and ourselves in and through this indeterminant present? What versions of uncertainty, reckoning, and hope alongside visions of the future might be intensified, disrupted, or otherwise transformed through disparate conceptualizations of resilience?

The emerging rationality of neoliberal governance that I term "promising pessimism" relies upon and reproduces an ontology of "vulnerability in uncertain times" as the "new normal" condition of twenty-first-century globalization in which the sources of disaster are too complex to name, much less resist. The key (pessimistic) promise of resilience thinking is that people can live more freely through uncertainty if they are able to comprehend crisis as opportunity: to innovatively adapt and, in this process, acquire resilience capital. To benefit from this promise requires a forward-looking temporality that disavows grief and nullifies losses of the past (Chandler 2014; Neocleous 2013). Through this lens, individuals, families, communities, populations, and nations most vulnerable to erupting "shocks" are urged to incorporate them—the loss of livelihoods, unprecedented military deployment, imposed austerity measures, debt peonage, the immediate and long-term effects of ecological catastrophe (including forced migration and even the threat of human extinction)—as the promising *source* of increased resilience. This is the biopolitical vision of a homo resilient infrastructure that sustains and extends exploitative capitalist ways of life in and through the precarity it produces. At the same time, those subjects who "dwell" in trauma (rather than moving toward what is referred to as "post-traumatic growth")—or who cannot or refuse to perform this adaptive function—are cast as impediments to the collective project of social (systemic) resilience more broadly.

Crucially, this shaping and governance of the historical present verifies its political authority by drawing upon knowledge about human and biospheric life circulated by two scientific fields: ecology and (positive) psychology. Throughout the 1970s and 1980s, within both domains, developing ideas about life as emergent and adaptable (rather than inherently knowable and thus "securable") prompted modification of the concept of resilience: from a narrow idea of "bouncing back," or returning to the original state and resuming linear normative development—to a novel conception of "bouncing forward," or transforming and perhaps even flourishing through disturbance (Walker and Cooper 2011, 143–45). According to these theories, if complex living systems develop resilience not as a result of being shielded from vulnerability but through innovative adaption to them, then the primary task of governing life (from people to forests) is to facilitate this coconstitutive process (Evans and Reid 2013). Direct intervention (to protect life, or resist creating vulnerability) is not only impossible in an uncertain world, but interferes with opportunities for what positive psychologists newly call "post-traumatic growth."

Within the United States, these scientifically authorized techniques for cultivating the "homo resilient" subject have infiltrated the wellness industrial complex and circulate widely within popular media. In this mushrooming literature, self-help "experts" regularly tout resilience as a practical, teachable, and learnable way to "flourish" within a noncalculable world. As one practitioner pair puts it, developing a "resilience lens" helps one to confront negative life events with "zest," turning trauma into a "win-win" (Padesky and Mooney 2012, 287). In light of COVID-19, this discourse has proliferated. For instance, in a recent *New York Times* article "4 Ways to Build Resilience in 2022," Dr. Stephen Southwick explains that the "extreme stress [of pandemic life]" might be embraced as a "prerequisite for post-traumatic growth" (Sohn 2021). Across this discourse is a naturalized account of precarity that postulates no sources, nor any agential way to intervene. "Since the holy war against boogeymen hasn't worked and isn't likely to any time soon," one self-help expert speculates cheekily, it may well be time to "roll with the waves instead of trying to stop the ocean" (Zolli 2012). To claim vulnerability or to dwell in loss, whether for the purposes of mourning, critical analysis of power, or resistance, is to adopt a maladaptive temporal strategy that impedes bouncing forward. Al Siebert barks emphatically in *The Resiliency Advantage* (2005), whether it be "executives, the government, self-serving politicians, administrators who lack emotional intelligence, cheap foreign labor, stock market managers, taxpayers, or any person or group," blaming others for ruining your life will keep you in a "non-resilient victim state" (3). *Managing at the Speed of Change: How Resilient Managers Succeed and Prosper While Others Fail* goes so far as to identify two types of people: dysfunctional *D*s who view disruption as danger, and thriving (*O*s) who incorporate crisis (Conner 2006). While there is some obvious compatibility here with the neoliberal subjects of flexibility, self-reliance, and personal responsibility, it is striking that homo resilient no longer optimistically "leans in" to her trials en route to a better, safer, or more prosperous life. Instead, and despite its aspirational resonance, the tautological promise of immunizing oneself with resilience is simply *more resilience*. This work on the self is not only the "ultimate art of living," as *Psychology Today* proclaims, but imperative for the health and survival of the larger social and political systems in which she is relationally embedded (Morano 2016). Because "resilience can radiate out from within," a pair of resiliency experts note, "the mental practices you cultivate, and how you respond to disruption truly shape the whole" (Zolli and Healy 2013, 275).

Within the United States alone, this vision of a homo resilient infrastructure dominates community, city, nonprofit, university, corporate, and national policy frameworks, including those governing public health, education, architecture, urban development, and climate crisis. It is so closely tied to national security that a US Department of Homeland Security official dubbed resilience the nation's new "immune system" in a world of "viral-like insecurity" (Schleifstein 2009). Indeed, from the Rockefeller Foundation's *100 Resilient Cities* to the National Institutes of Health's *Resilience Training Program*, countless mission statements promise to measure, track, inject, and booster-shot the adaptive responses of populations. But perhaps the most vivid illustration of this resilience-as-inoculation is the US military's "Ready and Resilient" campaign, called the "largest deliberate psychological experiment in U.S. history" (Lester et al. 2011, 77). Inspired by skyrocketing PTSD diagnoses among soldiers, the program deploys intensive resilience training aimed at teaching "cognitive reappraisal" techniques for seeing the endless horizon of war as a productive terrain of personal enhancement, transformation, and flourishing. For example, the "spiritual resiliency" module guides soldiers through creating preemptive eulogies for a "fallen friend" (or themselves) helping them to focus on the meta-significance of trauma to come. In the "emotional resiliency" module, soldiers work to retrain their neurons such that "adaptive" responses to crisis override "gratuitous negativity" (like anger or fear) and "impulsive actions" (from questioning a mission's purpose to suicide). Through the logic of promising pessimism, to approach war through any lens but resilience thinking is to act irresponsibly and to leave oneself, one's troop, and even the nation vulnerable: spoiling troop morale and the efficacy of the mission, threatening national security, and placing the economic burden for treating PTSD on the public (Howell 2016).

At the global level, organizations like the International Panel for Climate Change, the United Nations Development Program, USAID, the World Economic Forum, and the World Bank foreground promising pessimism in approaching global poverty and food insecurity, disaster risk reduction, migration and refugee planning, and ecological catastrophe. As former Chief of the World Humanitarian Summit Secretariat Dr. Jemilah Mahmood summarizes in the *Guardian*, since humanitarian funding of populations living within "fragile contexts" is "no longer enough," we must "increase people's resilience" in the face of shocks-to-come (2015). Recently, the World Bank announced that the private financing of resilience-based responses to climate crisis is the key priority of its 2025 Climate Change Target, while the Asian Development Bank affirms "climate-induced" migration as a "win-win" resilience strategy for economically developing countries—with the greatest risk posed by those "unwilling to relocate" (ADB 2012, 11). In another striking example, the USAID's *Building Resilience to Recurrent Crisis* report describes how "chronically-vulnerable" farmers in Burkina Faso have been weaned off of their "maladaptive" dependence upon rain-fed crops (and pastoral lifestyles), switching to drought-resistant (GMO-produced) onions and investing in irrigation systems (through privately financed micro-loans) and resilience insurance (2013, 10). The report features a farmer named Safieta, beaming widely: "I am resilient now [. . .] just like the onions'" (10).

Make This Desert Come Alive!
Or, On Making a Homo Resilient Species

These situated accounts of promising pessimism point toward a homo resilient infrastructure in the making—operating at every scale of governance, from the individual to the transnational. As vulnerable subjects of uncertain times, we are incited to pursue transformation in and through a hostile habitat, accepting that looming threat and resilience building are dialectically bound. Nowhere, however, is this dystopic imagination more apparent than in emerging propositions to render the human species itself more resilient through interplanetary colonization. The Mars Society's 2017 inspirational anthem aptly summarizes this mission:

> There are challenges before our eyes
> That nature never knew
> But the power of human enterprise
> Shall take us through and through!
> Come along raging nations
> Altogether hopeful spirits
> Bring an end to strife
> For our future lies beyond the skies
> Rise to Mars! Men and Women!
> Dare to dream! Dare to strive!
> Build a home for our children
> Make this desert come alive!
> Come along, altogether
> For our future
> Rise to Mars!

For decades, of course, environmental activist bumper stickers have actively admonished that "there is no Planet B." And indeed, permanent human habitation on other planets has been long relegated to the domain of speculative fiction. But as disquiet about humanity's future on Earth swells, as does real-life momentum toward colonizing deep space. What was once a "fanciful idea," renowned theoretical physicist Stephen Hawking confirms, is now both necessity and scientific fact (Knapton 2017). Superseding prior rationales of a global "space race" competition or quest to satiate natural human curiosity, the explicit aim of NASA's *Journey to Mars* mission (2017) is to promote "the resilience of the human species" (and the "entrepreneurial spirit") through establishing self-sustaining outposts on the Red Planet.

Deeply rooted in promising pessimism, NASA makes it clear that ecological devastation has fostered urgent exploration of Mars as humanity's adaptive and transformative response to the inevitable wasteland that is Planet A. On one hand, the journey offers the promise of staving off human extinction: through the possibility of escape to a new world and through technological experiments within Martian terrain that can be replicated on an inhospitable Earth. On the other hand, the mission is touted as an opportunity to use Earth's impending crisis to foster the resilience of the capitalist economy, through previously unthinkable commercial enterprises and defense-industrial expansion. In both cases, while neoliberal ways of life are rendering Earth inhospitable, it is the interplanetary extension of this very infrastructure that will make (some) life go on living—and even thrive.

NASA (2017) readily admits that this scientific imaginary presents severe stumbling blocks, not least among these that humanity's backup homeland is "hostile to life" in every way. But, informed by resilience-thinking, NASA cheerfully refers to such obstacles throughout its literature as an opportunity for transformative adaption: for the human species, scientific technology, and commerce. Its new Resilient ExtraTerrestrial Habitats Institute, for instance, details outpost plans for underground architecture, cosmic radiation-resistant ice domes, plastic-making machines, 3-D printing of food and construction materials, and extensive drilling for in-situ resources (Dyke 2019). As did "early European settlers coming to America," NASA scientists relay, "planetary pioneers" will need to learn to harvest raw materials (Granath 2016). The journey toward Mars colonization has also prompted extensive technocratic discussion about the plausibility of terraforming, or the (hypothetical) process of planetary engineering. This deliberate invasion and permanent modification of the atmospheric surface and climate of Mars (to create a more Earthlike environment), it is argued, might allow a wide variety of life forms, including humans, to flourish.

Importantly, such invasive adaptation strategies aimed at enabling interplanetary human resilience do not only target planetary bodies. NASA's current research is concerned with modifying a human body and mind capable of enduring the voyage to and life on Mars. These studies explore physiological reaction to long-duration space flight (the flight to Mars is six months), including bone and muscle loss, intracranial pressure changes, and declining immune function. In response, NASA is examining possibilities for manipulating astronaut DNA to make them more resilient to cosmic radiation, chronic lack of oxygen, and the effects of micro-gravity—known to cause dementia, blindness, and fertility problems. Additionally, psychological resilience training programs (developed in the military's Ready and Resilience experiment) will prepare astronauts to thrive through the challenges of isolation and confinement and to benefit from post-traumatic growth rather than suffer from PTSD (Heinicke 2017).

Importantly, these technologies for survival are equally directed toward fostering adaptive resilience on the ransacked Earth to come. One leading scientist offers enthusiastically, for example, that the 3-D printing of food will be "useful in future scenarios with food is scare" (Benson 2015) while experiments with underground silo-dwelling, oxygen suits, resilience-training, and even DNA manipulation will allow Earthlings to cope with toxic radiation levels. In the glow of this promising pessimism, however, political questions of who will have economic access to these resilient ways of life, and how these projects are intertwined with corporate interest get sidelined. As *Forbes* reports, there is likely a "fortune to be made on Mars" (Walker 2016), in the form of intellectual property rights (for commercially funded technologies developed on Mars) as well as privatized mining ventures, export of raw materials, and ownership over Martian terrain more broadly.

Indeed, NASA has initiated partnerships with billionaire-backed space companies like Blue Origin (Amazon tycoon Jeff Bezos), Virgin Galactic (business magnate Richard Branson), and SpaceX (Tesla CEO Elon Musk). Among these, Musk has been the most vocal, pro-active, and lucrative, recently winning a $1.4B contract from NASA for future Mars missions (fittingly, one of his rockets is called *Resilience*). While Musk concedes that founding a back-up human civilization is in part "extinction insurance," he is adamant that this promisingly pessimistic horizon offers unlimited opportunities for cosmic entrepreneurship. These braided ambitions, ubiquitously flaunted on SpaceX's OCCUPY MARS t-shirts and hats, take shape first as a Mars Colonial Transporter (a commercial convoy of "interplanetary *Mayflowers*," which Musk likens to the transcontinental railway) and eventually the establishment of a Martian city (Achenbach 2016). Musk emphasizes that the half-million-dollar trip will be accessible to anyone, given that people can take out loans and pay back the debt through a kind of indentured servitude on Mars. And as for the challenge of making what Musk calls a "fixer-upper" planet habitable? SpaceX's newest NUKE MARS t-shirt announces this terraforming fix: blasting its poles with nuclear missiles (ten thousand would be required) in order to release carbon dioxide stores under the surface.

No longer contained within science or science fiction literature, the prospect of becoming an interplanetary species as a solution to ecological disaster is rapidly infiltrating the popular imagination. NASA offers a hands-on STEAM curriculum for public school students called the Imagine Mars Project in which students work with NASA engineers to design a "model resilient community" on Mars. The stated aim of the project is to keep kids "focused on the reality of Mars, and not on a science-fiction idea of community on Mars" and features students from Los Angeles, New Orleans, and Chicago public housing communities drafting ideas for "bouncing forward" through constraints (NASA 2017). Inspired by SpaceX, newly released board games like *Terraforming Mars* feature players competing as corporations to transform Mars into a habitable planet as they "race for awards" (Fryx Games 2016). Will you be the company, the game's website asks hauntingly, to "lead the way into humanity's new Era?" Similarly, the 2022 video game *Occupy Mars* encourages individual colonists to dig for mining rigs and valuable resources in the "open sandbox" of Mars. Sure, you will need to "learn to cope with 'rapid unscheduled dissembly" (the euphemism for SpaceX's explosive landing)—as well as running out of air, water, and energy—but these are all opportunities for resilience thinking! Similarly, National Geographic's hybrid docuseries *Mars* (2016–), an unabashed infomercial for SpaceX, weaves Musk's real-world attempts to launch reusable rockets to Mars with a scripted drama of a 2033 Mars colony. In between these scenes, NASA scientists, historians, and the president of the Mars Society provide commentary on the urgency of these experiments for humankind, given the un-becoming of our own terrestrial existence. As producer Ron Howard explains, "The show is not posing the question, should we go to Mars? It's moving past that and instead offering audiences a sense of what it will be like" (Peplow 2018).

Faced with accelerated extinctions of animal species, rising temperatures, toxic epidemics, and dwindling resources, the prospect of ecological devastation looms large. Through promising pessimism logic, this Capitalocene tragedy nudges humanity to adapt, transform, and emerge a more resilient species. Indeed, with humanity and capitalist resilience firmly conjoined, and economic development naturalized as an inevitable facet of the horizon, the only solution to a dying Earth lies within the same technocratic "ingenuity" and colonizing "discovery" that is killing it: for global political and economic elites, world-making is to be performed through the extension of exploitative and extractivist logics into deep space. This is the privileging of technological becoming over political becoming, the terraforming of worlds over transforming the one we inhabit.

Parables of the Future, Liberating Resilience

Given this dark narrative, it is tempting to join emerging scholarly calls to "resist resilience" (Neocleous 2013; Evans and Reid 2014; Chandler 2014). Enjoinders like these carry deep emancipatory resonance, denoting a story in which "resistance" (as the essential property of activism) boldly confronts "resilience" (owned by power). But, such reductive judgment misses the point of critical reevaluation, and reactively forfeits a concept vital to the liberatory imagination. If the aim of showing how resilience is put to work as a neoliberal biopolitics is precisely to expose and unsettle the limits it imposes upon the political imagination, then these analyses might also fuel a subversive bid to liberate it from this labor—and reattach it to radical hope. One way of entering this contest is to apprehend the call to "Occupy Mars" as a kind of prefigurative storytelling, and to pit it against alternative speculative visions that are at once technologies of resistance. As Donna Haraway proposes in her lecture, *Anthropocene, Capitalocene, Cthulucene,* "it matters what stories tell stories, it matters what worlds world worlds. [. . .] It matters to destabilize worlds of thinking with other worlds of thinking" (2015, 160). In other words, the calling forth of a future rooted in the promising pessimism of the present—in which capitalism is made to survive and thrive at all costs—does not get the last word on resilience.

In her critical dystopian *Parable* series, Octavia Butler alerts us to the ways in which uncertainty and crisis—as chronic conditions of the world—can unmoor us from active engagement with the present, provoking nostalgic longing (for a past world, imagined prior security, or lost modes of struggle); aspirations of utopian exodus (another world, entirely); or pessimistic resignation (adapting to the world as is). Driven by despair, each of these orientations abandons the world. Against these tendencies, Butler invites us into a Black feminist-led world-making praxis—equal parts philosophical, spiritual, and pragmatic—that centers acknowledging, adapting to, and seizing the forces of change in service of resilient political struggle. In Butler's hands, vulnerability becomes the ground of possibility for inhabiting a collaborative sociality that refuses to buttress the individual modes of survival, lack of empathy, and unjust power relations that lock us into a self-destructing future.

Parable of the Sower plunges us into a postapocalyptic portrait of mid-2020s United States, in which chaos is the central feature. It is a futurity brought to us by a neoliberal biopolitics of resilience: individual efforts at adaption have run their course, the pessimistic promise of crisis has lost its rhetorical sheen, and vulnerability is laid bare (and quite literally pathologized). This "pox" terrain is populated by white supremacist fascism, corporate ruthlessness, corrupt police, homelessness, rape, drought, uncontrollable fires, debt slavery, and an eviscerated public sphere. The protagonist, an African American teenager named Lauren Olamina, lives in a Los Angeles gated community where her neighbors refuse to face the reality of a political order that has abandoned any pretense of safety or security. These "dying, denying, backward looking peoples," Lauren observes, cling to return narratives in which twentieth-century progress will soon be restored (Butler 2019a, 20).

In an effort to combat the historically escapist longings and political paralysis that surround her, Lauren develops a novel life philosophy called Earthseed that sacralizes impermanence itself as a permanent feature of the world. Far from defeatist, Earthseed's core tenet insists upon a radical entanglement of contingency, tenacious doing, and emergent becoming: "All that you touch You Change/All that you Change Changes you/The only Lasting truth is Change" (104). Notably, Butler does not portray the surrender of linear temporality, revolutionary dogma, reification of canonical ideas, or cruel optimism of a panacea as a painless paradigm shift. Lauren scribbles furiously, "God is Change. I hate God" (158). But as her solo journey transfigures into an emerging social movement, accruing a multiracial, intergenerational group of crisis refugees, Lauren becomes an activist and community organizer. Her personal musings take shape as a liberatory ethos of resilience, intended to sustain the mutual survival, radical hope, and collaborative seed-sowing practices of her aptly named "Acorn" community.

In particular, Lauren exhorts her community members to abandon a traditional conception of power/God as sovereign, omniscient, or static, a "big-daddy-God or a big-cop-God or a big-king-God" (Butler 2019a, 13). Such a security blanket view of authority, whether spiritual or political, converts the most vulnerable into "God's plaything, God's prey" (29). She cautions equally, however, against assenting to Change/uncertainty in ways that subordinate the creative and transformative potential of human action. While power cannot be permanently "stopped," the ground of struggle can be immanently shaped in order to "rig the game in our favor" (24). Resilience, in this sense, does not imply individual adaption as art of survival, "limping along, playing business as usual" (24), but the collaborative styling of new questions, relations, and modes of action through deep reflexivity.

Over time, Lauren begins to articulate the movement's future as an extrasolar Destiny, decentralized Acorn communities scattered amidst the stars. These new worlds, not requiring a "long, expensive umbilical cord to earth," would be cleansed of our planet's political failures, corporate economy, and tortured ecologies (79). In one sense, this longing might illustrate the pull of utopian exodus, another form of retreat from a heart-rending terrain. But it is equally clear that this aspirational horizon, "radical enough to make us become more than we ever have been," inspires transformative movement work on Earth. Earthseed's verses emphasize cultivating sustainable partnership between and among human and more-than-human life and the planet; these are the seeds for new modes of being and conditions for world-making worthy of interstellar transport. Accordingly, while Butler's protagonist lauds the prospect of space exploration, she is wary of its inevitable privatization and the pursuit of "dead" planets (like Mars) for profit alone. She muses that Mars is at once enticing and "too close within the reach of the people who've made such a hell of life on Earth" (21).

It might give us pause, then, that in 2021 NASA named a Mars rover landing site after Butler, declaring that her protagonists' "determination and inventiveness are a perfect fit for the Perseverance rover mission and its theme of overcoming challenges" (NASA 2021). It is certainly tempting to laud this (long-overdue) international recognition of a Black feminist science fiction writer, whose life work fuels radical hope in the possibility of another world. But this symbolic designation of US territory on Mars, quite literally in the name of Black feminist resilience, also raises an alarm. Most crucially, it detaches Butler's ideas of adaption, tenacity, and the value of an aspirational horizon from their activist aim: to transform humanity's values, relations, and ways of being or, as Lauren urges in *Parable of the Talents*, to become a radically new species. Mars colonization does not prefigure resilient (transformative) world building but resilient (replicative) world extension, its discourse shamelessly steeped in analogic frames of (settler) colonialism and extraction. At the same time, it signals world abandonment: Earthbound refugees and a wrecked planet left to adapt and transform to their death. In an interview, Butler herself warned about the unjust future of space technology in which the "few rich people who can afford to cut themselves off" will do so (Palwick 1999, 152). Perhaps she foresaw, in other words, how resilience might become an individually mandated art of existence for the vulnerable majority (on Earth), while available for purchase (as a kind of private life insurance) by the elite.

At a visceral level, resilience is braided with attachment to life. But the vital question foreclosed by promising pessimism is precisely the one Butler urges us to consider: To which praxes of survival, and ways of belonging to this (or any) world, do we desire to attach? Entering into this question with the humility, persistence, adaptivity, and intentionality that transformation requires means releasing the past as a cruelly optimistic banister for action, and being energetically awake to a mutable present. While we can scavenge ideas and warnings from prior political struggles, leaders, and thinkers, Butler cautions us, there is no one centralized strategy to be recuperated and re-rehearsed. Instead, there are "hundreds of projects" to be seized in the present, which might shape us as better human beings and help us practice a more liberatory future. Lauren writes, "The world is full of painful stories. Sometimes it seems as though there aren't any other kind and yet I found myself thinking how beautiful that glint of water was through the trees" (Butler 2019a, 235). It is by searching out the vastness for these glints, these unpredictable flashes of possibility—entangled as they are with loss and despair—that we sustain radical hope along this emergent journey. Butler harbors no illusions about the immense struggle that shaping a just Destiny ("Another Place! Another Way! Anything!") demands, nor about whether it is possible (2019b, 70). But that is, in fact, the point. What Butler teaches us is that resilience is found in solidarity of transformative purpose and that this purpose is in itself salvific, whether or not our visions come to fruition.

Note

1. This chapter was originally published as A. Olson, "Parables of Resilience: Promising Pessimism, Octavia Butler's 'Purpose,' and the Making of Worlds," *Feminist Theory* 25, no. 3 (2023): 436–453. Copyright © 2024 (Alix Olson). https://doi.org/10.1177/14647001231202134. Reprinted with Permission.

Works Cited

Asian Development Bank (ADB). 2012. *Addressing Climate Change and Migration in Asia and the Pacific*. Manila: Asian Development Bank.

Benson, T. 2015. "What We Learn from Living in the Harsh Conditions of Mars Will Help Us If We Fully Destroy Earth." *Fast Company*, May 29, 2015. https://www.fastcompany.com/3046766/what-we-learn-from-living-in-the-harsh-conditions-of-mars-will-help-us-if-we-fully-destroy-e.

Berlant, L. 2011. *Cruel Optimism*. Durham, NC: Duke University Press.

Berlant, L. 2016. "The Commons: Infrastructures for Troubling Times." *Environment and Planning D: Society and Space* 34, no. 3: 393–419.

Butler, O. 2019a [1993]. *Parable of the Sower*. London: Headline Publishing Group.

Butler, O. 2019b [1998]. *Parable of the Talents*. New York: Grand Central Publishing.

Chandler, D. 2014. *Resilience: The Governance of Complexity*. London: Routledge.

Dyke, Shirley J. 2019. "Resilient ExtraTerrestrial Habitats Institute. "*NASA*. May 22, 2019. https://www.nasa.gov/directorates/spacetech/strg/stri/stri_2018/resilient_extraterrestrial_habitats_institute_rethi/.

Evans, B., and J. Reid. 2014. *Resilient life: The Art of Living Dangerously*. Cambridge, MA: Polity Press.

Friedman, T. L. 2014. "Opinion: Memorial Day 2050." *New York Times*. May 24, 2014. https://www.nytimes.com/2014/05/25/opinion/sunday/friedman-memorial-day-2050.html.

Fryx Games. 2016. *Terrarforming Mars* [Board Game/Website]. Available at http://www.fryxgames.se/games/terraforming-mars/.

Granath, Bob. 2016. "Pioneering Space Requires Living Off the Land in the Solar System." *NASA*, September 30, 2016. https://www.nasa.gov/feature/pioneering-space-requires-living-off-the-land-in-the-solar-system.

Haraway, D. 2015. "Anthropocene, Capitalocene, Plantationocene, Chthulucene." *Environmental Humanities* 6: 159–65.

Holling, C. S. 1973. "Resilience and Stability of Ecological Systems." *Annual Review of Ecology and Systematics* 4: 1–23.

Howell, A. 2015. "Resilience, War and Austerity: The Ethics of Military Human Enhancement." *Security Dialogue* 46, no. 1: 15–31.

Mahmood, J. 2015. "Humanitarian Funding Is Not Enough: We Must Increase People's Resilience." *The Guardian.* June 19, 2015. https://www.theguardian.com/global-development/2015/jun/19/humanitarian-assistance-funding-record-levels-increase-resilience.

Marano, H. E. 2003. "The Art of Resilience." *Psychology Today*, May 1, 2013. https://www.psychologytoday.com/us/articles/200305/the-art-resilience.

Mars Society. 2017. "Mars Society Releases New Red Planet Anthem." http://www.marssociety.org/mars-society-releases-new-red-planet-anthem-rise-mars/.

Morris, D. 2017. "Elon Musk Reveals More Details about His Plan to Colonize Mars." *Fortune*, October 15, 2017. http://fortune.com/2017/10/15/elon-musk-reddit-spacex-mars/.

National Aeronautics and Space Administration (NASA). 2021. "NASA's Perseverance Drives on Mars Terrain." March 5, 2021. https://www.nasa.gov/press-release/nasa-s-perseverance-drives-on-mars-terrain-for-first-time.

National Aeronautics and Space Administration (NASA). 2015. "NASA's Journey to Mars: Pioneering Next Steps in Space Exploration." https://www.nasa.gov/sites/default/files/atoms/files/journey-to-mars-next-steps-20151008_508.pdf.

National Aeronautics and Space Administration and National Endowment for the Arts. 2009. The Imagine Mars Project, April 10, 2009. https://www.nasa.gov/audience/foreducators/k-4/features/F_Imagine_Mars_2006.html.

Neocleous, M. 2013. "Resisting Resilience." *Radical Philosophy* 178. https://www.radicalphilosophy.com/commentary/resisting-resilience.

Padesky, C. A., and K. A. Mooney. 2012. "Strengths-based Cognitive-Behavioural Therapy: A Four-Step Model to Build Resilience." *Clinical Psychology and Psychotherapy* 19: 283–90.

Palwick, S. 1999. "Imagining a Sustainable Way of Life: Interview with Octavia Butler." *Interdisciplinary Studies in Literature and Environment* 6, no. 2 (Summer): 149–58.

Pargament, K., and P. Sweeney. 2011. "Building Spiritual Fitness in the Army: An Innovative Approach to a Vital Aspect of Human Development." *American Psychologist* 66: 58–64.

Peplow, G. 2018. "Humans on Mars? That's Just the Beginning." *SkyNews*, November 8, 2018. https://news.sky.com/story/ron-howard-humans-on-mars-thats-just-the-beginning-\ 11546369.

Rockefeller Foundation (RF). 2013. "100 Resilient Cities." https://www.rockefellerfoundation.org/our-work/initiatives/100-resilient-cities/.

Schleifstein, M. 2015. "Disaster Response Should Mimic Human Immune Response, Thad Allen Says." *Times-Picayune*, June 2, 2015. http://www.nola.com/environment/index.ssf/2015/06/national_disaster_response_sho.html.

Siebert, A. 2005. *The Resilience Advantage: Master Change, Thrive Under Pressure, and Bounce.* San Francisco, CA: Berrett-Koehler.

Sohn, E. 2021. "4 Ways to Cultivate Resilience in 2022." *New York Times*, December 9, 2021. https://www.nytimes.com/2021/12/09/well/mind/emotional-resilience.html.

United Nations (UN). 2012. *Resilient People, Resilient Planet: A Future Worth Choosing.* http://archive.ipu.org/splz-e/rio+20/rpt-panel.pdf.

United States Department of the Army (US Army). 2014. Hunting the Good Stuff During Resiliency Training. December. https://www.army.mil/article/140671/hunting_the_good_stuff_during_resiliency_training.

Walker, J., and M. Cooper. 2011. "Genealogies of Resilience: From Systems Ecology to the Political Economy of Crisis Adaption." *Security Dialogue* 42, no. 2: 143–60.

Walker, R. 2016. "Is There a Fortune to be Made on Mars?" *Forbes*. September 26, 2016. https://www.forbes.com/sites/quora/2016/09/26/is-there-a-fortune-to-be-made-on-mars/?sh=3a36dcc56e28.

Zolli, A. and A. M. Healy. 2012. *Resilience: Why Things Bounce Back.* New York: Simon and Schuster.

Zolli, A. 2012. "Learning to Bounce Back." *New York Times*, November 2, 2012. https://www.nytimes.com/2012/11/03/opinion/forget-sustainability-its-about-resilience.html.

Chapter 7

"My Ovaries Ain't for You to Bully"

Trap Feminist Rappers and the Fight for Sexual Autonomy and Reproductive Justice

SHANTEE ROSADO

On Friday, June 24, 2022, a majority conservative Supreme Court overturned *Roe v. Wade* and *Planned Parenthood v. Casey*, effectively outlawing the federal protection of abortion in the US. While devasting to women's rights activists, and a cause for celebration among antiabortion activists, the decision to overturn *Roe* was not surprising. In fact, a memo had leaked about the Supreme Court decision months earlier, so many were waiting for the official ruling from the court to confirm their suspicions. When the ruling was released, though, protests were widespread.

That afternoon, a group of abortion rights activists gathered outside of Dallas City Hall to voice their opposition to the Supreme Court decisions (CBS Texas Staff 2022). In the video, which I encountered on Twitter/X, you see a group of women, most of whom look young and of different races, gathered on a hilltop. The video seems to have been filmed in the aftermath of a march, with protestors gathering to dance as part of their protest. The song being blasted was rapper Megan Thee Stallion's "Plan B." In the song, Megan expresses regret and anger about engaging with an undeserving man, claiming "Popping Plan B's 'cause I ain't plannin' to get stuck with you." The message in the song is clear—if a man does not treat you well, you should use contraception before, during, and/or after intercourse, or else you might get stuck raising a child with him. "Plan B" was the perfect sonic backdrop to the protest. It provided a scathing critique of unworthy men, while also offering a clear message of women's bodily autonomy—a woman's right to make decisions about her own body and reproductive functions (UN Working Group on the Issue of Discrimination against Women in Law and in Practice 2017).

Megan's song being the soundtrack to an abortion rights protest was not a random occurrence. Since the 2010s, Black women rappers have again been rising in popularity and clout. So much so that NPR referred to 2020 as "The Year that Female Rappers Dominated." Salient among this growing group of artists are Black women rappers like Megan Thee Stallion, who espouse a sex-positive, hood-conscious feminism, making them what Sesali Bowen (2021) calls *trap feminists*. Megan stands among many trap feminist rappers whose artistry and public commentary center women's independence in the face of misogynoir—the anti-Black misogyny experienced by Black women (Bailey and Trudy 2018).

In this chapter, I use a purposive case study method and critical discourse analysis to examine how trap feminist rappers, primarily Cardi B, Megan Thee Stallion, and Latto, have used their artistry and activism to creatively fight for women's bodily autonomy. Two main findings emerge from this analysis. First, that trap feminist rappers consistently address women's bodily and sexual autonomy in their work, making their artistry a fitting source of inspiration for reproductive rights activists today. And second, that trap feminist rappers' creative activism surrounding women's rights—evident in their lyrics, performances, and partnerships with non-profit organizations—reflects their strategic use of celebrity status to highlight how these political decisions impact all women, while centering the experiences of those most negatively impacted, poor Black women.

I argue that trap feminist rappers' artistry and activism, as well as the responses to these, offer a lens through which to understand the modern plight of poor Black women in the US, who, along with other women of color, will be the most negatively affected by the legal constriction of women's reproductive rights (Artiga et al. 2022).

Women's Bodily Autonomy and the Long Descent of *Roe v. Wade*

While political discussions surrounding reproductive rights and abortion tend to be presented as "race-neutral" and applying to all those capable of becoming pregnant, existing studies consistently reflect how race, class, sexuality, and other axes of oppression shape the impact of these issues. Before discussing these disparities, and how they are reflected in the artistry and activism of trap feminist rappers, a background on abortions rights is warranted.

Roe v. Wade (1973) enshrined in law the right to have abortions. Immediately following this decision, though, antiabortion religious groups began solidifying power in conservative politics. In the 1980s Evangelical Christians joined the fight against abortion, which had largely been the purview of Catholics. When attempts to challenge abortion rights at the federal level were unsuccessful (except for the Hyde Amendment [1976], which made it illegal to use federal Medicaid funds for abortions), pro-life groups began lobbying state-level politicians instead. From the 1980s onward, conservative politicians at the state level chipped away at the gains of past feminist movements by limiting abortion rights and access to contraceptives—the laws they passed included those requiring parental notification for minors seeking abortions, "informed consent," which included showing women materials about fetus development, and extended wait times for women seeking abortions (Holland 2019). In four states, politicians attempted to pass "heartbeat protection bills" that made it illegal for women to have an abortion if a fetus's heartbeat was detectable, usually six weeks after conception.

The conservative push to limit women's bodily autonomy was fast-tracked when former president Donald J. Trump appointed three ultra-conservative Supreme Court justices during his first term (2017–2021): Neil Gorsuch, Brett Kavanaugh, and Amy Coney Barrett. Of these three appointees, two claimed adamantly that they would uphold *Roe v. Wade* as the law of the land once on the bench. Yet, that promise was quickly reneged in 2022. The long game of antiabortion religious groups had paid off with the Supreme Court appointments—the court now had six conservative justices and three liberal justices, making it easier than ever to secure an overturning of *Roe*.

The overturning of *Roe v. Wade* outlawed federal protections for abortion and made it the purview of states to dictate policies surrounding pregnancy terminations. Sixteen states had "trigger bans" in place to restrict access to, or completely outlaw, abortion once *Roe* was overturned. This meant that the Supreme Court decision led to immediate and widespread consequences.

That said, the decision to overturn *Roe* was somewhat anticlimactic. In a context of extreme political partisanship, a persistent global pandemic, and on the heels of many tense summers of activism around the issue of police brutality, the overturning of *Roe* was met with less fire than anticipated. This might be partially attributed to the leaking of a Supreme Court memo months earlier, which detailed the overturning of *Roe* but did not confirm it. Or, perhaps women, and all those capable of becoming pregnant, were exhausted in the wake of an overwhelming news cycles.

Once *Roe* was overturned, organizations like Planned Parenthood received a huge influx of support, and networks of organizations, like the National Network of Abortion Funds, gathered donations and then spread funds to smaller clinics providing abortions and contraceptives. Among celebrities, we saw a widespread outcry from white feminists, who had already been using their platforms to highlight the negative impacts of sexual harassment and assault through the #MeToo movement.

Yet, as stated above, the impact of abortion and contraceptive bans would be felt most acutely by women of color, and Black and Indigenous women, in particular (Artiga et al. 2022). For one, women of color are more likely to have an abortion than white women. In 2019, nearly four in ten of abortions were among Black women (38 percent), one-third were among White women (33 percent), one in five among Hispanic women of all races (21 percent), and 7 percent among women of other racial and ethnic groups (Artiga et al. 2022). Women of color are also less wealthy than white women, which means they experience financial barriers in accessing abortion and other forms of reproductive care. According to the Kaiser Foundation, from 2016 to 2021, Black women were over three times as likely as white women to die during childbirth (Artiga et al. 2022). Further, a 2023 study from the National Bureau of Economic Research used birth and financial data in California from 2007 to 2016 and found that racial disparities in maternal health outcomes persisted regardless of women's income or financial status—wealthy Black women were still more likely to die during childbirth than wealthy white women.

A reproductive justice framework (Ross and Solinger 2017) specifically addresses these racial disparities in reproductive care by centering four rights: (1) the right to have children, (2) the right to not have children, (3) the right to raise children in healthy environments, and (4) the right to sexual autonomy and gender freedom for all humans. Here, I use the reproductive justice framework to highlight how trap feminist rappers are not only advocating for reproductive rights, but also doing so from a specific justice-oriented Black feminist perspective that acknowledges the importance of sexual autonomy in our struggle for equitable access to reproductive care.

After the overturning of *Roe v. Wade*, Black feminists voiced opposition to the ruling, while also highlighting the long history of reproductive injustice faced by Black women since slavery (Strongman 2022). These feminists showed how, historically, Black women have faced forced reproduction for the sake of capitalist profit-making during slavery, forced sterilization following emancipation and still occurring today, as well as exposure to a child welfare system that disproportionately finds Black mothers "unfit" to care for their own children, resulting in the removal of children from their households.

Black Women's Oppression and the Importance of Pleasure Politics

To fully understand the transgressive, activist potential of trap feminist rap for the reproductive justice movement, we must first examine the tools and mechanisms sustaining Black women's oppression. This context allows us to examine themes in these rappers' artistry, as well as how the public receives, interprets, and responds to their work. As reproductive justice scholar Loretta J. Ross states, "Countering caricatures of Black women's sexuality begins with deconstructing the racialized, misogynist discourse that pervades popular culture and social understandings" (2017, 290).

Black feminist literature in the social sciences and beyond has consistently shown how Black women are marginalized due to their race, gender, sexuality and more, in ways that intersect to produce specific forms of oppression unique to this group. Black feminist sociologist Patricia Hill Collins (2009) refers to this as a "matrix of domination," wherein Black women experience oppression that is informed by the interlocking mechanisms of racism, sexism, and classism. Legal scholar and Black feminist Kimberlé Crenshaw (1991) popularized the term "intersectionality" to address how racism and sexism intersected to exclude Black women in ways that were irreducible to just one facet of their identity (in other words, Black women are often marginalized due to their race *and* their gender, simultaneously).

The oppression of Black women takes many material forms, including exclusion from centers of power and racialized-gendered violence. Underlying Black women's oppression, though, is often a discursive engagement with stereotypes, or what Patricia Hill Collins (1986) calls "controlling images," that work to contain and restrain Black women's agency. Research in the social sciences has shown how controlling images can work to exclude Black women, especially poor Black women, from the political sphere. For instance, political scientist Ange-Marie Hancock (2004) shows how the controlling image of "the welfare queen" was mobilized to pass legislation that dismantled welfare in the 1990s, while simultaneously excluding Black women from the political realm. Black feminist sociologists have also shown how trap feminist rapper Cardi B was targeted by conservative politicians and pundits for her attempts at entering the political sphere (Green et al. 2024). This exclusion occurred through the framing of Cardi B as unintelligent and morally corrupt, both of which are also features of the "welfare queen" stereotype.

Two other controlling images are particularly helpful for understanding the public's perceptions and framing of trap feminist rappers: the Sapphire and the Jezebel. The Sapphire stereotype frames Black women as too assertive, too angry, and therefore, as "unfeminine" (Hill Collins 1986). Trap feminist rappers who work in a majority-male hip-hop industry—and where bravado and strength are central to the artistry of rappers—are often framed as Sapphires. These trap feminist rappers are often depicted as "too masculine" and "too aggressive" in their artistry and due to their commentary on sexism in the music industry.

The Jezebel stereotype, on the other hand, presents an image of Black women as hypersexual, promiscuous, and lacking morality (Hill Collins 2009). Given that trap feminist rappers are unapologetic in their engagement with the topics of sex, the erotic, and pleasure, they are frequently demeaned through the Jezebel stereotype. A recent example of the Jezebel stereotype is the controlling image of the "thot," short for "that hoe over there." Male rappers have used this term to refer to women that are not "wifey material" and are only good for casual sex. Rapper The Game's 2014 track "T.H.O.T." highlights the underlying sentiments behind this controlling image, stating, "You a thot, yeah I really know these bitches / Dick is all I owe these bitches for being themselves." A nuance of this controlling image is that it refers to a high-class, or "high value," "good girl" who is a Jezebel in disguise. In other words, Black women's deceptive attempts at disguising their "true" promiscuity or supposed "low value" are central to this controlling image.

Hill Collins also points out the ways in which Black women have challenged controlling images through the power of self-definition (Hill Collins 1986, 2009). When Black women wield the power of defining themselves, they challenge those with more power who have rendered them "Other." Further, self-definition works to undo the internalization of controlling images that psychologically harm Black women.

While the Black feminist scholarship on controlling images has been critical for understanding Black women's oppression, it does not always provide tools with which to understand Black women's sexual autonomy, particularly as it is negotiated in hip-hop. For example, Patricia Hill Collins explains how the controlling image of the Jezebel got mobilized as the figure of "the hoochie" in '90s hip-hop, arguing that rappers' use of this image normalized and condoned the subjugation of Black women (2009, 90). Yet, Collins does not provide readers with a framework for understanding women who love hip-hop, or women who are unapologetic about their desires for sex, despite being labeled as hypersexual.

Here, I use Joan Morgan's theory of pleasure politics (2015) to address gaps in previous Black feminist theorizing surrounding the topic of Black women's sexuality. Morgan points out how previous Black feminist scholarship frames Black women's sexuality as "a site of reoccurring trauma," where holding the US accountable for the violent histories of "legally and culturally sanctioned rape and gender violence against black women" is centered (36). She pushes Black feminist theorists to move past this centering of pain to "claim pleasure and a healthy erotic as fundamental rights" (36).

Morgan's theorization does not disagree with Audre Lorde's conception of the erotic as "an assertion of the life force of women" (2007, 55) but does disagree with Black feminist scholars who read Lorde's work through heteronormative and binary lenses. Here, she challenges Patricia Hill Collins's view that "the erotic" is completely separate from "sex (fucking)" and can only be manifest when expressed by "an honest body that is not alienated from itself" (2005, 287). In contrast, Morgan states, "My interest is in a capacious casting of the erotic that includes black women's variegated sexual and non-sexual engagements with deeply internal sites of power and pleasure . . . In other words, I want an erotic that demands space be made for honest bodies that like to also *fuck*" (2015, 40).

Trap feminist rappers are clearly aligned with this conception of the erotic, and their artistry should not be written off as simply exemplifying "the commodified sexuality that permeates hip-hop culture" (Collins 2005, 287). In fact, trap feminist rappers, most of whom are Black women who grew up impoverished, are consistently unapologetic in their lyrics, music videos, and performances, about their desire to fuck. Trap feminist rappers dare to clearly name their sexual desires, and it is this daring, in conjunction with their race, class, and gender, that has provoked both admiration and backlash from the public.

Trap Feminism and Its Challenge to Misogynoir

Though trap feminist rappers' music is central in popular culture today, trap feminist rappers themselves are still subject to the same stereotyping, silencing, and racialized gender violence that poor Black women face outside of the music industry. The marginalization of trap feminist rappers is evident in three realms: (1) the policing of poor Black women's creative and political expressions, (2) long-standing sexism and misogynoir in hip-hop, and (3) the specific policing of women's sex-positivity within hip-hop culture. Three substrands of Black feminist theorizing have emerged to bolster poor Black women generally and Black women rappers specifically: Hood Feminism, Hip-Hop Feminism, and Trap Feminism.

Hood Feminism (Kendall 2020) emerged to specifically address the marginalization of poor Black women in feminist movements. These women are often ignored in feminist movements and talked about in feminist literature without being considered part of the conversation as contributors. Hood Feminism challenges mainstream feminism by pointing out its exclusion of marginalized women (including trans women) and its lack of attention to poor women's needs for basic rights including groceries, rent, and healthcare. Given that hip-hop has historically been tied to Black people's lived experiences in poor neighborhoods, it is helpful to have a lens through which to understand the hood Black women who make it into mainstream hip-hop. Thus, Hood Feminism, while an explicit critique of the white, middle-class nature of mainstream feminism, also offers some space for understanding Black women rappers and their experiences.

Hip-Hop Feminism emerged as a tool for women in the post–civil rights generation to express their feminism in ways that allowed for sex-positivity, nuance, personal responsibility, and accountability. Joan Morgan (2000) coined the term "Hip-Hop Feminism" as an alternative to first and second wave feminism, as well as middle-class Black feminisms espoused in academia. She elaborates on the concept by stating that we need a feminism that, like hip-hop, centers "keeping it real" and acknowledges the messiness of living as a Black woman in the age of hip-hop. She states: "The keys that unlock the riches of contemporary black female identity lie not in choosing Latifah over Lil' Kim, or even Foxy Brown over Salt-N-Pepa. They lie at the magical intersection where those contrary voices meet—the juncture where 'truth' is no longer black and white but subtle, intriguing shades of gray" (2000, 62). Hip-Hop Feminism also differs from mainstream feminism by centering the welfare of Black women, the Black community, and Black love. Thus, it recognizes the importance of Black women working *with* Black men, rather than against them in the struggle against racism and sexism.

Later, groups like the Crunk Feminist Collective emerged from the intersection of academic and nonacademic spaces "[t]o create space where Black and Brown chicks who loved hip hop but didn't love sexism could say what needed to be said" (Cooper, Morris, and Boylorn 2017, 1). Pairing the specificity of Southern Crunk Hip-Hop with Black feminism, crunk feminists "are not invested in being polite, respectable, or politically digestible—because our very lives are on the line" (Cooper et al. 2017, 11).

Lastly, Trap Feminism, coined by Sesali Bowen (2021), emerged as a specific form of hip-hop feminism that not only supports poor Black women, but also those whose aesthetics, culture, and public engagement align with the trap. The "trap" is Atlanta slang for houses where illicit drugs are held, processed, and sold. The emergence of the trap house as a locale tied to music came about with rapper T.I.'s music. With the rise of Southern trap rap, we saw the usual story of a male-dominated group of rappers. Their lyrics spoke of similar topics as other hip-hop (e.g., life in poverty, the need to hustle to survive, the impact of drugs and poverty on loved ones and the self, and police brutality) but added a Southern inflection that made it stand apart from the rap styles of artists from the Northeast or Midwest. Today, though, trap music encompasses rappers from all over the country who include the same heavy bass, modified vocals, and gritty delivery as earlier Southern trap rappers.

Trap feminism, then, is shorthand for rachet girls who believe in gender equality and attempt to achieve it despite the constraints of poverty. They are sex-positive women who may or may not be affiliated with processing or selling drugs, but who are nevertheless aware of the hustle necessary to survive in the trap. Trap feminists also make space for queer and nonbinary hood chicks who not only decenter men in their feminism but might altogether exclude them. Not all trap feminists produce trap music, but they all unapologetically enjoy listening to trap rap and hip-hop more broadly. Trap feminist rappers, on the other hand, have taken that sex positive, unapologetically hood stance into the hip-hop industry, leading to the fame of rappers ranging from Lil' Kim and Trina to Cardi B and Megan Thee Stallion.

Trap Feminist Rap and the Creative Fight for Black Women's Sexual Autonomy

Patriarchal reactions to trap feminist rappers are often evident in the policing of their sexuality and sexual autonomy; the public policing of these rappers' sexual expression is tied to notions of "proper" behavior that women should exhibit. Yet, these (oftentimes outdated) social mores concerning women's public expressions of sexuality present a conundrum for trap feminist rappers. They are policed for being too sexual, while facing pressures to be more sexual by music executives who are aware that "sex sells." They are critiqued for rapping about their pussies, while having their bodies dissected by the public regardless of what they say or do. And, it is this type of policing, which can take the form of inter- or intraracial reactions and responses to these rappers, that underlies policy decisions aimed at limiting women's autonomy in the US.

Early Trap Feminist Rap and Women's Sexual Autonomy

In hip-hop we have witnessed women rappers being vocal about sexual liberation and autonomy through their lyrics, music videos, and performances. An early example of this was Lil' Kim, who entered the hip-hop scene as part of Junior Mafia, a crew of rappers including Notorious B.I.G. that was formed in Brooklyn in 1994. Lil' Kim's 1997 hit "Crush on You," featuring male rapper Lil' Cease, was an unapologetic ode to a man she was pursuing ("the only one thing I wanna do is freak you"). Exemplifying the erotic was part of her approach in the song's lyrics, where she assures the man she's pursuing that she would be waiting for him, "undressed in the bra or see-through." In the accompanying music video, Lil' Kim is the central focus for viewers—we see her shifting in looks through various scenes, wearing color-coordinated bikinis, or shorts and crop tops, paired with matching sunglasses, fur coats, and colored wigs. The background dancers in the video are equally divided among men and women, and, while their clothing is more modest than Lil' Kim's, their dance moves are clearly sexual throughout the video.

There's an interesting contrast, though, between the song's chorus and Lil' Kim's lyrics. The chorus is sung primarily by Biggie, though he doesn't appear as an artist on the song credits or in the video. He speaks about being seen as a player by his crush's friend group ("got a different girl every day of the week"). He then goes on to state that he has a crush on the woman but that it's something that needs to be kept secret ("keep this on the hush"). Overall, the video shows a clear attempt at achieving gender equality in the dating scene, while showing that men in powerful positions (in the videos, on the radio) are still likely to be players. Lil' Kim's response to this, though, is to require that any man propositioning her needs to provide for her as well, "You got to hit me off, buy this girl gifts of course." The song and video reflect many of the features of mainstream hip-hop in the '90s: grittiness paired with a discussion of relationship issues, and hood sensibilities paired with a desire for an elite, flashy lifestyle.

Another notable early contributor to trap feminism was Trina. In 2023, Trina completed a Tiny Desk concert for NPR, where she opened the set by declaring, "I wanna introduce you guys to the baddest bitch. The original baddest bitch." While Trina followed Lil Kim's entrée into the hip-hop scene, first releasing music in 1998 and dropping her debut album in 1999, she carved a unique lane for herself in the genre and is still producing music today. In her debut album, the title song, "Da Baddest Bitch" lays out how she refuses to have sex with men for nothing in return. She advises young women to "Sell the pussy by the grands / And in months you own a Benz." Unlike women rappers today, most of whom are known for being unabashed about their sexuality, Trina was rapping in an era of relative modesty for women in the music industry. Her approach was straightforward—women need to demand something in exchange for access to their bodies. While many read this sort of phrasing as indicative of a crude, transactional, approach to relationships, Trina's lyrics are a response to the realities of gendered-raced inequalities for Black women. In the US, where Black women are historically the least economically remunerated for their work (ASA Task Force on the State of the Art in Sociological Scholarship on Race 2023), it is imperative for these Black women to be strategic in their social and economic relationships.

The period between the 1990s and the 2020s was sprinkled with other trap feminist rappers, but none that rose to the prominence of Lil' Kim and Trina. Artists like Nicki Minaj and Cardi B reopened the doors to sexually liberatory rap lyrics leading up to 2020. Yet, these artists were constantly pitted against each other. In the hip-hop industry, there is a tendency to set women artists against each other, given their small numbers in the mainstream rap world, as well as the misogyny limiting women's entrance into the genre. Since 2020, though, trap feminist rappers have increased in number and prominence, and are more likely to collaborate. The days of only a few women rappers dueling for a coveted tokenized spot in the hip-hop game are over.

WAP Makes a Splash in Trap Feminist Rap

On August 7, 2020, Cardi B and Megan Thee Stallion released the single and music video for "WAP" ("Wet Ass Pussy"), marking a watershed moment in trap feminist rap. The single was released amid a flurry of social and political upheavals: the beginning of the COVID-19 pandemic, the police killing of George Floyd leading to global Black Lives Matter protests, and a pending presidential election following four years of Donald J. Trump's leadership, which was marked by trenchant political partisanship. Cardi B had been a stronghold in the rap game for years at this point, having released her chart-topping single "Bodak Yellow" in 2016 and her debut album, *Invasion of Privacy*, in 2018. Megan, in contrast, was a newer arrival to the mainstream hip-hop scene, having released mixtapes and EPs from 2016 onward, but charting for the first time in 2019, with her song "Big Ole Freak." In April 2020, Beyonce collaborated with Megan on the remix to her single "Savage," which topped the Billboard 100, making it Megan's first Billboard number one song in the US.

Amid Cardi B's continued success, Megan Thee Stallion's meteoric rise to fame, and the many notable social and political events of 2020, WAP made a huge splash on the music scene beyond hip-hop. WAP debuted at #1 on the Billboard Hot 100 Chart and broke the US record for most streams of a song within its first week of release, being streamed 93 million times across the country. The song opens with a sample of DJ Frank Ski's 1993 single "Whores in This House," and then alternates between verses by Cardi and Megan describing their sexual needs and prowess. The song is explicit, and unabashedly so, with Cardi asking her sexual partner to "bring a bucket and a mop, for this wet ass pussy" and Megan urging hers to "gobble me, swallow me, drip down the side of me." In this way, the song is simultaneously silly, clever, and an ode to women's confidence and sexual autonomy.

The song also reflects the importance of women's financial and social independence, while contending with the realities of gendered inequalities in relationships. Cardi proudly claims, "I don't cook, I don't clean / but let me tell you how I got this ring." Her statement reflects a challenge to gender norms that urge women to take on domestic chores, particularly while married. And yet, these lyrics also show a capitulation to gender norms that frame marriage as an end goal for women. These conflicting approaches to gendered norms are evident in many trap feminist rappers' lyrics.[1]

In contrast, Megan's lyrics in the song are unequivocally centered on women's independence from men. In the song she states, "I tell him where to put it, never tell him where I'm 'bout to be/ I run down on him 'fore I have a nigga running me." Here, Megan pairs her sexual demands with an insistence on not being controlled by the men she sleeps with. Throughout the song, Megan's centering of her sexual pleasure is always coupled with a demand to be free from the constrictions of patriarchy. She later clarifies "You ain't never gotta fuck him for a thing / He already made his mind up before he came." This lyric contrasts with Cardi's lyrics as well as with earlier examples of trap feminist rap lyrics, including Trina's 1999 hit "The Baddest Bitch," where she encourages women to exchange sexual acts for luxury goods. Here, Megan is pushing for an evolution in trap feminism, urging women to extract money and goods from men while withholding sexual access to their bodies. Her erotic power does not require exchanging sex at all, but rather offering the illusion that men will be able to access her body. Thus, these lyrics show how Megan is reappropriating the image of "the thot" (a promiscuous woman who enjoys expensive things), while also increasing its deceptive undertones. She's providing a rulebook for women on how to become successful hustlers while retaining power over their bodies.

Overall, trap feminist rappers have used their artistry to empower Black women, whether that be sexually, financially, or sociopolitically. Trap feminist rappers' lyrics espouse a politics of pleasure (Morgan 2015) that centers Black women's sexual desires while pushing for their freedom from patriarchal strictures. These lyrics also work to establish a self-definition that pushes back against controlling images of Black women as "thots." Trap feminist rappers instead reappropriate the image of the "thot," calling themselves the term (as Megan does in her 2021 hit "Thot Shit") and redefining it as a woman who is powerfully attuned to her sexual and financial needs. These features of trap feminist rap highlight why it has become a transgressive soundtrack to the modern-day fight for women's rights and reproductive justice.

Trap Feminist Rappers and the Fight for Reproductive Justice

When people think of protest anthems for the women's rights movement, they usually think of folk or punk songs—they rarely, if ever, think of hip-hop tracks, even though hip-hop emerged as a genre merely seven months after the passing of *Roe v. Wade* in 1973 (Carson 2022). Within hip-hop, the search for songs addressing abortion or reproductive rights yields few popular results, including Nas' "Keep Ya Head Up" and Lauryn Hill's "To Zion" (Harshaw 2022). Below, I examine how trap feminist rappers have entered the social, political, and artistic conversations surrounding reproductive rights, particularly in the lead up to the overturning of *Roe* in June 2022. I find that their activism has been evident in three realms—artistically in their song lyrics and music videos; socially in their live performances and commentary on social media sites like Twitter and Instagram; and politically through their direct partnerships with reproductive rights organizations.

Trap Feminist Rappers' Artistic Activism for Reproductive Justice

One clear example of a trap feminist rapper centering reproductive justice through their artistry is Latto's song "Pussy" (censored to "Pxssy" on YouTube and other sites). "Pussy" was released on July 15, 2022, less than a month after the Supreme Court decision to overturn *Roe v. Wade*. The song is geared toward men and women, with Latto reminding them, "Girls, you can do what the guys do / And still be a lady." Latto's lyrics in the chorus of "Pussy" point to the double standards applied to men and women who enjoy sex (later in the song, she directly refers to this, saying, "Fuck you and your double standards, pussy ain't for you to judge"). Rather than capitulate to "respectable," and oftentimes oppressive notions of being a lady, or what Patricia Hill Collins refers to as a the "cult of true womanhood" (2009), Latto makes space for women who are unapologetic about their sexual desires and still demand respect from outsiders.

The song samples Betty Wright's popular 1968 song "Girls Can't Do What the Boys Do," which reached #33 on the Billboard Top 100 Chart and #16 on the R&B Billboard Chart. In Wright's rendition, she warns women that, while men may make them cry, "Don't lose your self-respect / Trying to get revenge" because "Girls, you can't do with the guys do, no / And still be a lady, no." By contrast, Latto is assuring women that things have changed—she and other trap feminist rappers are the vanguard of a new moment in which women *can* do what men do, while still being a lady. Latto goes on to claim,

> Your misogynistic ways show the size of your dick
> Seen with the opposite sex and just decide that he hit
> I ain't your property, bitch, get mad and call me a bitch
> And if he make you split rent then he probably a bitch

Her lyrics are bold and righteously angry. Latto specifically challenges misogyny head-on and pushes back against men who claim to the public that they have slept with her simply because she has been on a date with them. She directly insults men who are misogynistic by referring to a primary marker of masculinity: penis size. She also insults those who do not provide financially for women by using the term most employed to degrade women, "bitch." Later in the song, Latto gets even more specific in holding men accountable for their misogynoir:

> The gender roles y'all projecting are hypocrisy (On God)
> Half of y'all pussy niggas owe your mama an apology (Haha)
> How you ain't got a pussy, but got opinions on pussy?
> That's pussy (Pussy), my ovaries ain't for you to bully
> Y'all the reason we make music, teaching bitches how to use you

Here, Latto starts by pointing out the hypocrisy of gender norms being espoused by men today. One reading of this is the persistent gendered view of men as providers and women as nurturers. Given the current manifestations of late neoliberal capitalism, most households today include multiple people who work to maintain the household. So, Latto here might be referring to the mismatch between men's desire for "traditional" heterosexual relationships where women are submissive, and the reality that men rarely occupy the traditional role of "sole provider" in the current economy. Latto then points out her frustration with men who have "opinions on pussy" without having to live with the daily realities of being a woman. Men, particularly in hip-hop, use "pussy" as an insult for other men who do not meet heteronormative standards of masculinity. Latto uses the term to further drive home the point that policing women's bodies is the epitome of being a pussy. While some might argue that this is an example of Latto trying to use the master's tools to dismantle the master's house (to reference Audre Lorde's famous essay), I read this as Latto's way to reach male listeners that would otherwise dismiss her. Latto is showing how, in a patriarchal society, the most effective means to reach a male listener might be to use terms that men employ to police the boundaries of masculinity.

Latto's statement, "my ovaries ain't for you to bully," present a clear trap feminist clarion call. While trap feminist rap centers women's pleasure and erotic power, it always does so within the constraints of a cis-hetero-patriarchal society in which men oppress women. The bully figure is one of inherent power imbalance—bullies choose targets who are vulnerable and lack social power, which makes their abuse more likely to succeed and be socially sanctioned. By noting that her ovaries are not for men to bully, Latto is implying that this is the goal of powerful men in a sexist society. She ends the verse with a reversal of power, stating "Y'all the reason we make music, teaching bitches how to use you." This lyric is another example of how trap feminist rappers reappropriate sexist stereotypes to challenge the unequal power dynamics between themselves and sexist men. As stated above, the controlling image of "the thot" is used in hip-hop and beyond to disparage (usually working class) women who enjoy an expensive lifestyle and pose as "good girls" while being promiscuous. In "Pussy," Latto is leaning into this controlling image, framing herself as someone who not only uses men (as a thot would), but also joins other trap feminist rappers in making music that teaches all women how to do the same. She then puts the onus of this contestation of power on men—if they were not trying to bully women's ovaries, women wouldn't need to resort to using them for money and luxury goods.

The video for "Pussy" further drives home the point of Latto's lyrics. The video begins with a shot of Latto lying elegantly on a chaise, watching TV. She tunes into a news report of abortion rights protests following the overturning of *Roe v. Wade*. From the jump, Latto is providing the impetus for her song—what better example of men trying to bully women's ovaries than the overturning of *Roe*?

While Latto is the only human depicted in the music video, she is in an apartment surrounded by cats. The use of cats in the video is a play on the multiple meanings of the term "Pussy." Yet, we might read another meaning into this artistic choice. The image of a woman sitting alone in an apartment with only the company of cats evokes the persona of the "crazy cat lady." The crazy cat lady could be termed a controlling image, as well. She is oftentimes a woman who is imagined as not being feminine or beautiful enough to gain the attention of a male partner—or, in turn, she is seen as someone who is too independent to prioritize a relationship with a man. She is then relegated to a life of "madness" where her only companions are pets, and where she lives a pitiable, sexless life.

The controlling image of the crazy cat lady is linked to recent political discussions within conservative circles. In July 2021, vice presidential candidate JD Vance went on Fox News' *Tucker Carlson Tonight* to discuss the state of the US government (O'Dell 2021). Vance argued that the country was being run by "a bunch of childless cat ladies" who "want to make the rest of the country miserable, too." He then went on to specify that he was referring to Democrat politicians Kamala Harris, Alexandria Ocasio-Cortez, and Pete Buttigieg, none of whom have biological children. He went on to say, "Maybe, if we want a healthy ruling class in this country . . . we should support more people who actually have kids." Vance's comments reflect how conservative ideology centers the traditional nuclear family as the only family formation that is "healthy" and worthy of representing the nation (Chervinsky 2021). By referencing this trope in her music video for "Pussy," Latto is reinscribing the power of the "crazy cat lady" as a woman who is independent, self-sufficient, and who demands respect from men.

Megan Thee Stallion has also used her artistry to advocate for reproductive justice. As noted above, her song "Plan B" refers to her use of the emergency contraceptive to avoid getting stuck raising children with unworthy men. She also refers to women's bodily autonomy in the song "Gift & A Curse" released in August 2022 as part of her album *Traumazine*.[2] Set to an energetic beat fit for a gym session, Megan raps:

> All dicks, please rise, let's praise the ass
> And all my real freak hoes, let's fuck some more (Ah)
> My motherfuckin' body, my choice (My choice)
> Ain't no lil' dick takin' my voice

Megan's lyrics here highlight two central and overlapping tenets of trap feminism—unapologetically centering Black women's pleasure and asserting women's right to do as they please without being constrained by patriarchy. While the phrase "my body, my choice" has been a common slogan of the women's rights movements since the passage of *Roe v. Wade* in the 1970s, Megan translates the term in the language of trap feminism. It's not just "my body," it's "my motherfuckin' body." It's not just about the choice to have a child or not, it's also about the choice to be a proud "freak hoe" and to "fuck some more" while you're at it. Like Latto, Megan also uses penis size, one of the metrics of masculinity in our patriarchal society, to disparage men who try "takin' my voice." One might argue that this line is about Megan policing men with small penises, but one could also argue that it is men's attempts to control women that make them "lil' dick" men in her perspective.

In addition to her music, Megan Thee Stallion penned an opinion piece in the *New York Times* titled "Why I Speak Up for Black Women" to point out the many challenges facing women like her in the lead up to the 2020 Presidential Election (Stallion 2020). After speaking about violence against women, both domestic violence and police brutality, Megan discussed racial inequities in maternal health outcomes in the US and the role of stereotypes in shaping the normalization of violence of against Black women. Decrying the public's "obsession with Black women's bodies," Megan speaks to the issue personally, stating,

> I would know. I've received quite a bit of attention for my appearance as well as my talent. I choose my own clothing. Let me repeat: I choose what I wear, not because I am trying to appeal to men, but because I am showing pride in my appearance, and a positive body image is central to who I am as a woman and a performer. I value compliments from women far more than from men. But the remarks about how I choose to present myself have often been judgmental and cruel, with many assuming that I'm dressing and performing for the male gaze. When women choose to capitalize on our sexuality, to reclaim our *own* power, like I have, we are vilified and disrespected.

Her words echo Patricia Hill Collins's analysis of controlling images, as well as Joan Morgan's acknowledgment of women's erotic power in hip-hop and call for a new pleasure politics. Megan's words also reflect how trap feminism encourages women to control *how* their sexuality is consumed by others as a means of reclaiming their power.

Trap Feminist Rappers' Social Activism for Reproductive Justice

Trap feminist rappers have taken their pro-choice stances outside of the booth and the music industry altogether. By using their platforms as influential artists, they have created room to voice the concerns of Black women who lack access to these spaces. Megan Thee Stallion, for example, has used her concert performances and social media posts to address and fight against the recent constriction of women's rights in the US. In September 2021, Texas passed a state law that would restrict abortion rights to those in the first six weeks of their pregnancy and would allow anyone to sue doctors who provide women abortions after those six weeks. The law made no exceptions for cases of incest or rape and would reward those who sued non-compliant doctors $10,000. Megan, who was born and raised in Houston, Texas, took to Instagram to vent about the law, stating "Y'all know I'm a Texas girl and we deserve better! Politicians want to cut off abortion access and control our bodies, lives, and futures—I'm speaking up" (Landen 2021). That evening, during her performance at *Austin City Limits*, she asked audience members to hold up their middle fingers, then stated, "This middle finger is also to these motherfucking men that want to tell us what the fuck to do with our body. 'Cause how the fuck you gonna tell me what to do with my motherfucking body? Drop that shit" (Landen 2021). The DJ then dropped the beat for her performance of "Plan B." Here, Megan boldly challenges politicians and all men who want to control women's bodies. Her statement, "I'm speaking up," bolsters not only her voice, but also the voices of women, and particularly working class and poor Black women, who do not have her platform.

After the overturning of *Roe*, Megan also used her performances to advocate for reproductive justice. The day after the Supreme Court ruling, Megan performed at the Glastonbury Music Festival in the UK and spoke to her fans in the crowd (Billboard 2022), stating, "You know it wouldn't be me if I didn't take a second to call out these stupid ass men. I mean, goddamn. What else you want?" She then specifically called out Texas, "Texas really embarrassing me right now—y'all know that's my home state." She continued, appealing to her fans, who she refers to as "hotties," "And I want to have it on the record that the motherfucking hot girls and the hot boys do not support this bullshit that y'all campaigning for." She drove the point home by asking the crowd to join her in chanting the trap feminist slogan and lyric from her song "Gift & A Curse," "My body, my motherfucking choice!"

Megan's use of live performances to call out politicians for attempting to control women's bodies shows how she uses her celebrity status to speak directly to centers of power. While she might not be standing in front of congress, she knows that her global fanbase can carry her message to those who pull the levers of power. She is also forging space for other "non-respectable" women to speak on political issues, and to be free to curse and twerk as they do so.

While Cardi B has not been as political in her lyrics, she has a long history of speaking on political issues on social media, to the press, and directly to politicians themselves, including President Joe Biden and Vermont Senator Bernie Sanders.[3] Several days after Texas passed its six-week abortion law, Cardi tweeted, "It's crazy how they only giving women 6 weeks I didn't even know I was pregnant till around 11. This country is soo damn backwards" (Twitter/X; @iamcardib; 09/04/2021). She included a meme with the post that read "Republican Logic" in bold letters at the top and with two drawn images below it, one of a surgical face mask, and the other a rendering of a uterus. Above the face mask were the words "my body, my choice," reflecting the conservative push for "freedom" from COVID-19 mask mandates. By contrast, the text above the uterus read, "your body, my choice," referring to Republicans' push for limiting reproductive rights. After the overturning of *Roe v. Wade*, Cardi again pointed to Republicans' hypocrisy concerning reproductive rights, tweeting, "If your pro-Life how come you believe in the death penalty?" (Twitter/X; @iamcardib; 06/29/2022). While she does not mention Republicans directly, it is clear who she is referring to, given that being pro-life and pro-death penalty are central in Republican political platforms.

Megan Thee Stallion's comments and social media posts about reproductive justice have been addressed more broadly to "men" and "politicians." In contrast, Cardi B has been very direct in naming Republican politicians and pundits for their role in limiting reproductive rights, while calling them out for their hypocrisy. Both trap feminist rappers, though, show the importance of social media for advancing their activism surrounding reproductive justice.

In the lead up to the 2024 Presidential Election, we witnessed the importance of trap feminist politics (Green et al. 2024) in action. Vice president and presidential hopeful Kamala Harris, who is of Indian and Black Jamaican ancestry, invited several trap feminist rappers to join her on the campaign trail. The first was Megan Thee Stallion, who performed at a Harris rally on July 30, 2024, introducing the slogan "Hotties for Harris" (Moorman and Robinson 2024). The performance set off a slew of disparaging remarks, claiming that Harris was pandering to Black voters and that Megan was not a "serious enough" entertainer to be part of a presidential race (Robinson 2024). In response, Megan said the following at her concert in Chicago two days later: "They was fake mad that I was popping it for Kamala. I don't think they heard what she said. Kamala said she wants a ceasefire. Kamala said she supports women's rights. Kamala said y'all tired of those high . . . gas prices. Kamala said, 'I'm for the people.' Tonight, I'm not giving y'all my lightest twerk. I'm giving y'all my hardest twerk in the . . . rain. It's Hotties for Harris!" (Robinson 2024).

Later in the campaign, and four days prior to the general election, Kamala Harris hosted a rally in Milwaukee that was clearly an ode to trap feminist rappers (Levy 2024). The presidential candidate invited a pioneer of Black women in rap, MC Lyte, to perform. This was followed by performances by upcomers Flo Milli and Glorilla. To top off the evening, she had Cardi B take the stage for a speech *and* to introduce her. Cardi delivered a passionate, ten-minute-long speech, which she had to read from her phone due to technical issues with the venue's teleprompter. Cardi began her remarks by drawing parallels between herself and the presidential candidate, stating that "Just like Kamala Harris, I, too, have been the underdog. I have been underestimated, my success belittled and discredited." While Cardi was mindful to make the parallel about how women are underestimated, the event and invitees were a clear nod toward Black women's power, in particular.

Later in the speech, Cardi railed on Donald J. Trump's comment that he would protect women "whether they like it or not." Cardi retorted, "If his definition of protection is making sure our daughters have fewer rights than our mothers, I don't want it. I don't want it!" The trap feminist rapper continued, "He's selling us bigotry, misogyny, division, chaos and confusion. And it's going to cost you your money, equal opportunity, affordable health care, and any rights you thought you had for your body. He's going to take it from you! Listen to me. He's going to take it. I'm not giving Donald Trump a second chance. I'm not taking any chances with my future and I damn sure am taking no chances for the future of my children!" (Levy 2024). Here, Cardi B takes full ownership of her role as an influential artist to advance her political aims, and that of many Black women. As a mother of three children who had to hustle her way to stardom from a hood in the Bronx, Cardi understands the real-world implications of politicians' policies. As she stated herself that evening, "I do not take lightly the call to show up, the call to speak up, the call to deliver a message that has been on my heart for a hot minute now."

Trap Feminist Rappers' Partnerships with Reproductive Rights Organizations

Prior to, and in the wake of, the overturning of *Roe v. Wade*, trap feminist rappers partnered directly with reproductive rights organization Planned Parenthood to raise awareness about the restrictions being placed on women's access to abortions and contraceptives.

Several hours after the Supreme Court decision, Megan Thee Stallion took to Twitter/X to share infographics from Planned Parenthood's "Ban Off Our Bodies" campaign with her 7.5 million fans on the site. Along with the infographic, she wrote: "The court has failed us all—but we won't back down. I'm going to keep fighting because everyone deserves access to the care they need. Join me and @PPact: BansOff.org. #BansOffOurBodies" (Twitter/X; @theestallion; 06/24/2022). Two of the four infographics shared "the facts" about the Supreme Court decision, another gave options for those interested to join the struggle, and the last infographic read "We will not be defeated. We will not back down" in bold pink letters. In addition, when she was awarded a Webby Artist of the Year Award on May 22, 2022, Megan used her acceptance speech to share Planned Parenthood's campaign slogan. She said, "They said make it short and sweet, so . . . Imma just say, take the bans off our bodies" (Twitter/X; @The WebbyAwards; 06/24/2022). Lastly, Megan used the popularity of her song "Plan B" to collect funds for Planned Parenthood after *Roe* was overturned in 2022. She released a t-shirt reading Ladies, Love Yourself, which is the opening line to the song's chorus, and funneled all the proceeds to Planned Parenthood (Guerra 2022). Megan's advocacy shows the importance of celebrities using every platform available to highlight sociopolitical issues of importance. And Megan's main social justice concern has always been the well-being of Black women and girls.[4]

Latto also partnered with Planned Parenthood to create a public service announcement in the wake of *Roe* being overturned (Peters 2022). The PSA was aired in late August 2022, as part of the lead-up to the MTV Music Awards, where Latto's music video for "Pussy" was nominated in the "Video for Good" category, as well as three other awards. The PSA is a 30-second clip, featuring a then 23-year-old Latto standing against a plain white background. She states,

> What's up y'all, it's Latto and I need y'all to pay attention to what's going on in this country. The Supreme Court took away our right to abortion so now politicians are banning abortions and billions [sic] of people live in states where it's illegal. I'm not okay with that. We have to decide whether and when we wanna be parents, but they wanna force us to give birth. That's why I'm joining with Planned Parenthood to fight to restore our rights and expand access to care.

Latto then provided information to viewers on how they could get involved in fighting for access to reproductive care. At the award show itself, Latto discussed the collaboration with a journalist on the red carpet, saying, "It's something that I'm passionate about. I'm a woman. It affects me, it affects you, it affects everybody" (Saunders 2022).

Latto's words in the PSA and on the MTV Music Awards red carpet were phrased to reach as broad of an audience as possible ("it affects everybody"). In a July 2022 statement obtained by *Billboard Magazine* (Peters 2022), though, Latto was more specific in her support for the cause, pointing out the need to address racial inequalities in reproductive care and abortion access. In the statement, which reflects a trap feminist ethos, she says,

> We already know who's going to be hurt the most by these ridiculous abortion bans: Black women, Brown women, the LGBTQ+ community, and communities with low incomes. Because of this country's history of racism and discrimination, these folks already have a hard time getting the health care they need. We all deserve to be safe and it's every person's right to make decisions about their own bodies. As an artist, I want to use my platform to let these politicians know: My body is for no one to control but me.

In October of 2022, weeks before the US Midterm Elections, Latto used a performance in Atlanta, Georgia, to further advocate for reproductive justice—and to encourage her fans to vote for candidates that supported the cause. During her performance for "Pussy," Latto surprised the audience by inviting Stacey Abrams—the Democratic candidate for governor of Georgia—to the stage, where the aspiring politician held a large sign reading My Body, My Choice (Abraham 2022). Once the song was done, Abrams addressed the crowd, saying, "I'm not going to interrupt your fun. I just want to remind you, if you believe 'it's my body, my choice,' I need your vote! You gotta show up. This is our time. This is our choice, and this is our year. I need your big energy [referring to Latto's hit song, 'Big Energy']! Let's get it done." Abrams's words showed how politicians are also engaging with trap feminist rappers to reach (often younger and more diverse) constituents—an approach that clearly informed Kamala Harris in her 2024 presidential campaign. Abrams's surprise appearance during Latto's set also reinforced a central tenet of trap feminism, the importance and value of Black women acting as sisters to protect each other in the face of oppression. As Megan Thee Stallion noted in her *New York Times* opinion piece in the lead up to the 2020 Presidential Election, "Black women are not naïve. We know that after the last ballot is cast and the vote is tallied, we are likely to go back to fighting for ourselves. Because at least for now, that's all we have" (Stallion 2020).

Conclusion

When a majority-conservative Supreme Court ruled to outlaw federal abortion rights in 2022, sex-positive Black women rappers like Cardi B, Megan Thee Stallion, and Latto, had been ranking high on music charts. In 2020, Megan Thee Stallion became the first woman to have three chart-topping singles in a year (with songs "Body," "Savage remix" ft. Beyonce, and "WAP," her collaboration with Cardi B). Cardi B had five Billboard number one singles under her belt by the end of 2021 ("I Like It," "Girls Like You," "Bodak Yellow," "WAP," and "Up"). And Latto, who entered the mainstream after Cardi and Megan, had her single "Big Energy" hit number three on the Billboard charts in late 2021. The contrast was stark—trap feminist rappers were not only becoming prominent, but topping music charts with their unapologetically sexual music, while the rights of women and many others to have a say over their own bodies was being severely restricted.

The popular music or artists of a given year are not necessarily those to whom activists turn in times of political contention. In other words, protest music is not always popular, and popular music is not always welcome at protests. This type of mismatch was evident at some of the protests following the overturning of *Roe v. Wade*, including the one in Dallas, Texas, with which I opened this chapter. Once video of the protests, and women twerking to Megan Thee Stallion's "Plan B" were released, reactions to the choice of song and the dance styles displayed were varied. In the comments beneath the video, you see clear manifestations of misogyny, respectability politics, and outright hatred toward the women present. One conservative pundit, Elijah Schaffer, quote tweeted the video adding, "Dallas women TWERKING for abortions. WTF," as well as a mocking attempt at a rap lyric describing the scene, "Shaking a** so we can kill our babies. Proud to be a hoe and not to be a ladies [sic]." The tweet garnered almost 13K likes and over 5K retweets. Others commented on the "unattractive" bodies of the women dancing and their supposed inability to twerk. And numerous otherwise sympathetic women in the comments argued that the twerking protestors were detracting from the seriousness of the day and the Supreme Court ruling. The irony of the matter was that online commenters were policing these protestors in ways that aligned with the Supreme Court's constriction of women's bodily autonomy.

What makes for a "proper" reproductive justice anthem, though? And what is the "appropriate" way to protest when the state has just determined your bodily autonomy is not going to be protected? To assess the place of trap feminist rap in the reproductive justice movement, we first need to address the role of sexual autonomy in the reproductive justice struggle. When feminists frame the conversation in binary terms of pro-choice vs. pro-life, or abortion vs. adoption, or contraceptives vs. family planning approaches, we often divorce ourselves from the reality that sex and pleasure are intimately implicated in these matters. In short, many folks fighting for women's rights are not centering sex and pleasure and instead center pregnancy, abortion, and contraceptives alone.

The findings above illuminate how trap feminist rappers engage topics of sexual freedom and bodily autonomy, which has led to their artistry being used as a transgressive soundtrack for reproductive justice advocates. Further, trap feminist rappers have directly engaged with the movement through their songs, music videos, commentary online, chants during their shows, and through partnerships with organizations like Planned Parenthood. Trap feminist rap has proven to be a powerful tool for enabling young women, particularly young and poor Black women, to reclaim their sexual and erotic power, challenge the hold of racist and sexist controlling images, and center a politics of pleasure within the reproductive rights movement.

Notes

1. In *The Sociology of Cardi B: A Trap Feminist Approach*, four co-authors and I examine how Cardi B's lyrics throughout the album *Invasion of Privacy* show Cardi grappling with the competing demands of traditional gender norms and a trap feminist ethos of independence (Green et al. 2024).

2. The themes mentioned here are also evident in Megan Thee Stallion's song "Rattle," the first track on her 2024 album *Megan*, where she raps, "Y'all why I'm standin' on business for pro-choice / 'Cause the niggas don't beef with the niggas / They scared of each other but beat on the women."

3. See "Chapter 6: Cardi B's Trap Feminist Politics," in *The Sociology of Cardi B* (2024) for a detailed analysis of Cardi B's political activism to date.

4. For example, Megan founded an organization called Southern Black Girls and Women's Consortium that works to increase philanthropy for organizations that empower young Black women and girls in the Southern US (https://www.southernblackgirls.org/), as well as a mental health initiative called *Bad Bitches Have Bad Days, Too*, to share mental health resources, including resources specific to Black and LGBTQIA people, with the general public (https://www.badbitches havebaddaystoo.com/).

Works Cited

Abraham, Mya. 2022. "Stacey Abrams Joins Latto For A Special 'PXSSY' Protest Performance." *VIBE.Com* (blog). October 24, 2022. https://www.vibe.com/ news/politics/stacey-abrams-latto-pxssy-performance-1234704733/.

Artiga, Samantha, Latoya Hill, Usha Ranji, and Ivette Gomez. 2022. "What Are the Implications of the Overturning of Roe v. Wade for Racial Disparities?" *KFF* (blog). July 15, 2022. https://www.kff.org/racial-equity-and-health-policy/ issue-brief/what-are-the-implications-of-the-overturning-of-roe-v-wade-for-racial-disparities/.

ASA Task Force on the State of the Art in Sociological Scholarship on Race. 2023. "Race and Racism in the United States: A Sociological Guide for the Public | American Sociological Association." https://www.asanet.org/for-press/press-releases/ race-and-racism-in-the-united-states-a-sociological-guide-for-the-public/.

Bailey, Moya and Trudy. 2018. "On Misogynoir: Citation, Erasure, and Plagiarism." *Feminist Media Studies* 18 (4): 762–68. https://doi.org/10.1080/1468 0777.2018.1447395.

Billboard, Ashley Iasimone. 2022. "Megan Thee Stallion Leads Crowd in 'My Body, My Motherf***ing Choice' Chant at Glastonbury." *The Hollywood Reporter* (blog). June 27, 2022. https://www.hollywoodreporter.com/news/music-news/ megan-thee-stallion-roe-v-wade-chant-glastonbury-1235172358/.

Bowen, Sesali. 2021. *Bad Fat Black Girl: Notes from a Trap Feminist*. New York, NY: Amistad.

Carson, A. D. 2022. "Roe v. Rap: Hip-Hop Artists Have Long Wrestled with Reproductive Rights." *The Conversation*. July 8, 2022. http://theconversation.com/roe-v-rap-hip-hop-artists-have-long-wrestled-with-reproductive-rights-186439.

CBS Texas Staff. 2022. "Protestors March in Support of Abortion Rights in Dallas." June 29, 2022. https://www.cbsnews.com/texas/news/protestors-march-support-abortion-rights-dallas/.

Chervinsky, Lindsay M. 2021. " 'Childless Cat Ladies' and the Long History of Regulating Who Counts as an American." Text. *The Hill* (blog). August 22, 2021. https://thehill.com/opinion/campaign/568876-childless-cat-ladies-and-the-long-history-of-regulating-who-counts-as-an/.

Collins, Patricia Hill. 2005. *Black Sexual Politics: African Americans, Gender, and the New Racism*. 1st ed. New York: Routledge.

Cooper, Brittney C., Susanna M. Morris, and Robin M. Boylorn. 2017. *The Crunk Feminist Collection*. New York: The Feminist Press. https://muse.jhu.edu/pub/90/edited_volume/book/49610.

Crenshaw, Kimberle. 1991. "Mapping the Margins: Intersectionality, Identity Politics, and Violence against Women of Color." *Stanford Law Review* 43, no. 6: 1241. https://doi.org/10.2307/1229039.

Green, Aaryn, Maretta McDonald, Veronica A. Newton, Candice C. Robinson, and Shantee Rosado. 2024. *The Sociology of Cardi B: A Trap Feminist Approach*. New York: Routledge.

Guerra, Joey. 2022. "Megan Thee Stallion's 'Ladies Love Yourself' T-Shirt Supports Planned Parenthood | Datebook." July 4, 2022. https://preview.houston-chronicle.com/music/megan-thee-stallion-s-ladies-love-yourself-17279619.

Hancock, Ange-Marie. 2004. *The Politics of Disgust*. New York: NYU Press.

Harshaw, Pendarvis. 2022. "How Hip-Hop Talks About Abortion in Ways Other Art Forms Can't." KQED. June 30, 2022. https://www.kqed.org/arts/13915289/hip-hop-songs-lyrics-abortion.

Hill Collins, Patricia. 1986. "Learning from the Outsider Within: The Sociological Significance of Black Feminist Thought." *Social Problems* 33 (6): 14–32. https://doi.org/10.2307/800672.

Hill Collins, Patricia. 2009. *Black Feminist Thought: Knowledge, Consciousness, and the Politics of Empowerment*. 2nd ed. Routledge Classics. New York: Routledge.

Holland, Jennifer L. 2019. "Abolishing Abortion: The History of the Pro-Life Movement in America—Organization of American Historians." August 23, 2019. https://www.oah.org/tah/november-3/abolishing-abortion-the-history-of-the-pro-life-movement-in-america/.

Kendall, Mikki. 2020. *Hood Feminism: Notes from the Women That a Movement Forgot*. Penguin.

Landen, Xander. 2021. "Texas Rapper Megan Thee Stallion Blasts State's Abortion Law." Newsweek. October 9, 2021. https://www.newsweek.com/texas-rapper-megan-thee-stallion-blasts-abortion-law-court-reinstates-it-1637338.

Levy, Piet. 2024. "From Cardi B to GloRilla, Highlights from Kamala Harris' Guests at Milwaukee Rally Friday." *Milwaukee Journal Sentinel*, November 1, 2024. https://www.jsonline.com/story/entertainment/music/2024/11/01/cardi-b-to-glorilla-highlights-from-harris-guests-at-milwaukee-rally/76000628007/.

Lorde, Audre. 2007. *Sister Outsider*. Crossing Press.

Moorman, Taijuan, and KiMi Robinson. 2024. "Megan Thee Stallion Performs 'Savage' at Kamala Harris Rally: 'Hotties for Harris.'" *USA TODAY*, 2024. https://www.usatoday.com/story/entertainment/celebrities/2024/07/30/megan-thee-stallion-kamala-harris-campaign-rally/74599637007/.

Morgan, Joan. 2000. *When Chickenheads Come Home to Roost: A Hip-Hop Feminist Breaks It Down*. Simon and Schuster.

Morgan, Joan. 2015. "Why We Get Off: Moving Towards a Black Feminist Politics of Pleasure." *The Black Scholar* 45, no. 4: 36–46. https://doi.org/10.1080/00064246.2015.1080915.

O'Dell, Liam, dir. 2021. *AOC and Buttigieg Are 'Childless Cat Ladies,' Says Republican Candidate JD Vance*. https://www.independent.co.uk/tv/news/aoc-and-buttigieg-are-childless-cat-ladies-says-republican-candidate-jd-vance-b2183420.html.

Peters, Mitchell. 2022. "Latto Teams Up With Planned Parenthood for Abortion Rights PSA: Watch." *Billboard* (blog). August 27, 2022. https://www.billboard.com/music/music-news/latto-planned-parenthood-psa-video-1235131819/.

Robinson, KiMi. 2024. "Megan Thee Stallion Hits Back at Kamala Harris Rally Performance Critics: 'Fake Mad.'" *USA TODAY*, August 2, 2024. https://www.usatoday.com/story/entertainment/celebrities/2024/08/02/megan-thee-stallion-kamala-harris-rally-backlash/74650656007/.

Ross, Loretta J. 2017. "Reproductive Justice as Intersectional Feminist Activism." *Souls* 19, no. 3: 286–314. https://doi.org/10.1080/10999949.2017.1389634.

Ross, Loretta, and Rickie Solinger. 2017. *Reproductive Justice: An Introduction*. 1st ed. Oakland: University of California Press.

Saunders, Angel. 2022. "Latto Teams up with Planned Parenthood in Support of Abortion Rights." *REVOLT* (blog). August 30, 2022. https://www.revolt.tv/article/2022-08-30/189033/latto-teams-up-with-planned-parenthood-in-support-of-abortion-rights/.

Stallion, Megan Thee. 2020. "Opinion | Megan Thee Stallion: Why I Speak Up for Black Women." *The New York Times*, October 13, 2020, https://www.nytimes.com/2020/10/13/opinion/megan-thee-stallion-black-women.html.

Strongman, SaraEllen. 2022. "Perspective | Despite Antiabortion Campaigns, Black Feminists Support Abortion Rights." *Washington Post*, June 29, 2022. https://www.washingtonpost.com/outlook/2022/06/29/despite-anti-abortion-campaigns-black-feminists-support-abortion-rights/.

UN Working Group on the Issue of Discrimination against Women in Law and in Practice. 2017. "Women's Autonomy, Equality and Reproductive Health in International Human Rights: Between Recognition, Backlash and Regressive Trends."

Chapter 8

Convicted by Our Humanity

Race and the Politics of Art

Utz McKnight and Jared Rodríguez

We live in a time when the struggle over the future of racial progress in this society is a popular contested politics. The claims to identity and difference are often overdetermined on the Right, and the claims to equality and difference are a source of fragmentation on the Left, both a function of attempting to change how the society considers race. Rather than being a vague intuition, the assertion that how goes race so goes the nation in the United States, is now an explicit concern for many. Somewhat portentously but also poignantly, it is useful to consider that we are all participants in this change and will therefore reap the consequences of what we do today. In three parts, this chapter explores some of the potentialities of the challenge that race creates for us as a society. Using theoretical arguments and examples of art to anchor the ideas being developed, each section provides the reader with the opportunity to speculate on an aspect of our contemporary race politics.

One Love

What are we to make of the portraits of Barack Obama, by Kehinde Whiley, and that of Michelle Obama by Amy Sherald side-by-side in a gallery, and then juxtaposed in the case of Barack Obama with the portraits of the other presidents of the United States, and for Michelle Obama with the other First Lady portraits. President John F. Kennedy was painted by Elaine Kooning with a palette of vivid colors, and the painting by John Singer Sargent of President Woodrow Wilson, of many presidential portraits, could serve as the perspective by which to favorably assess Barack Obama's portrait by Whiley. The portrait of Mary Todd Lincoln by Mathew Brady Studio, or of Frances Folsom Cleveland by Anders Zorn can similarly be compared to that of Michelle Obama by Amy Sherald.

In *Darker Than Blue*, Paul Gilroy provides a description of Bob Marley, youthful, serious, whose face is found on T-shirts sold around the world, as some thirty years after his death perceived by many as an "iconic, godly embodiment of a universal struggle for justice, peace, and human rights" (Gilroy 88). The idea of Marley as a political icon to be mobilized on behalf of these concepts does not depend solely on his music but on a description of the person, his portrait literally on t-shirts, that is shorn of references to more complex narratives of his life. Similarly, Barack and Michelle's portraits portray individuals on display for narratives about Black life that threaten the reification by the viewer of the distinction between archetype and the transformative politics in which both were engaged. To create a portrait is to cut them out of the flow of the time, their relationship to all of us today. What their success made possible, becomes instead an artifact of representation that deadens and mutes the political potential in Barack Obama's two terms as president.

The opportunity exists to read the portraits with a perspective distinguishing between their capacity to represent everyone who has ever sat for a portrait in these roles, the ability of race to provide a comprehensive description of America, and as a description of the place of the presidency and first lady within the democratic institutions that define specific narratives of life in America. Instead, let's bring to our analysis the challenge that race creates for us today, in an acknowledgment of the furor that occurred in the press over Michelle Obama's arms and clothes, her professional success prior to becoming first lady, together with the irritation caused by many in Barack Obama's articulate poise, both characterizations of their persons that are on full display in the portraits. This interpretative approach provides the opportunity to see the coalescing of a politics in his election, and in her elevation in status to fashion icon and the cover of *Vogue*, as similar to that of other historical aporetic moments in American society. What Gilroy writes about Marley, that his music and iconic presence allowed for a solidarity to be created that did not previously exist, the results of which remain open, is also true for the Obamas in their portraits and their professional political achievements (Gilroy 92).

The portraits are symbols for a new solidarity for many with an America not calcified into set pieces or formal positions, that simultaneously retains the narratives of the importance to its description of racial inferiority and misogyny. In fact, we could argue that what the portraits symbolize is the efficacy of a politics, a collective variegated mélange of forces and actors, whereby the pursuit of racial and gender equality requires that the meaning of America is never complete, always in question as a challenge to what democracy means for all of us every day. But this perspective elides the problem of how we should describe the changes in the society that the Obamas represent just in their being captured literally in these portraits, like the iconic Marley T-shirts seen around the world and on posters in college dorm rooms across the United States.

Captive Once More

Let us start our analysis of what it means to engage in the portraiture as both Whiley and Sherald have, with the authority and political presence of the first Black US president and first lady. Consider for a moment Foucault's well known description in *The Order of Things* of members of the Spanish royal family in Las Meninas, a painting by Diego Velazquez. As Foucault discusses the problem of perspective, suggesting that there are several different representational practices and ideas being rendered, to ask where the viewer is in relation to the painting's subjects, he is allowing for a narrative to develop of how we use norms and standards for artistic interpretation to make sense of the relationship of the painting to our own sense of the world (5). The place of the figures in the painting, and their obvious relationship to us, the human behaviors and practices on display, the query asked by the painter of how we are to make sense of a family depicted that is both larger than life, the expression of the political desires of a nation, and yet also only still always human. The description of the king's two bodies, human and more than human, and by extension that of his family, is depicted by Velazquez as something the viewer is invested in as well. The painter offers us a glimpse into the personal lives of those who otherwise remain representative of something larger than life itself. What is it be royal and yet to also be something more, to be the subject of a narrative about monarchy and the relationship to the viewer of the painting that is not theirs? The royal family has no need for more than the admiration that comes from necessary, absolute deference. In spite of the fact that the subject seems indifferent to our presence, why are we watching them so diligently, avidly?

Why do we care? What is it that brings us to desire or meditate on the thoughts contained in the minds of those within the two Obama portraits in question, except as a similar trope to that of Foucault's reading of Las Meninas, of temporary contingent availability and a necessary relationship between the subject of the paintings and the viewer? We are expected to not only be fascinated but eager to engage with both Obamas. To be in their presence. The portraits deliver on this promise, of grace and generosity and an extended companionship. We had better act proper, say the right thing, do the right thing. Just as they have.

At one remove, the relationship of viewer to the painters and the knowledge of their craft mediates this relationship of the portraits between viewer and the subjects as well. Giving us several layers of connection, if the idea that these two persons depicted are of historical importance as political icons is simply not enough to justify wanting a view. The comparison between Foucault's description of perspective and form in *The Order of Things* provides an initial approach to consider how both Obama paintings are connected to both historical practices, norms, and symbols but also connected to those who view the paintings. How the viewer is included in a dialogue with this image of Barack Obama, by the interest expressed on Barack Obama's face in who stands in front of the painting, in front of him, and that Michelle Obama appears to be considering what we just asked of her in person, or thinking of what she might say to us.

Typical of presidential and first lady portraits is the importance of a democratic connection to the populace, to the dress and interests of the audience to come. An American citizen beholding the portrait is supposed to consider the fact of the subject's political elevation through a courageous act of their own, a choice by the citizen viewer of who should govern. Even as the chosen individual is expected to remain interested and invested in the ideas that might come from a democratic populace. They are expected to be someone we could have a beer with, sit with at dinner and share a meal: someone who will listen and understand our successes and sympathize with our discontent. The president and first lady are supposed to be those we select to run a government that we actively assist in forming, and in this sense we share in the corporeal assignments of the body politic. We are both citizen and individual. The Obamas in this sense are mirrors to our own democratic ambition for the society. In this capacity it is possible to perceive the portraits of the Obamas as representing the solution for generations of people of what June Jordan laments in 1992, "I know my parents would have wanted to say, 'Thanks, America!' if only there had been some way, some public recognition and welcome of their presence, here, and then some really big shot to whom their gratitude might matter" (5). The portraits fulfill a promise, of an America that has now arrived in a place where African Americans can say, as Michelle Obama did, that we are proud to be American.

The above perspective on the portrait, of a presidential interlocutor for the democratic populace, Barack Obama as the personification of the people's constitutional compact or contract with one another, and the idealization thereby of the racial politics that allowed for the election of the first Black president, substitutes a solipsistic flawed understanding for the complex difficult politics of what is actually required to address the reproduction of racial inequality in the society. The portrait collapses the complexity of the inequalities that define racial difference in society to the simple problem of voting and electoral outcomes. Through this framing, racial politics itself becomes captured, momentarily titrated down into disambiguity—captured in the gaze that Barack directs at us from the portrait.

Erased in this portrayal is the extensive security apparatus US international and domestic institutions use to create racial injustice. The otherwise seemingly comprehensive racial inequalities in the domestic banking and housing market, educational system, and employment structural processes are contrasted with the exceptional figures in color, of Barack and Michelle Obama. The portraits of both president and first lady are in this counter-perspective rife with the attempt to obscure, through the explicit representation in art of the connection between their personal and public success as examples of what is possible now in America, of what it still means to be an American if you are Black. The paintings themselves display for us, symbols of nativity and national pride, the capacity to engage the work of famous artists: the implication that now the office of the president and first lady, though occupied by Black persons, is free of the imperative to inscribe racial difference throughout society. Even as the portraits of both are different from those presidents and first ladies that have come before, this difference is framed in this perspective as something unique, but unproblematic. Race is merely an artifact in paint, a visual cultural exoticism like the flower placed in the portrait to represent Barack Obama's Kenyan ancestry, or the quilting references, perhaps evoking the triumphant legacy of the quilters of Gee's Bend, Alabama in the dress worn by Michelle Obama, a new welcome introduction to the melting pot that is now with his election fully democratic and equal for all Americans.

There are two interpretations that arise from studying the portraits in this manner. The first is that of how as a society we should address the relationship between the exceptional success of some Black persons relative to the description of inequality experienced by all Black people. The second is whether the differences between Black people allow for a claim against the idea of racial difference and can class, ethnicity, or culture successfully attenuate the determination of racial inequality. To address these two perspectives, the discussion briefly turns to the work of Paul Gilroy and, at greater length, to that of Stuart Hall, respectively.

Exceptionalism and Articulation

As Paul Gilroy points out, with reference to Condoleezza Rice and her work as national security advisor and secretary of state under the administration of President G. W. Bush, it is too easy to translate the terms for Black exceptionalism, of which Barack and Michelle Obama are ideal examples, into the argument that while race was a thing of the past, today racial inequalities are a matter of individual choices and cultural divisions as a privileged explanation of local, national, and geo-political conflicts (163). While the portraits are an impressive and important moment in Black individual achievement, both for the Obamas and the artists, how can the portraits assist in addressing the politics of exceptionalism and obscurantism that their very success as iconic and representative of Black life brings in their wake?

What we should do is see in these portraits the limits of the efficacy of a politics of racial representation to define future success in the definition of racial equality in the US. The portraits make obvious what was true with the election of President Barack Obama: another politics of racial justice must be pursued to continue to develop the democratic potential in the US polity.

In the article "New Ethnicities," Hall posits that a solution to the problem of resolving the contradictions in Black popular culture, and the possibility of a politics of racial justice that it generates, depends on perceiving the production of culture as a contested strategic space (252–53). Asking for a consideration by researchers of the idea of ethnicity as a definition of the scope of the range of cultural descriptions of Black politics, the sheer multiplicity of desires and needs that arise from Black individuals, the variegation of collective demands, Hall in this early article contrasts this idea with that of a distinction of racial difference across the color line.

Through the introduction of the problem of ethnicity present in the idea of Blackness as a thing in itself, Hall correctly points out in the article that the description of what a racial difference allows internal to the grouping into a discrete population does not describe a subject position able to address the problem of the relationship between races, the color line itself, such that the idea of racial hierarchy is attenuated and challenged. What Hall attempts is the integration of the politics of racial difference with the problem of ethnicity as migration and culture ("Multicultural"). The problem with this approach by Hall is obvious if we consider for a moment how we might answer a similar query today with reference to the subjects of the two portraits, what are the ethnicities of the Obamas, and how does this apperception of difference of social geography and family by them relate to the description of the processes by which these differences are elaborated, and attenuate the description of both the everyday and collective political determination of racial hierarchy? Following Hall's analysis we should not ignore in our consideration of the politics of race and the portraits, the two popular criticisms of Barack Obama, of whether he was Black enough, and whether he was American enough, in the electoral contests that ensued when he ran for president.

As the changing standards, norms, and behaviors determine the description of the discursive elements of racial articulation in everyday life, Hall reminds us in this article of the need to be attentive to the layered discordance and conjuncture that exists between old and new descriptions of racial difference, and not understand these descriptions as progress nor as a difference between a new ethnic multiculturalism, a definition of diversity as defeating the former definition of race as immutable and allowing for predation. The claim of individual difference exists within and affirms the comprehensive conviction that race retains on each of us in the society. Simply, the question Hall sought to answer in "New Ethnicities" was that of how does the diversity of experiences and material relationships adjacent to and imbricated in the social definition of race attenuate the impact that race has on our lives? How do we describe the problem of racism, while also allowing for its variegated description?

If we consider the problem of race as that of defining what difference is supposed to make a difference, when that difference isn't necessary to human flourishing, its persistence today as an idea that matters, begs the question of how, not why, it is used. To support the possibility of its attenuation requires that we elaborate on what we mean by necessity, not truth. The attempt to distinguish race from ethnicity as a criticism fails to distinguish what is important to preserve in our social relationships, as

Hall notes in his article "What is the 'Black' in Black Popular Culture" (88).

Gilroy's description of Marley also contains this distinction of the importance of difference within racial categories when he suggests that Marley's ethnic characteristics as a Black person may have made it easier to develop his particular musical style and perspective (103). The problem of this strategic ethnic mobilization is further addressed by Paul Gilroy, of this theme of relationships as alternatives to that of racial difference and its possible attenuation, when he speaks not simply of Black consumerism, but of how specific consumption of automobiles provides a relationship between persons alongside or against racial collective descriptions. As Gilroy writes, "Today, the decay of those formations has helped to deliver us to the historic point where blackness can easily become less an index of hurt, resistance, or solidarity in the face of persistence and systemic inequality, than one more faintly exotic lifestyle "option" conferred by the multicultural alchemy of heavily branded commodities and the presealed, "ethnic" identities that apparently match them in a world where globalization is, to all intents and purposes, a process of (North) Americanisation"" (25). In this description, hierarchy becomes embedded in the desire for duplication and acquisition, to want what is otherwise unexpected, to in countering the cultural symbols or material reproduction of racial difference, refine or reinforce the importance of the artifacts by which racial difference was only nominally given.

There are few things more explicitly affirming of racial hierarchy than having those who are excluded demand to belong, to state a desire to mimic and own what is defined as important by those to which they can never belong. The authority to set the norms of desire, is distinct from making the demand of racial difference one's own through the capacity to follow the desires of those always signified as superior. "To acquire objects rather than rights," to consume differently, to create cultural artifacts that cannot change the terms by which whites decide their superiority, is not to make these gestures of difference unimportant, but to affirm their importance, their political inefficacy as Black people to everyone (Gilroy 33). Retreating in our criticism of racial difference in society into a demand for social equality leaves us pessimistic and vulnerable in these gestures to the accommodation and coordination of racial hierarchy in our criticism. We accept the terms for our conviction and await further elaboration of what this idea pessimistically might have in store for us. An unfortunate ontology and boundary to which to acquiesce.

What must be remembered in this moment is that this is not a new problem, this distinction between accepting the terms of inferiority, here described as a demand for social equality, and on the other hand a demand for a political equality that constantly requires the disruption of the consolidation of racial difference as an extensive category for processes that are believed necessary for the polity. This distinction between a racial ontological pessimism and its conviction of the possibilities individuals could envision for societal change and the complexity of a politics instead, and the subsequent individual struggle to arrive at an understanding of this problem, one that disrupts the concession by pessimism to the terms given by racial hierarchy, has been something to refuse in African American writing since Maria Stewart, Frances Harper, and Frederick Douglass, for those who must perforce of race live in that space between the demand for social belonging and the need for a politics of refusal. Reading Baldwin's *Another Country*, Toni Morrison's *Home*, Jesmyn Ward's *Sing Unburied Sing*, and Kiese Laymon's *Heavy*, we should not be surprised by how these writers attempt to build up for the reader a reservoir of resistance to the idea of a difference between persons that could require mere social claims on us, in contrast to those that are political, larger than the descriptions given by the account of the lives of solitary individuals.

In the context of this important historical record of artistic production, the portraits of Barack Obama and Michelle Obama offer us hope. Optimism for the visible capacity in the portraits to remain open to what might still be possible, against the temptation to argue that one person's success can occlude, stand, or substitute for the suffering of the many. In fact, the record of Obama's administrations is a testimony to how Barack's political success is no more than a statement of what must still be accomplished to achieve racial equality in the society. Even as this record is also that of continuing the legacies of the security state and American foreign policy, reifying them through Barack Obama's tenure as US president as always still important to the definition of Black American life. That the latter is similar to the legacy of generations of Black soldiering for the US government, and the role of Black Americans in the development of the economy over centuries is merely to remind us of the price of accepting the ticket of political activism. If we look closely, it is possible to see this ambivalent call to action, for the democratic polity and for each of us, in both portraits.

This interpretation of the portraits requires a subjectivity be which to act that is described simultaneously in the many processes by which race is defined. Many of which are not accessible as everyday perceptions. The prohibition of explicit social racism, the slur, the stare, and the calling for a public lynching on the street in the US today, is a change in how race is described on an everyday basis from those descriptions available several decades ago. This prohibition defines a democratic politics of infinite regression, contained, given by the knowledge that simply reacting to the description for difference in our lives, be this through collective protest or the individual refusal to acquiesce, is not sufficient for its attenuation. Rather, we are required by this acknowledgment of the force of the exceptionalism of the Obamas and in our apperception of their portraits, to accept how our refusal of racial conviction has also to avoid reproducing this distinction of race in other processes and practices.

It is worth spending a little time here to discuss the particularities of Stuart Hall's definition of the problem that race poses for social theory. In his classic formulation on race, in the article "Race, Articulation, and Societies Structured in Dominance," Hall reminds us that class identifications arise from their structural relations to the means of production and not ideological or political positions and that what matters are the articulating mechanisms and modes of dominance that comprise what we mean when we speak of race (185). By articulating mechanisms, Hall means a complex set of relations, united "as much by their differences as their similarities" (196). These combinations of things create in their relation a structure, structures that in turn are in dominance or subordination to one another. The resultant social formations, here African Americans and European American populations, are defined from this complex unity and differentiation of structured material, ideological, and political relations.

This nonreductive description is for Hall sufficient to posit that criticism of race in society should be historically specific, an analysis of particular relations and not approached as evidence of a universal structure for all societies, as "racism in general" (210, 214). According to Hall, we should show how racism is "reorganized and re-articulated with the relations of new modes off production" (211). To put it factitiously, as Hall points out, racism is not required for slavery to exist, and according to our analysis of the two portraits above, the election of the first Black US president does not signal an end to racism in the United States (212). For Hall, race and class exist in relation to one another, and when discussing Black labor "race is the modality in which class is "lived," the medium through which class relations are experienced, the form in which it is appropriated and "fought through" (216). Racism is not for Hall therefore simply ideological or political, but rather articulated in relations wherein race matters.

The three sections of this chapter should be understood as offering an optical window through which to view each of the relations of race being described. Together, they explore Black life as a force that holds society accountable; the commodification of Black art; and how the politics of change must navigate the tension between narratives of pathos and the exception that exists to quell or dampen those relations that might otherwise produce racial equality.

Two People

In Titus Kaphar's painting *Analogous Colours*, used as a cover for a *TIME Magazine* special issue on the protests following the murder of George Floyd in Minneapolis, we perceive the problem of a political consolidation to be elided. Focusing on a kind of enervation thought to be analogous to the unruly breadth of cultural descriptions of Black politics, we are made acutely aware of the complexity of a description of levels of truth regimes, and the possibility of a conflict or aporia between relations of creative production and structures of hierarchical necessity, between diversity and difference, and between conviction and the politics of accommodation. What Titus Kaphar suggests in the film *Shut Up and Paint* is that instead of valuing primarily the economic wealth he acquires as his art has caught the attention of wealthy collectors, he seeks the acknowledgment of his art as contributing to an understanding of the experience by Black people of what his paintings depict. His wealth is beside the point, when the work he creates for the exhibit *Unseen*, and in others, is conceived by him as part of the discursive relations that equate contemporary racism with the death of Black youth and accompanying sorrow of Black mothers.

In *Shut Up and Paint*, Kaphar works with, among others, Dwayne Betts and Jason Stanley to describe the consequences of working on the edge of a constant opportunity to cross back and forth over this boundary of a problematic absolute essence and exception. The signal that institutions are always open to those who rise above the norms, standard, and behaviors that define Black life creates a space without resonance or acknowledgment by those who remain invisible, ambiguously Black, as though Black life is merely a definitional problem for society, and not abundant and meager, requiring that instead everyone respond affirmatively to the call to action. Kaphar with this paintings, and Betts with his poetry, in the short film argue that their pursuit of art is explained by this idea of ambiguity and refusal, of representing the experience that race provides even as this does not convict them. The creation of art for Kaphar is (to paraphrase what he discusses in the film) how he refuses the constraints and difficulties that racism creates for Black people. He therefore wants Black people to see the art, just as Betts has a nonprofit to bring books and poetry to the prisons to allow the Black victims of mass incarceration the opportunity to see themselves in that space of discontent and possibility they establish by their art as well.

Children

But what about the art? In *Analogous Colours* we experience the three degrees of separation, the near miss, the sure possibility of our being next, and the common and also particular loss. What is it to lose a child? If we look at his previous work *Asphalt and Chalk: Michael Brown, Sean Bell, Amadou Diallo, Trayvon Martin*, from 2014, Kaphar creates art that acknowledges our collective loss but also realizes for us the injustice of each death. In its depiction of the faces of the men, their outline in chalk, the asphalt in which they lay upon death, just as in the short film as we hear the words, "breathe, breathe," we are reminded of Erica Gardner lying down in the outline made by the police of her father's body on the pavement in New York. Kaphar's art offers us a reconstruction, redefinition even as it limns the terms for our future. What does the mother do with the absence in her arms? For which we are responsible? What should we do about the sorrow we experience with each death that we see by violent racism? For it is a visual perspective that Kaphar offers, in paintings and in film.

As we look at *Analogous Colours* we have to wonder, with all this loss, what is the inheritance left by each death? There is no recovery, retrieval of persons, of our past lives possible. Instead we look to the future and refuse to allow each loss to convince us of the futility of refusing the terms whereby Black people can be killed, incarcerated, and suffer the predation of racism in the society. Every person lost, becomes in Kaphar's art a reason for solidarity and resolution. The mother still embraces the idea of a child, in another painting a mother pushes the empty stroller, in each painting in that series Kaphar offers us resolve, a commitment to change the terms by which we must mourn the absence of our children due to racism. George Floyd becomes in the painting our son, our brother, our cousin, lost to injustice. In the painting we see through the eyes of the painter Kaphar, and his message to us is trenchant and poignant.

I
can not
sell

you
this

painting. . . .

Is this what it means for us? . . .

Do
not
ask
me
to be
hopeful. . . .

One
Black
mother's
loss
WILL
be
memorialized.
This time
I will not let her go.

I
can not
sell
you
this
painting.

Kaphar's painting and poem in response to protests surrounding George
Floyd provide an example of the capacity to create in the politics of refusing

conviction, something that points beyond the local truth to something not yet attained but possible. It points to what life after the disaster of the murder of George Floyd and many others might look like for us, to what life in the context of the juxtaposition of the murder of Trayvon Martin and the successes of the Obamas might look like.

The title of the poem itself, *I cannot sell you this painting* in its redundancy and contradiction opens up our understanding of the complexity of racial politics. The painter cannot sell this painting which is the cover of a magazine, and as consumers of both the magazine and the fact of the disaster of the murders of Black people, we are not buying the truth of this America. We refuse the truth that the painting is offering us, as a cover, and as a limit to what is possible for this society. Something must be done instead, something must change, if we are to agree rather than refuse the conditions by which race is described. Kaphar offers us the following set of contradictory truths to consider:

- I can't sell you this thing that is selling you this thing
- You can't see this Black Mother I'm showing you
- Do not ask me to be hopeful as I refuse despair
- We must burn but we can live

Crying and Laughter

While Stuart Hall provides a useful frame for discussing the Obama portraits, as his analysis remains focused on the problem of structure and hierarchy, and the contradictions within society as a description of the relations between race and class. To study the relationship between the mothers' loss, a Black life as requiring resolve, and the problem Kaphar identifies with the relationship his exceptional success allows to the concerns of regular Black people, we have to turn to another perspective. Zora Neale Hurston was both a writer and anthropologist of Black life, and in her work conceptualizes not only the relationship between the Black vernacular and class relations, but also provides us with a description of gender relations. As Alice Walker writes, "Only after she died penniless, still laboring at her craft, still immersed in her work, still following *her* vision and *her* road, did it begin to seem to some that yes, perhaps this woman *was* a serious artist after all, since artists are known to live poor an die broke" (4).

The contemporary description of politics, art, and race reminds us of the heyday of the Harlem Renaissance, when a community of Black writers, artists, activists, and scholars formed a loose but important creative moment of Black artistic life in the US. Robert Hemenway provides a description of how Hurston perceived her desire to collect folklore among the regular Black folk, in contrast to creating fiction in Harlem (Hemenway 81–82). She eschewed the collection of materials as her one time boss Woodson desired. As a historian, Woodson valued the importance of double checking sources and verifying the accuracy of what was provided by locals against written documents. Instead, Hurston sought out a tape recorder to record the oral traditions that many thought were fast disappearing in the move from country and the South during the great migration. The source material she would gather over the thirty years that she was considered the most prolific Black woman writer in the US, is a profound collection of materials on the Black vernacular, folklore, stories, and popular myths.

But rather than describe Hurston as the quintessential rebel with a cause, it is also valuable to understand that to discard many of the scholarly traditions and the commercial structures that support the publicity of the professional creative process, is to literally remain outside of the reward system that exists for most artists, most writers. The argument could be made that had she done what was asked of her by the people and benefactors around her to achieve financial wealth, we would not today describe her writings as reflecting the everyday depictions of Black life. Why should artists be any different, experience a reprieve from the conditions by which Black success is determined, by the terms through which racial hierarchy develops, persists, and reproduces itself as a system of norms and standards in society? Kaphar is explicit in the film about this desire to not produce for the market that exists, on its terms, as though he is aware of definite representational racial signifiers, tropes, narratives within which it is possible to be successful as an artist. Kaphar says he wants to produce art for the people, even as he also wants his art to be legible and of interest to those who can pay significant amounts of money for a piece of his work. Like Hurston, Kaphar wants something more from his art in a society where race matters, where being Black matters, than wealth.

If we think of a perfect example of exceptional success in the person of Barack Obama, how did his elections and two administrations alter the capacity of race to determine the lives of everyday people in the society? When candidate Barack Obama was accused of not being an American, and it was a sufficiently robust political claim to launch the political career of Donald Trump? Hurston, similar to Frances Harper a half century before, in spite of her prolific writing and the energy that she brought to her field work, was not rewarded economically for her temerity in challenging the institutions that defined Black professional success.

This is the sentiment that motivates Kaphar criticism of the museum art exhibition practices of today. In the film *Shut Up and Paint,* Kaphar complains that those who he wants to view his art remain unwelcome, though through no necessary fault of the directors of the museums in question, in the gallery spaces where his art now is displayed. The art is also too expensive for most Black people to purchase. Hurston's difference with regard to established scholarly methods and her struggle against the requirements of the patronage and financial recognition by white elites, are exactly the tensions that Kaphar discusses in relation to his own art. Hurston describes this problem of how Black people struggle with the choices for professional success on the terms given by US society, when she explains in her autobiography *Dust Tracks On The Road,* how some Black people felt that a college education was wasted on Black folks who could do nothing with it, and others wanted to push ahead (185). This interpretative conflict for Black people between the refusal and acceptance of racism defines Kaphar's art and poem, and the film. To put it more succinctly, one might ask, of what value is art if it forms the means for one's own oppression, if the conditions for success of a sort demand racial complicity? Hurston famously made this question of the academic and creative artistic process by which Black people were simultaneously to be objects of ridicule and scorn, reinforcing and seeming to confirm the table of societal evaluation wherein Black people could be defined as categorically inferior to white people, and also represent the capacity of the creature that is the human being to upset, disrupt, and challenge the word to world fit of racial categories.

How else should we make sense of the anger Kaphar expresses when told in the film by a gallery owner that he is being too political in his art, making people uncomfortable with his demand that the buyers understand the criticism of racism in society that his art seeks to convey? Hurston describes this problem as one of a refusal to see Black people as exactly the same as everyone else, as not contained by the seemingly comprehensive description of race in their lives, and therefore as a society we should acknowledge the moral values we confirm in the act of racial injustice ("White Publishers," 146). Why would you mistreat, create a supposedly necessary and important demarcation of racial difference, only to wound your own community, your own family, your own children? In the context of this claim on us, the painting *Analogous Colours* is a powerful statement of how it is one thing to feel sadness at the injustice on display, the cruelty and disregard for Black lives, but it is another thing to be reminded of your own implication in this act of violence against another human being, by the artist's poem, and by Kaphar's comments to the gallery owner in the film *Shut Up And Paint*. As Hurston writes, "Show some folks a genuine bit of Negroness and they rear and pitch like a mule in a tin stable. 'But where is the misplaced preposition?' they wail. 'Where is the Am it and I'se?'" ("You Don't Know," 109).

What Kaphar doesn't do in his work is criticize the work of other Black artists, as Hurston often did (Lowe 185). Instead with Dwayne Betts reading his poetry in key moments of the film, and Jason Stanley equating his writing on fascism with Kaphar's art, we get the sense that Kaphar is trying to serve as a spokesperson for the need of art and the artists to ask for more than a framing of exotism and pathos from buyers and viewers. As Hurston writes, "What *is* actually known about us? Very little" ("You Don't Know," 111). What Kaphar desires in his art is not solely to challenge the conditions for financial success as an artist. Instead, as for Dwayne Betts as well, the MacArthur Fellows Program genius grant provides the professional visibility, as does the Yale academic pedigree, to ask what are actually very traditional questions of the role of art and artistic production in the politics of social change.

The *TIME* cover is an explicit political claim in the direction of making available to a large audience an experience of the consequences of racism for Black life. The frustration Kaphar feels at his buyers not getting the message he is trying to communicate through art: this is the justification for the creation of the film. To reach more people than just those who can purchase one of his pieces is to challenge the claims made by buyers of what his art should ask of them as a politics about racial injustice. To paraphrase Kaphar, he does not want his art to be just an economic investment. He does not want his buyers to be incurious but rather wants them to see his art as a window into a variegated and complex experience of Black life. Yes, there is violence, a remembrance provided by the names on the borders of the painting. But there are also the beautiful layers of the painting, the rich colors: suggesting life, possibility, and the memory of the care of a parent for their child. In the many elements of the painting we are asked to consider our own relationship to the deaths of those Black people killed in recent years by vigilantes, armed citizens, and the police because of racism.

Kaphar wants us to read his poem alongside the painting, to understand how sorrow and joy are coincident not only in Black lives, but in the lives of everyone. Like analogous colors, near one another, the rewards of fame and professional success do not alienate individuals from the problem of violence against other people. This violence should not be hidden but made plain for everyone to see. Just as Kaphar explains in the film that he still returns home, and therein confirms his present and future measure in the community of Black people that matter to him, so too do all of us need to acknowledge through the consideration of his art, our implication in, and proximity to, racial injustice.

It is useful here to consider a reading of *Their Eyes Were Watching God* that suggests Janie's experience in the novel as the condition of her emancipation over time from the pull of economic striving and success measured within institutions that demeaned her as a Black person and a woman. The particular engagement Janie has with gender roles in her relationships with her husbands and with the women in her life, describe a space for a self-realization that while she does require economic resources, she has to interrogate the relations that the attendant social expectations and gender roles require for their achievement. What she cannot do is to allow the measure of security and success defined by the developing Black community economy to overwhelm the description of a life that she might live. In an understanding about the role of financial expectations that is important in the context of Kaphar's explication of the problem of artistic creation, Janie literally works through the different normative expectations of what is required by the gender conventions in a Black community that has to form around other norms to thrive.

Kaphar offers us a similar message. While not eschewing financial success, this cannot become the sole measure by which to find value in his creation of art, in our appreciation of his art to describe norms for a sustainable Black life in the society. For Kaphar, the politics of artistic representation, the force of the activity of the artist should not merely confirm the exception to the rule propagated otherwise of the inferiority of Black people. Instead, like Barack and Michelle Obama have done in their own professional lives, Kaphar uses his own success to provide for an alternative description of a financial relationship with a new community, one that in his NXHAVEN art space provides for the literal transfer of the rewards of his financial success to other artists, providing for the resources that other artists might need.

Hurston the Black anthropologist, more than any other Black artist, scholar, and writer reminds us in her work that it is laughter and ease, people being social with one another, crude, funny, dull, and passionate, which allows for the possibility of sustained critique, and providing for the flourishing of this generative space should also be the measure of the success for art (Hurston). These values we view in the film in the banter between Kaphar and his friend, when they discuss how much money a piece of his has sold for, and between Kaphar and Betts and Stanley when they talk to him, that connects the viewer to the challenge of not falling victim to the greed and racism that otherwise threaten to overwhelm our capacity to define a better world. It is not the perception of sorrow alone, but also joy, irreverence, the vernacular language by which we express what we expect of this democratic society and from one another, that which best captures, holds close, the human imagination. This idea, of what we should expect of this society, as a claim against everyone, is what *Analogous Colours*, the poem, and the film *Shut Up and Paint* try to convey. As Hurston writes, "At any rate, very few grief-hackled bodies have been found" ("You Don't Know," 115).

Black Barons

Rickwood Field, in Birmingham, Alabama, is the oldest professional baseball field in the United States. It was famously home to the Black Barons, a Negro League team that included the likes of Satchel Page and Willie Mays. Today it is a regular field used by local high school teams. In honor of Juneteenth and as part of a campaign to play games at unusual places, the Giants and Cardinals will play a game there on June 20, 2024. In the picture (fig. 8.1) we see a young man walking across the scene, the diamond beyond him, complete with older-style advertising signs marking the homerun boundary. What captures the attention are the bleachers in the foreground, the juxtaposition between the large area between the player, the distant fences, and the tower of lights in the background. The older seating, the lack of care taken with the bleachers, the older signs

Figure 8.1. "Rickwood Field." Digital Photo, 2023. *Source:* Photo by Nicholas Simpson. Used with permission.

all leave us with the feeling of deterioration, of something worn down by use, and yet as we see with the player, still of value. In 1910, when the stadium was first opened, Birmingham was still a relatively new city compared to an old slave trading city such as Montgomery. A product of mining, iron, and steel interests developed after the Civil War, Birmingham's economic development is traditionally described as symbolic of the transition from cotton and plantation industrial success using slave labor in the Old South to the new industrial age using wage labor. Birmingham reflected the capacity of a nation to forge a new description of racial relations after slavery, with rigid legal codes of segregation reinforcing social relations between persons. As Charles Chesnutt describes in *The Marrow of Tradition*, it is not hard to imagine an alternative historical development in the US, where Black political activity overcomes the intransigence of those who wished, and sought, to use race as an idea that would prevail as a major societal concept. As he points out in the novel, it was simply too easy, too convenient, too necessary for those who had been defined as white for generations to find a confirmation of this idea through the creation of new legal and social norms. That many people, Black and white, sought to replace racial difference with new ways of living and working together in the decades following the Civil War is obvious when we read the writing of that period. Writers such as Frances Harper, Ida Wells-Barnett, Pauline Hopkins, and Anna Julia Cooper contributed important ideas at the time about what would be required of the society to achieve relations where race was not always overdetermined for everyone in daily life. The debates fought in the public eye between Booker T. Washington and W. E. B. Dubois served to frame some aspects of the development of Black educational, economic, and social institutions during these early decades after slavery had been replaced, but each suffered in their imagination from the illusion that what was lacking in society was leadership. The evidence we have is that racial separation and punishment for transgressions—as a primary mode for defining race in the everyday lives of those in society—was not due to the absence of sufficient collective resistance or public awareness of alternative ideas for social organization.

What was established did not have to make sense in terms of an objective measure of differences across human populations, scientific racism was always an addendum, rather than the main argument, in the decision to define race through different social systems. A politics by which race matters everywhere was the ambition of those who built Birmingham. That the Barons and the Black Barons played on separate days of the week at Rickwood was exactly the point. To make the idea of racial difference so pervasive in all aspects, all relations within which an individual described their lives, such that there was no alternative. That this baseball field is where so many amazing Black baseball players regularly played, is not evident in the photograph, but the art reveals to us the promise of a past, a story about ourselves if we are willing to spend the time to understand how playing the game professionally was segregated.

For generations any indication socially that race was not important was prohibited, individuals in both developing discrete population were reprimanded. The idea of a difference that no matter what a human being was capable of doing, was always a difference that mattered. There are few aspects of the polity that had a similar role in the foundation of relations in US society in the period from 1880s to the 1960s. In 1910, with the establishment of Rickwood Field, the need to provide for two discrete baseball events, the one for whites only, and the other for Blacks, was a requirement of Birmingham society. The cost of racial distinction was calculated in as the price of progress. Relationships between persons were policed for adherence to the color line, institutional rules and norms such as hiring practices, employment responsibilities, rules of promotion, purchasing and consumption, wholesale marketing, construction and leasing, city zoning ordinances, public policing, prison population control, academic admissions, publishing, pastorage, voting, these processes and many more were all assigned to the standards of racial difference. The third aspect of racial separation was the decision itself, the promulgation of the necessity of hierarchy. This last can be observed in the insistence that racial separation was required for moral purity, civilization, and safety. The terms of this hierarchy in housing, education, employment and social status were attached to the possibility of a democratic, progressive, flourishing America. That those defined as Black did not accept the constant litany of inferiority and culpability for their own subordination and exclusion was often taken as proof not of its fallacy, its unjust imposition on an always equal human population, but of the inability of Black people to understand their situation, taken as evidence of an incapacity that must not be allowed to impede societal progress.

Onward to Victory

While we often consider the 1960s in the US as a period where only specific instances of racial description as separation were challenged, two possible alternative explanations exist. How about if we consider the events of the period of civil rights protest as part of the collapse of the decision of racial difference itself. The necessity of racial separation as a societal good in this as a thing of the past is often spoken of today as a reason to no longer investigate possible incidents of racial discrimination. Attributing evidence of inequality to artifacts of the older system, the query then becomes how long should society police the artifacts of processes that are no longer important to the success of the polity. The decades of critical discussion of the problem of racial inequality are no longer relevant according to this narrative, this assumption of a new societal regime without race having come into existence by a form of the power of the will. Another possibility is that institutional descriptions of race, of process and the decision of hierarchy, are really problems of individual beliefs in racial difference. If human beings could be educated in the truth of human equality, learn the dangers of implicit bias and the injustice of overt racism, the problem of race will disappear. Regardless of interpretation, the collapse of the Negro Leagues, and the subsequent shift in use of the Rickwood Field, is now just a part of this history of change in US society.

To speak of the persistence of the evidence of racial hierarchy as distinct from processes, and as also different than social behaviors, is to echo the intuition we have from generations of research on race and its description in society, that there is a difference between the definition of racial categories through everyday practices, and the idea that these categories must be true as a foundational moment for US society. The relationship between how race in this sense "works" in our lives and the inability to access as a query the continued importance of race as a difference that matters in society is what Stuart Hall was trying to address in his theoretical writing on the importance of Gramsci, race, and ethnicity. In "Gramsci's Relevance for the Study of Race and Ethnicity," Hall writes, "We need to understand better the tensions and contradictions generated by the uneven tempos and directions of historical development. Racism and racist practices and structures frequently occur in some but not all sectors of the social formation" (322). This statement is made in the context of a complex argument for a history specific description of racial relations, the absence of a homogenous class subject, the distinction between economic, ideological, and political dimensions of society, and the relationship between state and civil society. This perspective is what provides the basis for his later claim in *The Fateful Triangle* that racial identities are not secured by complete discursive practices, but remain open to "infinite sliding among signifiers," the play of class, gender, and sexuality "into and across the discourses of race, ethnicity, and cultural differences" (171).

Consider for a moment Michel Foucault's similar well-known argument for the development in Europe of the description of races of populations as "permanently, ceaselessly infiltrating the social body, or which is, rather, constantly being re-created in and by the social fabric" (*Society* 61). He goes on to argue in the lecture that because of this constant struggle, the politics of race will come to occupy the discourse of power itself, and did so in Europe from the sixteenth century (69). That Foucault then contextualizes this description in his later lectures on the state, territory, biopolitics, and the relationship between government and the individual, confirms a concern similar to that of Hall. Each attempts to explain how the idea of race persists as a problem for society in spite of the effort by individuals, collective political actors, and policies to mitigate its hold on our lives. The common thread in these descriptions of race is the problem of history, of how change occurs in the everyday definition of race.

Convicted of Our Humanity

Looking at the photograph of the store front (fig. 8.2) we can feel the implied collapse of time, the failure to succeed, the genealogy of human enterprise on display in the layers of paint, the designs on the windows,

Figure 8.2. "BB King." Digital Photo, 2023. *Source:* Photo by Nicholas Simpson. Used with permission.

the empty light fixtures, a bent parking barrier. When did a car back into it? The storefront is barred, a single chair suggests that someone would sit in front of the store and watch cars and people walking by. As we look at the photograph do we also watch for a sign of life, of possible human activity, beyond the painted designs and a half visible sign on a wall? The textures of the building's surfaces, the colors, the painted curb to make sure someone can see the accessible walkway, show a care and human attention to detail. Someone spent time to add their own creative ideas to this environment. To make sure we know that they care about our attention, that they want our regard, that we are welcome to ignore the metal bars on the doors and enter.

Did the store owner realize that the store was to become their measure, a burden of little profit and a form of social ministry to the customers who frequented its environs, or was it the promise of something better? How many generations were raised behind the counters and stocking shelves? We can't say that the success of being the owner of your own store, is qualitatively different from that of being an award winning artist, or president of the United States. All share the democratizing dream of an America where anything is possible. Is this enough racial justice, or is something still missing? What do we still want, of this America where we live?

While located near Rickwood Field, in Birmingham, Alabama, as a part of a series of photographs taken by a local artist, the store might be confused for the one in Ferguson, Missouri, where the police first began pursuing Mike Brown after he was accused of shoplifting, or the store in Minneapolis, where after trying to purchase something using a counterfeit twenty dollar bill, George Floyd was killed by the police. The similarity between the photos of the field and the store, as our shared history, of loss and a form of studied, resilient human endurance is obvious. The difference in subject matter of the Obama portraits, and the painting, poem, and film by Kaphar, and these photographs is obvious. But at the same time, we can perceive that there is a relationship in how race works throughout each piece of art. The exceptionalism of the Obamas, while also present in Kaphar's art, is mediated by a self-consciousness by Kaphar of what that success might cost the artists in a conversation about racial injustice and the capacity to form a political subject able to address the problems of race in society. This concern is all the more poignant and disturbing when considered in the context of the terrifying message of loss and desire in the painting *Analogous Colours*.

The photographs of the store and Rickwood Field provide us with an understanding of what Kaphar is trying to say in the film and in the poem, when he demands that his art resonate with those at home, with a past and present that remind all of us of what remains unaccomplished in the struggle for racial equality. The Obama portraits don't avoid the description of hard use, the long hours and dedication to the task at hand, which is also symbolic of both the baseball diamond, its history of the Black Barons, and the store front and sidewalk. The Obama portraits instead laud the successes, pay homage to the end goal of democratic elections in the US, a previously unimagined victory for someone Black, even as Rickwood Field was where Willie Mays first played, and where other Black baseball greats such as Hank Aaron could be seen playing as well. Kaphar's painting of the mother and child shares with the photographs a demand upon us, to ask what we still desire from one another, what is missing from our lives? What still remains to be done?

The sense of imperative, of having to make something afterwards, and the loss of vision, perspective that occurs when we seek to confirm a prophetic politics in this way, means we fall back upon our reliance of the everyday. We speak of science and technology, as though these regimes of truth will pull us forward, allow us to discover more than simply the astute reaction to the latest racial description of difference (Rose 2007, 138). We paint portraits, make films, and commemorate a past neglected glory through a signature baseball game to be held in the future. Around us, every day, are these elements of a language of transformation. The question we should ask is how our ideas of equality and justice develop, if not in these complicated relational practices, where the success of an individual, an artistic achievement, a creative work, a store, a presidency provides an opportunity for us to acknowledge what we do together?

Rather than constantly measure ourselves against a totalizing discourse of difference, the study of each of the art pieces suggests the importance of taking advantage of human capacity to work both within the lines we draw and to constantly exceed these categories as limits of the description of ourselves. The earlier discussion of Hurston's writing on the vernacular and the purposive and tumultuousness of everyday Black lives, provides the perspective on the political needed here. What is the self we are cultivating, such that it should always limn the provisions for the constancy of a description of Black inferiority? Between the argument for race as pathos and a totalizing human difference, if we struggle against the architecture of racial hierarchy we are never free, but we also are not convicted by our humanity.

Works Cited

Foucault, Michel. *"Society Must Be Defended," Lectures at the Collège de France 1975–1976*, edited by Mauro Bertani and Alessandro Fontana. Translated by David Macey. New York: Picador, 2003.

Foucault, Michel. *The Order of Things: An Archaeology of the Human Sciences.* New York: Vintage Books, 1994.

Gilroy, Paul. *Darker then Blue: On the Moral Economies of Black Atlantic Culture.* Cambridge, MA: Belknap Press, 2010.

Hall, Stuart. "Gramsci's Relevance for the Study of Race and Ethnicity [1986]." In *Selected Writings on Race and Difference*, edited by Paul Gilroy and Ruth Wilson Gilmore. Durham, NC: Duke University Press, 2021.

Hall, Stuart. "New Ethnicities [1988]." In *Selected Writings on Race and Difference*, edited by Paul Gilroy and Ruth Wilson Gilmore. Durham, NC: Duke University Press, 2021.

Hall, Stuart. "Race, Articulation and Societies Structured in Dominance [1980]." In *Selected Writings on Race and Difference*, edited by Paul Gilroy and Ruth Wilson Gilmore. Durham, NC: Duke University Press, 2021.

Hall, Stuart. *The Fateful Triangle: Race, Ethnicity, Nation*, edited by Kobena Mercer. Cambridge, MA: Harvard University Press, 2017.

Hall, Stuart. "The Multicultural Question [2000]." In *Essential Essays, Volume 2*, edited by David Morley. Durham, NC: Duke University Press, 2019.

Hall, Stuart. "What Is This 'Black' in Black Popular Culture? [1992]." In *Essential Essays, Volume 2*, edited by David Morley. Durham, NC: Duke University Press, 2019.

Hemenway, Robert. *Zora Neale Hurston: A Literary Biography.* Chicago: University of Illinois Press, 1977.

Hurston, Zora Neale. *Dust Tracks on a Road.* Philadelphia: JB Lippincott, 1942.

Hurston, Zora Neale. *Their Eyes Were Watching God.* Philadelphia: JB Lippincott, 1937.

Hurston, Zora Neale. "What White Publishers Won't Print." In *You Don't Know Us Negroes and Other Essays*, edited by Genevieve West and Henry LouisGates, Jr. New York: HarperCollins, 2022.

Hurston, Zora Neale. "You Don't Know Us Negroes." In *You Don't Know Us Negroes and Other Essays*, edited by Genevieve West and Henry Louise Gates, Jr. New York: HarperCollins, 2022.

Jordan, June. "For My American Family." In *Technical Difficulties: African American Notes on the State of the Union.* New York: Pantheon Books, 1992.

Kaphar, Titus. "I Cannot Sell You This Painting." *TIME Magazine*, June 15, 2020.

Kaphar, Titus, and Alex Mallis, dirs. *Shut Up and Paint.* DCTV and Revolution Ready, 2022.

Lowe, John. *Jump at the Sun: Zora Neale Hurston's Cosmic Comedy*. Chicago: University of Illinois Press, 1997.

Rose, Nikolas. *The Politics of Life Itself: Biomedicine, Power, and Subjectivity in the Twenty-First Century*. Princeton: Princeton University Press, 2007.

Walker, Alice, ed. *I Love Myself When I Am Laughing . . . And Then Again When I Am Looking Mean and Impressive: A Zora Neale Hurston Reader*. Old Westbury, NY: The Feminist Press, 1979.

Contributors

Maxwell G. Burkey is assistant professor of political science at Kean University in New Jersey. His research concerns American political thought and social movements. His writing has been published in *The Star-Ledger*, *The Nation*, and *The Baffler*, as well as in scholarly encyclopedias, journals, and edited volumes.

Julian C. Chambliss is a professor of English and the Val Berryman Curator of History at the MSU Museum at Michigan State University. In addition, he is a codirector for the Department of English Digital Humanities and Literary Cognition Lab (DHLC) and a core participant in the MSU College of Arts & Letters' Consortium for Critical Diversity in a Digital Age Research (CEDAR). An interdisciplinary scholar, his work is shaped by Black Digital Humanities and a Critical Afrofuturist framework that seeks to bridge teaching, scholarship, and service to understand space, place, and identity. His reader on Afrofuturism, *Mapping Afrofuturism: Understanding Black Speculative Practice* (2024) offers students a comprehensive exploration of Afrofuturism theory and practice. His co-edited primary document reader, *Cities Imagined: The African Diaspora in Media and History* (2018), highlights the differing ideologies informing our understanding of black space. He co-produced, directed, and hosted *Afrofantastic: The Transformative World of Afrofuturism*, a documentary exploring Afrofuturism for WKAR PBS. He has worked on several exhibitions examining Afrofuturism and visual culture, including *Transfiguration: A Black Speculative Vision of Freedom* at Philip and Patricia Frost Art Museum at Florida International University and *A Past Unremembered: The Transformative Legacy of the Black Speculative Imagination* at the Zora Neale Hurston National Museum of Fine

Arts. He was featured on the Terrestrial Space Panel at the Smithsonian National Air and Space Museum, Claiming Space Symposium in 2022. Chambliss co-produced and hosted *Every Tongue Got to Confess*, a podcast examining communities of color from 2017 to 2022. *Every Tongue* won the 2019 Hampton Dunn New Media Award from the Florida Historical Society. In addition, he won the Hampton Dunn Internet Award in 2019 for *Advocated Recovered*, a project that digitally reconstructed a gilded-age Black newspaper in Central Florida. He produced and hosted Reframing History, a podcast exploring humanities theory and practice in the United States. The second season of Reframing History inspired the publication of *Reframing Digital Humanities: Conversations with Digital Humanists*(2021), collecting conversations from leading DH scholars.

Scot A. French is an associate professor of digital and public history, director of public history, and associate director of the Center for Humanities and Digital Research at the University of Central Florida. He is author of *The Rebellious Slave: Nat Turner in American Memory* (2004) and has contributed essays on African American history and memory to numerous edited volumes, including *Jeffersonian Legacies* (1993); *Media, Culture, and the Modern African American Freedom Struggle* (2001); *Pride Overcomes Prejudice: A History of Charlottesville's African American School* (2013); and *Marked, Unmarked, Remembered: A Geography of American Memory* (2017). A public and digital humanities scholar, his work crosses genres and disciplinary boundaries. He served as lead author/principal investigator on *Booker T. Washington Elementary School and Segregated Education in Virginia* (2007), a Historic Resource Study for the National Park Service. His film project on urban renewal in Charlottesville, Virginia—"That World is Gone: Race and Displacement in a Southern Town" (2010)—won Audience Favorite, Best Short Documentary, at the 2010 Virginia Film Festival. His recent work on Eatonville, Florida, and its historic Hungerford School has appeared in *Winter Park Magazine*, the Zora Neale Hurston National Museum of Fine Arts, WUCF's Central Florida Road Trip, Florida Frontiers: The Weekly Radio Magazine of the Florida Historical Society, and *CBS Sunday Morning*. In addition to his scholarly collaborations, he has published an essay, "Social Preservation and Moral Capitalism in the Historic Black Township of Eatonville, Fl.: A Case Study in Reverse Gentrification'" in *Change Over Time: A Journal of Conservation and the Built Environment* and is completing work on a monograph.

Jane Anna Gordon is professor of political science and social and critical inquiry, with affiliations in American Studies, El Instituto, Global Affairs, Philosophy, and Women's, Gender, and Sexuality Studies, at the University of Connecticut. Gordon is author of *Statelessness and Contemporary Enslavement* (2020), *Creolizing Political Theory: Reading Rousseau through Frantz Fanon* (2014), and *Why They Couldn't Wait: A Critique of the Black-Jewish Conflict over Community Control in Ocean Hill-Brownsville* (2001), co-author of *Of Divine Warning: Reading Disaster in the Modern Age* (2009), and, most recently, co-editor (with Drucilla Cornell) of *Creolizing Rosa Luxemburg* (2021) and (with Cyrus E. Zirakzadeh) of *The Politics of Richard Wright: Perspectives on Resistance* (2019). President of the Caribbean Philosophical Association (CPA) from 2014 to 2016, she continues to direct the CPA Summer School and to co-edit the *Creolizing the Canon* and *Global Critical Caribbean Thought* book series. With Lewis R. Gordon, she edits the open-access journal, *Philosophy and Global Affairs*.

Utz McKnight is the chair of the Department of Gender and Race Studies as well as the associate dean of strategic initiatives, recruitment, and retention in the College of Arts and Sciences at the University of Alabama. He is a political theorist of democracy, race, and society. His most recent book is *Frances E. W. Harper: Call to Conscience* (Polity, Dec. 2020).

Amanda Millis is a lifelong ballet dancer and instructor for several years. She is currently a J.D. candidate at William & Mary Law School, having graduated from William & Mary's Government Department in 2023. She serves as an associate editor on the William & Mary *Bill of Rights Journal* focused on constitutional and sociopolitical law and legal systems.

Alix Lindsey Olson is associate professor of women's, gender and sexuality studies at Emory University's Oxford College. She is the co-author of *The Ends of Resistance: Making and Unmaking Democracy* (2024). Her scholarly writing has appeared in *Feminist Theory*, *The Journal for a New Political Science*, *Wagadu: A Journal of Transnational Women's and Gender Studies*, *Contemporary Political Theory*, *The Review of Politics*, and in numerous scholarly collections. Olson is an associate editor of *The Journal for a New Political Science*. Prior to Olson's academic life, she toured internationally as a spoken word artist. Her poetry has been published in dozens of anthologies and journals, featured in media outlets like HBO's

Def Poetry Jam, Air America, *Ms. Magazine*, NPR, and is the focus of the multi award-winning documentary film *Left Lane: On the Road with Folk Poet Alix Olson*. Olson is the editor of *Word Warriors: 35 Women Leaders in the Spoken Word Revolution* (2007).

Simon Stow is the John Marshall Professor of Government and American Studies at William & Mary. A political theorist, he works and teaches at the intersection of theory, American politics, literature, and culture, paying particular attention to issues of race. Professor Stow is the author of *American Mourning: Tragedy, Democracy, Resilience* (2017) and *Republic of Readers? The Literary Turn in Political Thought and Analysis* (2007) and is the co-editor of *A Political Companion to John Steinbeck* (2013). He has published articles in the *American Political Science Review, American Political Thought, Perspectives on Politics, Philosophy and Literature, Theory & Event, Post-45, ANQ,* and elsewhere. He has also published chapters in several edited volumes, including *The Democratic Arts of Mourning: Political Theory and Loss, Literature After 9/11, Histories of Postmodernism, A Political Companion to Philip Roth, Isn't It Ironic? Irony in Contemporary Popular Culture,* and *American Television During a Television Presidency.*

Dr. Jared Rodríguez, PhD, is an assistant professor in the Department of Gender and Race Studies at the University of Alabama. Their work traces diasporic routes of Black Study under the disciplinary boundaries of Philosophy, Religious Studies, and History. They are currently completing a manuscript examining the conditions of possibility that Black Study offers for interrupting Racialized Modernity's religions of colonialism and Anti-blackness. Their projects also include an account of the Christian Coloniality of Data and Algorithims as Reproductive Political Technologies of Anti-blackness in the United States.

Shantee Rosado is assistant professor of Africana studies and Latino and Caribbean studies at Rutgers University-New Brunswick.

Alex Zamalin is professor of Africana studies and political science at Rutgers University-New Brunswick. He is the author of six books, "African American Political Thought and American Culture: The Nation's Struggle for Racial Justice" (2015), "Struggle on their Minds: The Political Thought of African American Resistance" (2017), "Antiracism: An Introduction" (NYU Press, 2019) and "Black Utopia: The History of an Idea from Black

Nationalism to Afrofuturism" (2019), which was named a 2020 Choice Outstanding Title by the American Library Association. "Against Civility: The Hidden Racism in Our Obsession with Civility (Beacon, 2021)," and "All is Not Lost: 20 Ways to Revolutionize Disaster" (2022). He is co-editor for a collection of scholarly essays aimed at reinterpreting the American political tradition, "American Political Thought: An Alternative View" (2017). His scholarly essays have appeared in various edited book collections and journals like *New Political Science*, *Contemporary Political Theory* and *Political Theory*. Zamalin has been a guest on NPR and MSNBC and his work has been featured in *The Guardian*, ESPN's *Undefeated*, the *Christian Science Monitor* and *YES!* magazine.

Index